CONTEMPORARY CHALLENGES IN SOCIAL SCIENCE MANAGEMENT

CONTEMPORARY STUDIES IN ECONOMICS AND FINANCIAL ANALYSIS

Series Editor: Simon Grima

CONTEMPORARY STUDIES IN ECONOMIC AND
FINANCIAL ANALYSIS   VOLUME 112A

CONTEMPORARY CHALLENGES IN SOCIAL SCIENCE MANAGEMENT: SKILLS GAPS AND SHORTAGES IN THE LABOUR MARKET

EDITED BY

ANNE MARIE THAKE
University of Malta, Malta

KIRAN SOOD
Chitkara Business School, Chitkara University, Punjab, India

ERCAN ÖZEN
University of Uşak, Turkey

SIMON GRIMA
University of Malta, Malta

United Kingdom – North America – Japan
India – Malaysia – China

Emerald Publishing Limited
Emerald Publishing, Floor 5, Northspring, 21-23 Wellington Street, Leeds LS1 4DL.

First edition 2024

Reprints and permissions service
Contact: www.copyright.com

British Library Cataloguing in Publication Data
A catalogue record for this book is available from the British Library

ISBN: 978-1-83753-165-3 (Print)
ISBN: 978-1-83753-164-6 (Online)
ISBN: 978-1-83753-166-0 (Epub)

ISSN: 1569-3759 (Series)

Printed and bound by CPI Group (UK) Ltd, Croydon, CR0 4YY

INVESTOR IN PEOPLE

CONTENTS

ABOUT THE EDITORS

Dr. Anne Marie Thake, BA (Hons) Public Administration (Melit.), MSc Human Resource Development (Manc.), PhD Social and Policy Sciences (Bath) is a Senior Lecturer at the University of Malta at Faculty of Economics, Management, and Accountancy. She specialises in human resources, public policy, employability, labour markets, and governance. She has made significant contributions in various sectors, including the Office of the Prime Minister of Malta, Bank of Valletta, and Deloitte. Her influence extends to her appointments on boards related to human resource policy, education funding, and fellowships. Dr Thake's international engagements span across Erasmus lectureships in and collaboration with the Universities of Coimbra, Portugal, Irvine, California, USA, and Trinity College, Dublin, Ireland, Polytechnic Institute of Braganca, Portugal, the European Parliament - Directorate General for Research in Luxembourg. She was also involved with the European Commission's Joint Research Centre related to the Future of Government 2030+. Recognised as a Salzburg Global Fellow for talent and skills, Dr. Thake received prestigious scholarships, including the 2021 Study of the U.S. Institutes for Scholars program in Montana. Dr. Thake is part of the EU-SEAS project Tourquooise – a joint master educational programme across European universities.

Kiran Sood is a Professor at Chitkara Business School, Chitkara University, Punjab, India. She is also an Affiliate Professor at the University of Malta. She received her undergraduate and postgraduate degrees in commerce from Panjab University, in 2002 and 2004, respectively. She earned her Master of Philosophy degree in 2008 and Doctor of Philosophy in Commerce with a concentration on Product Portfolio Performance of General Insurance Companies in 2017 from Panjabi University, Patiala, India. Before joining Chitkara University in July 2019, Kiran had served four organisations with a total experience of 19 years. She has published various articles in various journals and presented papers at various international conferences. She serves as an Editor for the refereed journals, particularly the *International Journal of BioSciences and Technology*, the *International Journal of Research Culture Society* and *The Journal of Corporate Governance, Insurance, and Risk Management*. Her research mainly focuses on regulations, marketing and finance in insurance, insurance management, economics and management of innovation in insurance. She has edited more than ten books with various international publishers such as Emerald, CRC, Taylors & Francis, AAP, WILEY Scrivener, IET, Rivers Publishers, and IEEE.

Simon Grima is the the Deputy Dean of the Faculty of Economics, Management and Accountancy, Associate Professor and the Head of the Department of Insurance and Risk Management which he set up in 2015 and started and coordinates the MA and MSc Insurance and Risk Management degrees together with the B.Com in Insurance at the University of Malta. He is also a Professor at the University of Latvia, Faculty of Business, Management and Economics and a Visiting Professor at UNICATT Milan. He served as the President of the Malta Association of Risk Management (MARM) and President of the Malta Association of Compliance Officers (MACO) between 2013 and 2015 and between 2016 and 2018, respectively. Moreover, he is the Chairman of the Scientific Education Committee of the Public Risk Management Organization (PRIMO) and the Federation of European Risk Managers (FERMA). His research focus is on Governance, Regulations and Internal Controls and has over 30 years of experience varied between financial services, academia, and public entities. He has acted as co-chair and is a member of the scientific program committee on some international conferences and is a chief editor, editor, and review editor of some journals and book series. He has been awarded outstanding reviewer for *Journal of Financial Regulation and Compliance* in the 2017 and 2022 Emerald Literati Awards. He acts as an Independent Director for Financial Services Firms, sits on Risk, Compliance, Procurement, Investment and Audit Committees and carries out duties as a Compliance Officer, Internal Auditor, and Risk Manager.

Ercan Özen received his BSc in Public Finance (1994), MSc in Business-Accounting (1997), and PhD in Business Finance (2008) from University of Afyonkocatepe. Now he is Professor of Finance in the Department of Finance and Banking, Faculty of Applied Sciences, University of Uşak, Turkey. His current research interests include different aspects of Finance. He served as Co-editor for more than 15 books by eminent international publishing houses, has publications of more than 100 papers, and participated in many international conferences. He is Board Member of 5 International conferences and workshops. Besides, he is Chair of International Applied Social Sciences Congress, Co-editor of 2 international journals (Journal of Corporate Governance, Insurance, and Risk Management (JCGIRM) and Opportunities and Challenges in Sustainability (OCS)). He is also a Certificated Accountant, Member of Agean Finance Association and Member of TEMA (Türkiye Combating Soil Erosion, for Reforestation and the Protection of Natural Resources Foundation).

ABOUT THE CONTRIBUTORS

Rashmi Aggarwal is a Professor and Dean Commerce UG Programs at Chitkara Business School, Chitkara University, Punjab, India. She is PhD, M.Phil, M.Com, and UGC-NET qualified, with a vast experience of 22 years in the teaching and administration at various positions. She has also worked at the position of Deputy Dean of Students' Welfare handling all the activities related with the students at the University level and outside. She has an expertise in accounting, management, business, human values and professional ethics, and research methodology.

She has publications in many reputable journals and has excellent research orientation. She also has many patents and copyrights to her credit. She has been awarded with the Excellence Award for Most Collaborating Employee. She also got the letters of appreciation for strenuous and meticulous efforts by her in guiding and mentoring the students.

Mallik Arjun Ahluwalia is a Student at Yadavindra Public School, Patiala. With a penchant for Economics and a Faculty for writing, he has won several accolades for his exemplary performance at international and national debate and writing competitions. He secured AIR 3 in the Unified International English Olympiad (2022–2023) and was ranked among the top 5 scholars at the Nha Trang Global Round of the World Scholar's Cup (2022). He has several hours of community service to his credit and is also the Editor of his School Magazine and Newsletter. His areas of interest include Identity Economics and Politics.

Ahmad Al Yakin is an Assistant Professor at Universitas Al Asyariah Mandar in West Sulawesi, Indonesia. He is a Lecturer, a National Speaker, and a Leader in Politics. He was the Chairman of the Civic Education Department at the Teacher Training and Education Faculty, and he was Assistant Dean at her university, to name a few of her accomplishments at her university. He is now Vice Rector 1. In the current year, he is active as a Lecturer, Researcher, and National Coordinator of Merdeka Belajar Kampus Merdeka. He is also Active as a Member of the Indonesian Association of Pancasila and the Civic Education.

M. Anand Shankar Raja works with the Department of Commerce, at Kumaraguru College of Liberal Arts and Science, Coimbatore, TN, India. He holds a PhD in Commerce from SRM University (SRM Institute of Science and Technology), Chennai, TN. His area of focus is on mystery shopping and mystery shoppers' profession. His doctoral dissertation was on enhancing job satisfaction through motivation and emotional intelligence, a study concerning mystery shoppers. His other research focus is on work-life balance, gig economy, consumer purchase behaviour, etc. He has presented his research article in AMA American Marketing Association Conference as an extended feather to his cap.

P. S. Anuradha is currently a Professor in the Department of Commerce, Christ University, Bengaluru, Karnataka, India. She joined the University in 1997. Though her specialisation lies in the areas of Accounting, Taxation and Finance. Her passion is towards women's empowerment and sustainable development aspects.

Rupali Arora is working as Professor with Chandigarh University since 2012 presently handling the role of Doctoral Research Coordinator. She is an MBA from Punjab Technical University, UGC-Net Qualified, and PhD from Kurukshetra University. She is the Founder Editor of Bi-annual refereed management journal *Management Edge* and on the Advisory and Review Board of various national and international journals. She has conducted MDPs for various organisations. She has more than 40 publications to her credit in various national and international journals and her leading Scopus publications are in World Review of Entrepreneurship and Sustainable Development (Inderscience Publishers-Listed C as per ABDC), Springer publications, and UGC listed journals.

Andi Asrifan, S.Pd., M.Pd., is a Lecturer in the Faculty of Teachers Training and Education, Universitas Muhammadiyah Sidenreng Rappang (UMS Rappang) in South Sulawesi, Indonesia. He is also the Head of Students and Alumni Affairs of Universitas Muhammadiyah Sidenreng Rappang (UMS Rappang). He received his PhD (Language Education, Concentration in English Language) and the M.Pd. (Master Pendidikan/Master of Education) from the State University of Makassar, South Sulawesi, Indonesia in 2018 and 2011, respectively. He received his Bachelor's degree (S.Pd.) in Faculty of Teachers Training and Education from Universitas Muhammadiyah Parepare, South Sulawesi, Indonesia, in 2007. He got a sandwich-like scholarship at Northern Illinois University, Dekalb, IL, USA, in 2015. He has published some research articles in leading journals and conference proceedings, including Scopus, and Thomson Reuters.

Theranda Beqiri is Head of Master in HRM in Faculty of Business in 'Haxhi Zeka' University in Kosovo. Her special fields of research are labour market, business environment, HRM. She has conducted a research in University van Amsterdam for HRM, she worked for the different Project for UNDP, World Bank, European Training Foundation (ETF). She worked as Lecturer at the University of Pristina and, Adjunct Faculty Member at Arizona State University. She has a Master in Economics for Business Analysis from Staffordshire University UK, and a PhD from the South East European University.

Ishfaq Hussain Bhat is working as an Assistant Professor at the School of Commerce, Narsee Monjee Institute of Management Studies (NMIMS), Navi Mumbai Campus, Navi-Mumbai, Maharashtra. His area of research is consumer behaviour, branding, and social media marketing.

Luís Cardoso holds a PhD in Modern Languages and Literatures from the University of Coimbra, Portugal. He was Dean of the School of Education and Social Sciences of the Polytechnic Institute of Portalegre, Portugal, between 2010 and 2018. He was President of ARIPESE, Association of Reflection and Intervention in the Educational Policy of Higher Education Schools in Portugal (2015–2018). Adjunct Professor at the Department of Language and Communication Sciences at the School of Education and Social Sciences of the Polytechnic Institute of Portalegre, he is a Researcher at the Centre for Comparative Studies at the University of Lisbon.

Reetika Dadheech is currently a Research Scholar in the School of Management Studies at Punjabi University, Patiala. She received her MBA degree in the year 2011 from Panjab University, Chandigarh. She has four years of academic experience. She has six research articles or papers to her credit in reputed journals and books. She has reviewed three research papers for reputed journals and is striving to do more. Her area of interest is people from underprivileged backgrounds, women labourers, and the informal sector. ORCID: https://orcid.org/0000-0001-9551-9398

Manju Dahiya is working as an Associate Professor, Economics, School of Liberal Education, Galgotias University, Greater Noida, India. She has done MA, MPhil, MBA (Finance), and PhD (Economics). She is an Economist and currently working at Galgotias University. Her previous work organisations include – Noida International University, Roots Global Education, FIIT, and Gautam Buddha University. She has 13 years of teaching and research experience in different capacities with an exposure of corporate as well as research. She has contributed numerous articles, book chapters, and edited books in leading journals, seminars, and conference proceedings. She has presented her research papers in various national and international conferences and seminars.

Swati Dwivedi is currently pursuing a PhD in Marketing Management, Department of Management Studies, Graphic Era University, Dehradun. She has done her postgraduation in International Business and Marketing. Her focus of work and research interests are on Green Marketing and Sustainable Development in Indian scenarios. She has presented two papers in international conferences and some research papers are under process. Presently, she is working as PGT Marketing in a New Delhi based School.

Ashulekha Gupta is a Professor of Management and Economics in the Department of Management Studies at Graphic Era deemed to be University, Dehradun, Uttarakhand, India. She is an Avid Researcher in the diverse field of International Business, Economics, and Marketing Management. She has more than 21 years of rich experience in teaching, research, and Industry. She has published a number of research publications in national and international journals of reputed and presented more than 30 research papers in national and international conferences that includes Bangkok, Thailand, and contributed various Chapters in edited books. Her recent research interest in the area of Environmental Economics is published as a book chapter in the edited book of Springer Nature, Singapore. She has published 14 patents at the national levels.

Shilpi Gupta is working as an Associate Professor at the Chitkara Business School, Chitkara University, Punjab, India. Her area of research is organisational behaviour and human resource management.

Sandra Jekabsone, Doctor of Economics, Professor at the University of Latvia Faculty of Business, Management and Economics, Department of Economics, Head of LU study field Economics (since 2019) LU Economics Bachelor's and Master's study program Director (since 2014). PhD thesis entitled *Adaption of the Fiscal and Monetary Policy in the Development of the Economy of Latvia*. The main research directions are macroeconomics, economics policy, national economy of Latvia, structural and investment policy, labour market, and development of regional and social economy. Number of scientific publications in the last 6 years: 51 (including 10 in the Scopus and Web of Science database).

Purmalis Karlis, Doctor of Economics, Associate Professor at the University of Latvia Faculty of Business, Management and Economics, Department of Management Sciences. PhD thesis entitled *Analysis of the Labour Market of Latvia and Its Development Possibilities*. The main research directions are labour economics, entrepreneurship, labour market, innovations, development of regional and social economy, and cost efficiency analysis in medicine. Number of scientific publications in the last 6 years: 9 (including 5 in the Scopus and Web of Science database).

Simranjeet Kaur is pursuing a PhD in Human Resource Management from Chandigarh University, UGC-Net Qualified, Awarded with Degree of Bachelors of Commerce and M.com in Management Honors from Panjab University, Chandigarh. She is certificated Cost Management Accountant (Qualified ICWA intermediate). She has over three years of teaching experience. She has been a high achiever throughout her educational career. She has authored many research articles and book chapters in various national and international journals listed in Scopus and UGC. Attended numerous national and international conferences, she has been participant to many workshops and conferences. Her Interested areas are human resource and finance.

Ashish Kumar is Senior Research Fellow in HSS in Motilal Nehru National Institute of Technology Allahabad, Prayagraj, India. He has published more than 5 research paper in reputed global journals in Scopus, ABDC listed journal. He has also published 2 edited book chapters in Springer Nature and Emerald Publishing. He has also attended several international conferences and workshop in reputed institutions.

Muhammad Masyat graduates from Universitas Sebelas Maret, Indonesia, who took the study program 'Mass Communication' at the Faculty of Social Sciences were declared graduated on 4 November 2003. It doesn't stop there. Persistence to continue to increase knowledge finally brought Massyat back to being a student at Hasanuddin University Makassar by choosing the Master of Communication Studies program and graduating on 13 May 2013. After graduating from UNHAS with a Masters in Communication Studies, Muhammad's Career, the masses were getting more and more brilliant until they were finally chosen and appointed as the Dean of one of the leading universities in West Sulawesi, which is none other than the Dean of FISIP at Al Asy'ariah Mandar University, commonly abbreviated as UNASMAN.

Muthmainnah is Assistant Professor at Universitas Al Asyariah Mandar West Sulawesi, Indonesia. She is a Lecturer, Global Speaker, and International Leader. Now, she is Deputy Director of Language and Character Development Institute at her university. In the current year, she is active as International Member, International Coordinator Conference and International Trainer. She is also the author of 36 national and international books – Springer, Emerald, and Taylor and Francis (https://sinta.kemdikbud.go.id/profile/books). She is also as International Board for Professors and Expert of Scientific Innovation Research Group, EGYPT (www.sirg.club), International Board of TEFL Kuwait (Member of Large) representing ASIAN. She is also as Country Head, Ambassador, and Country Director for many international organisation representing Indonesia.

L. Mynavathi is currently an Associate Professor in the Department of Commerce, Christ University, Bengaluru, Karnataka, India. She joined the University in 2007. Earlier to that she was working in The Oxford College of Business Management. She had undertaken minor research on cultural dissonance among international students during the year 2013–2014. Her major research project entitled. Efficacy of Women Entrepreneurship Schemes in the states of Karnataka and Tamil Nadu was conducted between 2016 and 2019.

Dhiraj Sharma is currently working at Punjabi University, Patiala in the School of Management Studies Department. He has successfully supervised 20 PhDs and currently 6 candidates are pursuing their research under his supervision. He has 14 books and more than 70 articles/papers published to his credit. For the last 25 years, he is actively involved in writing, teaching, and research in the diverse areas of Business Management. ORCID: https://orcid.org/0000-0002-1786-9998; Scopus ID: 37007864700.

Ritu Singh is a Young Researcher who is pursuing her Bachelors of Arts with Economics specialisation from Galgotias University. She stands out as a student who is really engaged in her study and committed to them. Her skills have allowed her to carry out several studies on a range of subjects. She has also completed a number of courses and certifications which include but are not limited to stock valuation with comparable companies' analysis, Financial Markets, Microeconomics: The Power of Market, and Non-Violent Communication. She also has command on econometrics software like Eviews.

Irina Skribane, Master of Economics, Lecturer at the University of Latvia Faculty of Business, Management and Economics, Department of Economics, Analyst at the Ministry of Economy of the Republic of Latvia. The main research directions are macroeconomics, national economy of Latvia, structural and investment policy.

Ravindra Tripathi is an Associate Professor and Head of the Humanities and Social Science Department and an Expert in Microfinance, at Motilal Nehru National Institute of Technology Allahabad, Prayagraj, India. He has guided more than 10 PhD students and 35 research publications to date, 6 edited book chapters, 3 books editor, and he has directed 2 projects provided by ICSSR.

Uma Shankar Yadav is working in Humanities and Social Science as a Senior Research Fellow at Motilal Nehru National Institutes of Technology Allahabad, Prayagraj, India. He has published more than 50 research papers in reputed global journals, and in the Ministry of MSME. He has submitted his project as a Research Associate under the Directorship of Dr. Ravindra Tripathi, he is currently Deputy Editor in Chief in *Bank and Policy Journal* and *Science Education and Innovation in Modern Prospects*, and Associate Editor in 12 international journals, Editorial Board Member in 15 international journals at the global level. He is a Reviewer in many reputed Scopus Indexed, ABDC B Listed, journals like AER, JAST, SEDME, RMI, FIIB, and Vision (All are SAGE Publication Scopus Journal). He is serving as a pioneer in the handicraft industry in the District of Prayagraj, India. He has 3 book chapters in the Taylor Francis Group, Palgrave Macmillan. He has also published 1 book on the proposal of Global Handicraft Index publisher is Lambert Academic Publishing Maldoa.

FOREWORD

Labour market performance represents a topical subject nowadays due to its notable economic and societal impact. As geopolitical crises, global shocks, technological innovation and digitalization disrupt society even more profoundly, concerns are growing about the spillover impacts on skills, jobs, wages, and labour productivity. Therefore, tailored and comprehensive labour market strategies are considered by policy makers, economists, and business representatives that render global the keen need to address the nowadays risks, challenges, and emerging opportunities.In this complex framework, the book entitled *Contemporary Challenges in Social Science Management: Skills Gaps and Shortages in the Labour Market* stands as a notable scientific research output devoted to a highly relevant and complex topic, with profound economic, but also social and political consequences. The book brings together diverse strands of thought and robust theoretical and empirical shreds of evidence to provide a coordinated response to contemporary societal and labour market challenges.

The book offers valuable insights into skill development and the types of skills required for increasing the employability of the labour force in a globalized digital economy, with a keen focus on youth and the transition from higher education to employment. Later in the text, the skill shortages and labour market rigidity are considered in an international outlook. Another interesting perspective presents the skills gaps in the workplace and their challenges in hospitality and tourism organizations, but also in the IT sector. Furthermore, the book inquires into SMEs' constraints and skill shortages in several emerging economies, since SMEs play an essential role in economic development. On these lines, the specific ways in which experiential learning leads to corporate change are considered next, along with the skill gap that exists between students' expectations and employers' expectations and requirements. Finally, the book discusses the effects of self-efficacy among teachers and management faculty members.

I am confident the readers will benefit from an insightful reading experience of this book that stands out through its scientific merit and practical value, the quality of argumentation, and the accuracy of analyses, bringing notable value to the literature in this scientific field.

Prof. Dr. Graţiela Georgiana NOJA
Vice-Dean of the Faculty of Economics and Business Administration
West University of Timisoara, Romania

PREFACE

The digital revolution and automation are accelerating the transformation of the labour market and the skills required in the workplace. These are also affected by changes in the international economy and employment opportunities. These factors present a policy challenge for all nations and economies. Individuals strive to acquire relevant skills and maintain transferable skills in the workplace in order to be employable and maintain employment. This book titled *Contemporary Challenges in Social Science Management: Skills Gaps and Shortages in the Labour Market, Vol 112 in Contemporary Studies in Economics and Financial Analysis* will delve into issues, such as education, religion, gender, marital status, culture, discrimination, training, regulations, standards, policies, health, taxation, etc. All of which may have a direct and indirect effect on skills gaps and shortages in the labour market.

It begins with skills shortfalls and gaps in labour markets. It explains the theoretical competency framework that is used to fill these gaps and meet the needs in different fields and areas. The factors that cause change around the world will be looked at, and the opportunities and challenges for skill growth will be looked into. The transition from education to employment in knowledge-based sectors in different countries are explored. The book gives a broad European context giving different viewpoints. The book is multidirectional where it can potentially be disseminated to EU institutions.

The subject matter is relevant and pertinent. Policy makers in the field of education, skills, and employment, higher education institutions, employers, research institutions, and professional associations are extremely interested in the topic. This publication serves as a resource for policy makers and business students. Employers with a keen interest in best practices in other nations and any lessons that can be learned in relation to this pertinent area of research would also find this book useful. The book is enriched and bolstered with European case studies of real-world situations that provide a practical and business-oriented dimension.

The book mainly covers:

- An overview of the evolution of the labour market and workplace skills.
- Diverse country perspectives on skills shortages and labour market dynamics.
- Skill shortages and gaps in European businesses.
- Adaptation to changing skill requirements.
- European case studies illustrating how employers attempt to reduce skill gaps and address skill shortages.

KIRAN SOOD
Chitkara Business School, Chitkara University, Punjab, India

SIMON GRIMA
University of Malta, Malta

CHAPTER 1

A STUDY OF THE 21ST CENTURY 4Cs SKILL GAP IN THE INDIAN PRIVATE SECTOR

Ishfaq Hussain Bhat[a] and Shilpi Gupta[b]

[a]School of Commerce, SVKM's Narsee Monjee Institute of Management Studies (NMIMS, Deemed-to-University), Navi-Mumbai, Maharashtra, India
[b]Chitkara Business School, Chitkara University, Punjab, India

ABSTRACT

Purpose: *This study aims to evaluate, explore, and characterise the perceptions of the Indian private sector employers on the 21st century 4Cs (critical thinking, communication, creativity, and collaboration) skills gap, which affects their productivity.*

Need for Study: *This research aims to shed light on the significant issue of the soft skills gap, precisely the 4Cs skills in India. Soft skills, including the 4Cs, are complex and crucial for organisations, and the shortage of these skills among the workforce is a growing concern. This research addresses enterprises' challenges in bridging this gap by exploring different ways to utilise these skills.*

Methodology: *Fifty-six respondents were interviewed based on cluster sampling. An invitation was sent to 40 private sector organisations from five different industries. Only 15 organisations agreed to participate in the interview process.*

Findings: *A total of seven were generated from the data, which included: (1) explicit and timely feedback; (2) compassion and understanding; (3) motivation deficiency; (4) lack of collaboration synergies; (5) lack of practical knowledge; (6) interpersonal skills; and (7) creating team culture.*

Contemporary Challenges in Social Science Management
Skills Gaps and Shortages in the Labour Market
Contemporary Studies in Economic and Financial Analysis, Volume 112A, 1–15
Copyright © 2024 by Ishfaq Hussain Bhat and Shilpi Gupta
Published under exclusive licence by Emerald Publishing Limited
ISSN: 1569-3759/doi:10.1108/S1569-37592024000112A014

Implication: *Given the prevalent skills gap, it is challenging for Indian industries and organisations to remain competitive in the global market. Investing in the education system, providing students with the necessary academic and vocational skills, and equipping them with soft skills, such as the 21st century 4Cs skills is essential to address this issue. Investment is necessary to prepare the workforce to meet the demands of emerging businesses and technologies, ensuring that industries and organisations remain competitive.*

Keywords: Skill gap; creativity; higher education; problem-solving; 4Cs; collaboration; skills

INTRODUCTION

In recent years, industries such as those related to information technology, data sciences, and financial services have emerged and have expanded. These industries have created new white-collar work opportunities for the Indian youth. Although there appears to be no problem with the demand and supply of graduates in terms of number, in reality, all graduates are unable to find suitable employment, and the industry struggles to find qualified candidates (Enriquez et al., 2018; Pambudi & Harjanto, 2020). This circumstance can be linked to employability or a lack of skills. The phenomenon in which workers' skill levels are insufficient to match the criteria of their current position is referred to as the skill gap (Hora, 2019; Rios et al., 2020).

Skill gaps are a significant motivating factor in organisations and employees' training expenditure decisions. They affect firm-level productivity since the average worker's productivity tends to be lower due to significant skill gaps. This reduction in productivity can result in inflated labour costs for firms, as they require more workers per unit of output to compensate for the lack of skills. As a result, addressing skill gaps is crucial for improving the overall productivity and cost-effectiveness of firms, which ultimately contributes to the long-term growth and sustainability of the organisation (Kenayathulla et al., 2019; Rios et al., 2020).

Skill gaps negatively influence a company's profitability due to increased training and recruitment expenditures. There is a growing desire for college graduates to be 'workplace-ready'. Not only is the present job market becoming more competitive, but it is also less likely to offer training programs for its new employees.

The labour market has a growing impact on global trends in higher education (Kenayathulla et al., 2019). States have realised the importance of education in establishing a robust and competitive socioeconomic base (Rios et al., 2020). Improved skills enhance employability because they help workers execute their tasks more efficiently, utilise new technology, and innovate (Li et al., 2021), enabling enterprises to progress up value chains.

Graduate employability is also considered a long-term strategy for enhancing university students' professional well-being and career growth (Singh Dubey et al., 2021). This multifaceted issue is becoming a top priority for the government, colleges and universities, students, and businesses (Hora et al., 2019). Since the 1990s, research studies have repeatedly demonstrated the significance of soft skills for the workforce and organisations' performance (Baral et al., 2022). Klaus Schwab, Founder and Executive Chairman of the World Economic Forum, says that rising technologies are altering everything: our relationships with one another, the way we work, the way our economies and governments operate, and even what it means to be human (Singh Dubey et al., 2021). Research studies also indicate that programs that develop soft skills have an important place in our society (Kenayathulla et al., 2019; Trajkovski et al., 2022).

Being prepared for the workplace requires the development of both hard (academic and technical) and soft (personality traits and habits) abilities (Baral et al., 2022). The areas of soft skill development, such as teamwork, initiative, critical thinking, and communication, are frequently untested for graduates entering the workforce, despite educators supplying knowledge and emphasising hard skill preparation (Trajkovski et al., 2022).

The study aims to explore the perceptions of private sector employers on the 21st century 4Cs skills and examine how they align with the targeted productivity and professional growth of business and industry. This alignment will serve as a starting point for further investigation of the 4Cs skills gap and its impact on organisational productivity and growth.

Furthermore, the study provides insights into organisations' challenges in addressing the 4Cs skill gaps by examining these perceptions. This will also help to identify potential solutions to bridge this gap (Baral et al., 2022).

Higher education's challenge is to prepare graduates for quickly changing employment settings. A few years ago, current job markets were still unheard of (Trajkovski et al., 2022). Globalisation and economic diversity compel educators to reevaluate what is most important for pupils to learn and how to prepare them for developing responsibilities in new job contexts. According to Adepoju and Aigbavboa (2021), workers without the necessary skills and education may struggle to adapt to a changing workplace and find it difficult to compete for jobs. This has been evident in the United States economy in the past decade, with high unemployment rates and an increasing number of individuals returning to school to acquire the essential skills required for ensuring their employability.

The Partnership for 21st Century Skills (P21) framework defines soft skills as life and career skills, learning and innovation, information, media, technology, critical thinking, problem-solving, communication, and teamwork. These skills are essential for success in the modern workplace, enabling individuals to adapt to changing environments and work effectively in teams. Investing in developing soft skills is crucial for individuals to remain employable and for organisations to remain competitive in the global marketplace (Thorvaldsen & Madsen, 2021). Developing 21st century abilities is paramount (Kenayathulla et al., 2019; Rios et al., 2020). Employers expect college graduates to be 'employment ready' with the requisite hard and soft skills to be effective in the workplace. Meeting the challenges of our society requires educational excellence, and our school systems must adapt better to an ever-changing world. Educators can help students make connections between learning and real life and provide them with the skills necessary for future success.

LITERATURE REVIEW

Social Constructivist Theory

The social constructivist theory provides a framework for understanding how learners in a social setting detect patterns, organise thoughts, engage and communicate with others, and construct or reconstruct knowledge through interactions. According to Ghosheh Wahbeh et al. (2021), learners in a social setting alter their realities by constructing or reconstructing knowledge, which is a crucial aspect of the learning process.

Internships provide a social learning setting in which communities of practitioners engage a student intern in active inquiry and collaboration to understand their work environment. This collaborative learning approach allows students to participate in the activities of the expert supervising them for the semester. However, as noted by Perumal (2022), the terminology used in the workplace may be unfamiliar to the student, necessitating clarification by the supervisor. During internships, students and supervisors collaborate to interpret information, develop meaning, and propose solutions to real-world problems using a recursive building process. This approach allows the learner to continually construct their understanding of the work environment and the industry-specific terminology. Overall, internships provide a valuable learning opportunity for students to develop their soft skills and become more knowledgeable through interactions with experts in their field (Al-Qaysi et al., 2021). Internships can be tailored to individual student interests, allowing for a unique learning experience. Since each student perceives information differently, the social constructivist approach promotes self-regulated learning, where students take an active role in and responsibility for their learning (Banihashem et al., 2021). As students interact more frequently with others in the workplace, they become more comfortable questioning and reflecting on their learning processes. Overall, internship-based social constructivist learning provides students a valuable opportunity to develop their soft skills, gain hands-on experience in their field of interest, and become more knowledgeable through interactions with experts. The approach promotes self-regulated learning and encourages students to participate actively in their education.

Employability and Skills

Employability is a concept that depends on integrating a wide variety of variables (Bala & Singh, 2021; Vignoli et al., 2021), some of which are under the control of the higher education institutions (HEI) and others that are not. Jung (2022) proposed that HEIs prioritise the development of graduates' work-related skills to encourage and promote their employability. Cheng et al. (2021) emphasised that employability should be the prime focus of higher education, focusing on skill development possibilities. Lavi et al. (2021) also acknowledged the need to create, implement, and distribute strategies for integrating generic skills into the professional curriculum. Numerous researchers have produced diverse employability models from various ideological and disciplinary standpoints (Bala & Singh, 2021; Lavi et al., 2021; Vignoli et al., 2021). Tarshis et al. (2022) analysed various ideological and disciplinary employability perspectives from prior literature (Cheng et al., 2021; Lavi et al., 2021). Alternately, Singh (2022) emphasised employability-related generic abilities.

Soft Skills

According to research conducted over the previous two decades, employers struggle to locate well-rounded college graduates with both hard and soft abilities (Adepoju & Aigbavboa, 2021; Baral et al., 2022; Ghosheh Wahbeh et al., 2021). McCaig et al. (2022) surveyed 30 company executives and recruiting managers from various private, public, and not-for-profit companies. The poll revealed that employers see a significant gap between essential learning outcomes (mostly soft skills literacy) and recent college graduates' preparation. This indicates a substantial soft skills gap between the critical learning outcomes employers tend to prioritise and the low levels of readiness that they notice in recent graduates. The soft skills gap between expectations and reality impacts recent graduates' employability (Li et al., 2021). Critical thinking is a crucial skill that involves an individual's ability to use their general cognitive processing skills to engage in higher-order thinking, such as analysis, evaluation, and creativity (Sasson et al., 2022). This skill enables individuals to think deeply, approach unfamiliar problems in various ways, and construct new ideas or solutions. Critical thinking is a process that involves gathering, interpreting, and evaluating information in a thoughtful, reasonable, and rational manner. It requires individuals to question assumptions, identify biases, and consider alternative perspectives. Critical thinking is essential for individuals to make informed decisions, solve complex problems, and communicate effectively in various contexts. Developing necessary thinking skills requires practice and intentional effort. Education and training programs allow individuals to learn and practise critical thinking skills in multiple contexts, such as the workplace, academic settings, and everyday life. Through these experiences, individuals can develop their necessary thinking abilities and apply them in different situations to enhance their problem-solving and decision-making capabilities (Hamdan et al., 2019; Miedijensky et al., 2021). In the classroom, students must be taught practical critical thinking and problem-solving skills to compare facts, assess conflicting ideas, and make intelligent judgements. Collaboration abilities, such as working effectively with various teams, making necessary concessions to achieve a common objective, and adopting shared responsibility for collaborative work, are closely related to communication skills (Adepoju & Aigbavboa, 2021). Globalisation and technological advancement require students and employees to work in collaboration. When the students work collaboratively, the group can develop more knowledge, making cooperation a crucial factor for student achievement in the global society of today (Sasson et al., 2022). Moreover, creativity is not the result of individuals thinking and working independently but of individuals cooperating and collaborating to draw on current information to produce new knowledge.

METHODOLOGY

This study used inductive and deductive methods to collect and analyse data to find patterns and themes about the subject (Bhat et al., 2022). Interviews were carried out with 56 respondents from 15 private sector organisations in India. The interviews consisted of open-ended questions that were structured keeping in mind the objectives of the study, which were conducted for approximately 30 minutes.

Table 1.1 shows the characteristics of the respondents. There were 4 respondents each from 11 organisations and 3 respondents from 4 organisations, respectively. It was decided that 56 interviews were sufficient to generalise since qualitative saturation had been reached at 49 interviews and it was noticed that extra interviews did not add any more value to our research objectives.

DATA ANALYSIS

To ensure that the meaning and interpretations drawn from the interview process were accurate, the researchers in this study used a qualitative method approach. The data was analysed on the production, development, and confirmation of concepts within 21st century 4Cs skills and related professions. The data collected from 56 respondents were transcribed into Microsoft Word documents. Once all transcripts were collected and validated, they were transferred to Microsoft Excel for coding. The data were divided into seven themes: (1) explicit and timely feedback; (2) compassion and understanding; (3) motivation deficiency; (4) lack of collaboration synergies; (5) lack of practical knowledge; (6) interpersonal skills; and (7) creating team culture (see Fig. 1.1). These themes are discussed below:

Table 1.1. *Demographic Details of Respondents.*

Particulars (N = 56)		Number	Percentage
Gender	Male	38	67.86
	Female	18	32.14
Years of experience	5–10 years	7	12.50
	11–15 years	24	42.86
	15–20 years	17	30.36
	20 years and above	8	14.29
Position held	Manager	17	30.36
	Senior manager	33	58.93
	CEO	6	10.71

Source: Author's compilation.

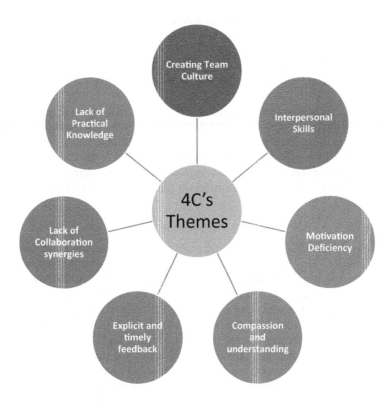

Fig. 1.1. Thematic Analysis of 4C's. *Source:* Author compilation.

RESULTS AND DISCUSSION

Interpersonal Skills

Most interviewees (48) mentioned that human connection skills are essential for graduates entering the private sector, whether with clients or co-workers. Specifically, they said that human connection would be crucial for generating insights that would lead to improved customer service, novel solutions/ outcomes, and strategic differentiation – all of which contribute to increased profits, expanded opportunities for professional development, and the continued viability of the business. Hora (2019) echoes this, arguing that humanism and the ability to connect with people in the face of rapidly evolving technology will be essential in the workplace of the future.

To better interact with their co-workers and clients, interviewees (43) emphasised the importance of 'soft skills' for future university graduates. They noted that many put a premium on interpersonal connections, seeing them as the critical differentiator between human beings and emerging technologies like AI and robots.

They continue to note that employers seek candidates with 'human' soft skills, such as conflict resolution, problem-solving, idea generation, teamwork, and critical thinking. However, although this technology area is still in its infancy having these skill competencies is crucial to providing technical services efficiently. This corroborates to the findings of Rios et al. (2020) and Kenayathulla et al. (2019).

In almost every interview, interviewees (51) mentioned that a recent graduate should fully grasp the basics of being human. They note that businesses believe employees are more effective when their technical skills and humanity are intertwined. Soft skills in their opinion highlight the importance of interpersonal connections in the private sector jobs and how employees can benefit from developing their interpersonal skills. This corroborates with the findings by Singh Dubey et al. (2021).

Lack of Practical Knowledge

Most interviewees (47) said that young graduates need more practical experience and knowledge. They highlight that companies need to ensure that new hires go through an extensive orientation and training program prior to allowing them to commence full-time work. They note that a lack of soft skill projects, training, and activities in higher education exacerbates the already low likelihood of finding a job after graduation (Adepoju & Aigbavboa, 2021; Baral et al., 2022).

All respondents (56) agreed that there is a constant and acute need for graduate employees. They say that, it is difficult to identify a suitable candidate with the necessary professional knowledge and personality level. Respondents agreed (56) that a solid college education is crucial for successful employment, and they understood from personal experience the difficulties associated with a lack of soft skills that could have eased the adjusting process. They find that graduates often lack the essential knowledge and expertise in their chosen fields, but this varies significantly from company to company.

As per findings by Ghosheh Wahbeh et al. (2021), Kenayathulla et al. (2019) and García and Weiss (2019), P1–31 respondents (49) note that employers value 'soft skills' (communication), 'thinking skills' (analysis, critical thinking, and problem-solving), 'the ability to offer innovative approaches to work', and 'discovery-based skills', which include critical thinking and reasoning. According to Ghosheh Wahbeh et al. (2021), skill mismatches are the leading cause of business inefficiency and the shortage of productivity.

Respondents (44) highlight that although universities play a significant role in developing graduates' marketable skills, numerous reports from various employers showed that employers needed help finding employees with the necessary skill set. This finding corroborates with the findings by Ghosheh Wahbeh et al. (2021), Perumal (2022), and García and Weiss (2019), who agree that recruiters often struggle to find qualified candidates.

Supena et al. (2021) also agree and found that communication skills is the ability to question established truths, and analytical and problem-solving prowess ranked highest on the list of desirable traits. Furthermore, Triana et al. (2020) and Erdoğan (2019) agree that a skill gap exists when hiring managers who cannot fill positions with qualified applicants. Hora (2019) similarly agreed and coined this term to emphasise the importance of education in boosting students' employability before employment, independent of any further employee development that might occur within an organisation. Hora (2019) coined another economic term, skills shortage, which refers to a lack of graduates with the necessary skills for specific occupations.

Absence of Motivation

According to respondents (46), business professionals continue to point fingers at their employees' lack of work commitment and organisational commitment. Organisational and managerial worry and complaints about employees, groups, and societal lack of motivation are nothing new. They find that this is an ongoing issue within businesses. The lack of work and organisational commitment directly impacts team performance, as revealed through interviews with organisation professionals. Many business experts also blamed people who needed a long-term perspective for their inability to set and work towards meaningful goals. This is agreed by Triana et al. (2020), Erdoğan (2019), and García and Weiss (2019), P1–31 who show that students' and workers' lack of motivation are common and educational institutions and employers must address a problem in today's labour market. Personal interest and professional aspirations should serve as the driving force behind the development of motivational abilities. The employees can effectively apply their critical thinking, creativity, and communication skills in the workplace to be more effective. There is a lack of skills and, more importantly, motivation among younger generations entering the labour market (Hamdan et al., 2019). Graduates, regardless of whether they plan to enter the workforce immediately, enrol in a vocational program, or continue their education to earn a master's degree, will need to demonstrate specific abilities, skills, and personal motivation inspired by personal goals to be productive members of an organisation (Hora, 2019; Li et al., 2021).

Lack of Collaboration Synergies

Some interviewees (36) stated that there needs to be more systematic cooperation between organisations and universities. This is also suggested by Singh Dubey et al. (2021). These interviewees (36) agreed that partnership effectiveness and interdisciplinary research collaboration were of particular interest. They suggested that relationships between local employers and educational leaders need more systematic, collaborative synergies. They complained that they need help to have their voices heard in creating graduate curricula.

Most of the reviewees (51) suggested that organisations do not collaborate with regional HEIs to improve students' soft skills, and this lack of communication and interaction is apparent. University advisory boards representing various industry sectors are vital to fostering this mutually beneficial interaction. Business owners do not serve on academic advisory boards, suggesting their knowledge needs to be disseminated. These findings are in line with the findings by Trajkovski et al. (2022) and Adepoju and Aigbavboa (2021).

Compassion and Understanding

As one respondent put it, the ability

> to understand the emotions that a person is going through is a crucial skill for problem-solvers. With this frame of mind, we can find ways to improve things like better customer service and the usability of new software. Companies are looking for recent graduates who can use human qualities like empathy and compassion in the workplace to help the company achieve its goals.

This statement in one way or another is agreed by other interviewees (44) and corroborates to the findings of García and Weiss (2019), P1–31.

Thirty-eight respondents in line with findings by Supena et al. (2021), and Triana et al. (2020) emphasised the importance of future customer service executives, engineers, technologists, and salespersons having empathy and technical competencies when providing services to customers and colleagues. They suggested skills such as hospitality, grooming, retailing, and empathising with customers. They state that the ability to put oneself in another person's shoes is a skill that will be essential for the future success of students and businesses alike.

Explicit and Timely Feedback

From the point of view of some interviewees (43), the ability to effectively communicate with co-workers and lay the groundwork for a cohesive team is also crucial. The success of any team rests on its members' ability to form and sustain positive relationships with one another. Team and team-relatedness can only be effective if members are personally connected. Not making assumptions and asking more questions to gain clarity are additional factors contributing to team effectiveness and productivity through effective, clear, and precise communication. Communication without collaboration creates an unworkable atmosphere, and most participants in the study stressed the importance of asking questions and avoiding assumptions to prevent costly breakdowns in equipment, scheduling, on-time deliveries, and productivity. The findings by England et al. (2020) and Miedijensky et al. (2021) corroborate to these views.

This problem was highlighted by Devedzic et al. (2018), who argued that collaboration and communication were complementary skills necessary for successful education in the 21st century. The national standards for speaking and listening have been raised to a higher level among schools to meet this national need, as stated by Ghosheh Wahbeh et al. (2021). These abilities are crucial for students' success because they form the basis of oral communication, the medium through which ideas are exchanged and teams are formed (Adepoju & Aigbavboa, 2021; Perumal, 2022). Collaboration, creative expression, and critical thought are all only possible with the ability to effectively convey one's ideas to others (Perumal, 2022). Students in the modern era need to learn how to effectively express themselves verbally and in writing and use symbols, images, and other forms of digital media in their communication (Pambudi & Harjanto, 2020). As a result, the ease and success of teamwork and collaboration depend increasingly on digital communication (Baturina & Simakov, 2023; Devedzic et al., 2018; Juliana et al., 2022; Sood et al., 2022).

Creating Team Culture

Another common thread that emerged from the interviews (46) was the importance of creating a team environment, which is something that modern businesses want to emphasise because of the four critical competencies (or 'Cs') of the 21st century. Results by Supena et al. (2021) support this. Interviewees (41) similar to Hamdan et al. (2019) and Enriquez et al. (2018) suggest that employees are expected to think critically, communicate effectively, make original contributions, and work together to solve problems, as envisioned by the organisation's management. Similarly to Hora (2019), Kenayathulla et al. (2019) found, interviewees (41) stated that the success of any team depends on its members' ability to work together towards a common goal. Team building is among the most common organisational development change interventions. Given that team cohesion and mutual understanding are crucial to team-building success, corporate development experts agree that interpersonal relationships among team members are an essential factor in the process.

Interviewees (47) lamented the lack of teamwork, yet individuals have expressed a desire to participate in team efforts not merely in the legal capacity of a team member but also in the more informal one represented by a willingness to engage others. Li et al. (2021) highlighted the value of team building as a collaborative process between companies and their employees. Collaboration here is an ongoing process with no clear conclusion in sight. As England et al. (2020, pp. 106–114) put it, 'There is the work of building relationships, engendering trust, and setting an agenda built on the mission, vision, core values, and a strategic plan'.

DISCUSSION

One of the most significant difficulties for developing nations is the skills gap between education and employment. There is an issue with the quality of education at many state and private universities across India (Hora, 2019; Rashid et al., 2021). Textbooks and pedagogical practices need to be updated. Faculty and students agree that there need to be more up-to-date scholarly materials, which poses a challenge for those students who are fluent in their mother tongue. The non-alignment between academia and employment is a challenge. The business community is not involved in education. Professionals have stated that this mismatch has led to a situation where there are many graduates and postgraduates with outdated skills and no jobs for them to do (Bhat & Gupta, 2019; Pambudi & Harjanto, 2020). This has a chilling effect on the pace of development of the economy. The purpose of education extends well beyond simply equipping the workforce with the knowledge and abilities they need to thrive in the modern economy. It also involves developing individuals into contributing members of society and encouraging their continued development throughout their lives (Adepoju & Aigbavboa, 2021; Bhat & Singh, 2018; Trajkovski et al., 2022). The strategy emphasises the importance of identifying and incorporating into education the skills and competencies that will best serve the purposes of the economic development of the country. The skills must be closely aligned with educational curricula to help find the best fit for employment (Hora, 2019).

In today's competitive business environment, it is clear that companies need employees who can use a particular set of functional abilities. Workforce development specialists call these abilities 'Survival Skills' for the modern workplace (Bhat & Singh, 2018; Supena et al., 2021). Jung (2022) states that companies have begun investing more time and money into soft skills training for their staff as they have come to appreciate the importance of doing so. Using technology, these methods can produce an all-encompassing classroom conducive to developing 21st century abilities (Bala & Singh, 2021; Cheng et al., 2021). From this study's findings, we can deduce several pedagogical ideas and strategies that educators can employ to integrate the 4Cs and soft skills into their curricula. Students must be encouraged to think critically and problem-solve, to compare facts, assess conflicting ideas, and make intelligent judgements (Cheng et al., 2021; Lavi et al., 2021). Collaboration abilities, such as working effectively with various teams, making necessary concessions to achieve a common objective, and adopting shared responsibility for collaborative work, are closely related to communication skills (Bhat et al., 2022; Singh, 2022). Globalisation and technological advancement require students and employees to collaborate. As a result of students working collaboratively, the group can develop more knowledge, making cooperation a crucial factor for student achievement in the global society of today (Erdoğan, 2019; Supena et al., 2021). Creativity is not the result of solitary thought and effort but cooperation and collaboration to build on current information and generate new knowledge.

IMPLICATIONS

The study contributes theoretically and practically to the existing research on skill gaps. It has established that synergy is required to combat the soft skills gap. Employers must interact with academic institutions and their internal customers to foster involvement and consumer advocacy, facilitating cooperative synergy. Universities that seek to integrate soft skills into undergraduate and master's courses must understand the skills expected of students, how these talents can be transferred to the industry, and why this development is crucial to students' career success. Educators should encourage the development of these talents to help students catch up to the 21st century in terms of education and employment by providing them with the resources and environments they need to learn more about themselves. This will help students to make the best decisions for their future.

CONCLUSION

The educational system needs to adapt to the business world. As a result of the current situation concerning employment skills, numerous changes are expected. They must be able to think critically, solve problems, communicate effectively, work together, rapidly and effectively locate relevant information, and effectively use technology. However, rapidly developing technology provides them with new tools to work with. As a result, teachers play a crucial role in shaping students' experiences in the classroom. They need to be able to evaluate various teaching resources and select the most effective one for students. The educational environment is equally important in educating students with 21st century skills. Efforts are intensifying to construct and inform pupils in such educational environments worldwide. These learning settings include workshops, laboratories, enriched libraries, and active learning classrooms. The educational background in India is still using traditional classroom order. This consists of dynamic rote-learning conditions where the teacher and the students are passive listeners. Therefore, it is evident that pupils learning in these educational contexts cannot be effective in the 21st century.

Consequently, significant modifications must be made to educational environments. These environments must be updated so that all courses and activities are geared specifically to deliver 21st century skills. These are indicated when the designed activities are carried out in classrooms where students can freely express themselves and actively participate. In addition, educational environments must integrate the appropriate technological infrastructure so that students may access knowledge swiftly and securely in the technological era. The teachers in the classroom should act as guides to assist students in utilising the available equipment and materials correctly and effectively.

LIMITATIONS AND FURTHER RESEARCH

This study's main drawback is that it used only practitioners in India to identify the need for skills in today's business world. Future research can be carried out by taking into consideration students and academicians. The study did not take into consideration the culture or the structure of society into consideration which may have an impact on the skills acquired. Therefore, future studies can be carried out by considering the nature of culture and the structure of society in India. Moreover, different subjects need different types of skills; therefore, future studies are needed to assess the value of a subject-specific education with a particular focus on how the financial and professional rewards of these subjects may stack up. Finally, the study uses a qualitative approach; future studies can be conducted using a quantitative approach to yield better results.

REFERENCES

Adepoju, O. O., & Aigbavboa, C. O. (2021). Assessing knowledge and skills gap for construction 4.0 in a developing economy. *Journal of Public Affairs, 21*(3), e2264.

Al-Qaysi, N., Mohamad-Nordin, N., & Al-Emran, M. (2021). Developing an educational framework for using WhatsApp based on social constructivism theory. In M. Al-Emran, K. Shaalan, & A. E. Hassanien (Eds.), *Recent advances in intelligent systems and smart applications* (pp. 243–252). Springer.

Bala, R., & Singh, S. (2021). Employability skills of management students: A study of teacher's view-point. *Materials Today: Proceedings*, *57*(1), 1–10. https://doi.org/10.1016/j.matpr.2021.05.473

Banihashem, S. K., Farrokhnia, M., Badali, M., & Noroozi, O. (2021). The impacts of constructivist learning design and learning analytics on students' engagement and self-regulation. *Innovations in Education and Teaching International*, *59*(4), 442–452. doi: 10.1080/14703297.2021.1890634

Baral, S. K., Rath, R. C., Goel, R., & Singh, T. (2022, March). Role of digital technology and artificial intel-ligence for monitoring talent strategies to bridge the skill gap. *2022 International mobile and embed-ded technology conference (MECON)* (pp. 582–587). doi: 10.1109/MECON53876.2022.9751837.

Baturina, L., & Simakov, A. (2023). Students' attitude towards e-learning in Russia after the pandemic. *Education Science Management*, *1*(1), 1–6.

Bhat, G. M., Bhat, I. H., Shahdad, S., Rashid, S., Khan, M. A., & Patloo, A. A. (2022). Analysis of fea-sibility and acceptability of an e-learning module in anatomy. *Anatomical Sciences Education*, *15*(2), 376–391.

Bhat, I. H., & Gupta, S. (2019). The mediating effect of student engagement on social network sites and academic performance of medical students. *International Journal of Sociology and Social Policy*, *39*(9/10), 899–910. https://doi.org/10.1108/IJSSP-05-2019-0093

Bhat, I. H., & Singh, S. (2018). Analysing the moderating effect of entrepreneurship education on the antecedents of entrepreneurial intention. *Journal of Entrepreneurship Education*, *21*(1), 1–10.

Cheng, M., Adekola, O., Albia, J., & Cai, S. (2021). Employability in higher education: A review of key stakeholders' perspectives. *Higher Education Evaluation and Development*, *16*(1), 16–31. https://doi.org/10.1108/HEED-03-2021-0025

Devedzic, V., Tomic, B., Jovanovic, J., Kelly, M., Milikic, N., Dimitrijevic, S., ... & Sevarac, Z. (2018). Metrics for students' soft skills. *Applied Measurement in Education*, *31*(4), 283–296.

England, T. K., Nagel, G. L., & Salter, S. P. (2020). Using collaborative learning to develop students' soft skills. *Journal of Education for Business*, *95*(2), 106–114.

Enriquez, L. E., Morales Hernandez, M., & Ro, A. (2018). Deconstructing immigrant illegality: A mixed-methods investigation of stress and health among undocumented college students. *Race and Social Problems*, *10*(3), 193–208.

Erdoğan, V. (2019). Integrating 4C skills of the 21st century into 4 language skills in EFL classes. *International Journal of Education and Research*, *7*(11), 113–124.

García, E., & Weiss, E. (2019). US schools struggle to hire and retain teachers. The Second Report in "The Perfect Storm in the Teacher Labor Market" Series. Economic Policy Institute.

Ghosheh Wahbeh, D., Najjar, E. A., Sartawi, A. F., Abuzant, M., & Daher, W. (2021). The role of project-based language learning in developing students' life skills. *Sustainability*, *13*(12), 6518.

Hamdan, N., Kiong, T. T., Heong, Y. M., Masran, S. H., Yunos, J. M., Mohamad, M. M., Azid, N., Othman, W., Hanapi, Z., Nor, M., Hairol, M., Haris, M., & Shafei, S. (2019). An effec-tiveness of high order thinking skills (HOTS) self-instructional manual for students' assign-ment achievement. *Journal of Technical Education and Training*, *11*(1), 63–72. doi: https://doi.org/10.30880/jtet.2019.11.01.008

Hora, M. T. (2019). *Beyond the skills gap: Preparing college students for life and work*. Harvard Education Press.

Hora, M. T., Zi, C., Parrott, E., & Her, P. (2019). Problematizing college internships: Exploring issues with access, program design, and developmental outcomes in three US colleges. Retrieved from University of Wisconsin-Madison, Wisconsin Center for Education Research. http://www.wcer.wisc.edu/publications/working-papers

Juliana, A. P., Lemy, D. M., Pramono, R., Djakasaputra, A., & Purwanto, A. (2022). Hotel perfor-mance in the digital era: Roles of digital marketing, perceived quality and trust. *Journal of Intelligent Management Decision*, *1*(1), 36–45.

Jung, J. (2022). Working on learning and learning to work: Research on higher education and the world of work. *Higher Education Research & Development*, *41*(1), 92–106.

Kenayathulla, H. B., Ahmad, N. A., & Idris, A. R. (2019). Gaps between competence and importance of employability skills: Evidence from Malaysia. *Higher Education Evaluation and Development*, *13*(2), 97–112.

Lavi, R., Tal, M., & Dori, Y. J. (2021). Perceptions of STEM alumni and students on developing 21st-cen-tury skills through methods of teaching and learning. *Studies in Educational Evaluation*, *70*, 101002.

Li, G., Yuan, C., Kamarthi, S., Moghaddam, M., & Jin, X. (2021). Data science skills and domain knowledge requirements in the manufacturing industry: A gap analysis. *Journal of Manufacturing Systems, 60,* 692–706.

McCaig, M., Rezania, D., & Lightheart, D. (2022). Examining talent management practices in a Canadian not-for-profit context: A theory-driven template analysis. *Relations Industrielles/ Industrial Relations, 77*(2), 1–23. https://doi.org/10.7202/1091592ar

Miedijensky, S., Sasson, I., & Yehuda, I. (2021). Teachers' learning communities for developing high order thinking skills—A case study of a School Pedagogical change. *Interchange, 52*(4), 577–598.

Pambudi, N. A., & Harjanto, B. (2020). Vocational education in Indonesia: History, development, opportunities, and challenges. *Children and Youth Services Review, 115,* 105092.

Perumal, K. (2022). A descriptive study on the effect of blogs on writing skill development using social constructivism as a theory. *Theory and Practice in Language Studies, 12*(8), 1537–1544.

Rashid, S., Hassan, A. U., Bhat, I. H., & Bhat, G. M. (2021). Analysing the attitude of medical students toward class absenteeism. *National Journal of Clinical Anatomy, 10*(4), 226.

Rios, J. A., Ling, G., Pugh, R., Becker, D., & Bacall, A. (2020). Identifying critical 21st-century skills for workplace success: A content analysis of job advertisements. *Educational Researcher, 49*(2), 80–89.

Sasson, I., Yehuda, I., Miedijensky, S., & Malkinson, N. (2022). Designing new learning environments: An innovative pedagogical perspective. *The Curriculum Journal, 33*(1), 61–81.

Singh, J. K. N. (2022). A Malaysian Research University's Initiative to develop international students' employability skills. In *Graduate employability across contexts* (pp. 187–205). Springer.

Singh Dubey, R., Paul, J., & Tewari, V. (2021). The soft skills gap: A bottleneck in the talent supply in emerging economies. *The International Journal of Human Resource Management, 33*(13), 2630–2661.

Sood, K., Kaur, B., & Grima, S. (2022). Revamping Indian Non-Life Insurance Industry with a trusted network: Blockchain technology. In K. Sood, R. K. Dhanaraj, B. Balamurugan, S. Grima, & R. Uma Maheshwari (Eds.), *Big Data: A game changer for insurance industry* (pp. 213–228). Emerald Publishing Limited.

Supena, I., Darmuki, A., & Hariyadi, A. (2021). The influence of 4C (constructive, critical, creativity, collaborative) learning model on students' learning outcomes. *International Journal of Instruction, 14*(3), 873–892.

Tarshis, S., Scott-Marshall, H., & Alaggia, R. (2022). An analysis of comparative perspectives on economic empowerment among employment-seeking survivors of intimate partner violence (IPV) and service providers. *Societies, 12*(1), 16.

Thorvaldsen, S., & Madsen, S. S. (2021). Decoding the digital gap in teacher education: Three perspectives across the globe. In *Teacher education in the 21st century-emerging skills for a changing world* (pp. 1–16).

Trajkovski, G., Killian, R. L., & Coen, S. (2022). Bridging the gaps between higher education, industry, and the learner: The skills-first approach. In S. Ramlall, T. Cross, & M. Love (Eds.), *Handbook of research on future of work and education: Implications for curriculum delivery and work design* (pp. 282–298). IGI Global.

Triana, D., Anggraito, Y. U., & Ridlo, S. (2020). Effectiveness of environmental change learning tools based on STEM-PjBL towards 4C skills of students. *Journal of Innovative Science Education, 9*(2), 181–187.

Vignoli, M., Alcover, C. M., & Mazzetti, G. (2021). Sustainable employability in the mid and late career: An integrative review. *Revista de Psicología del Trabajo y de las Organizaciones, 37*(3), 157–174.

CHAPTER 2

STRATEGICALLY ADDRESSING SKILL GAPS AND IMBALANCES AMONG HEALTH EMPLOYEES

Swati Dwivedi and Ashulekha Gupta

Department of Management Studies, Graphic Era University, Dehradun, Uttarakhand, India

ABSTRACT

Purpose: *Significant structural changes are currently occurring in the Indian labour sector. Artificial intelligence (AI) and other emerging technologies are redefining the activities and skill requirements for various jobs in the healthcare sector. These adjustments have been accelerated by the economic crisis brought on by COVID-19, along with other considerations.*

Need for the Study: *Skills shortages, job transitions, and the deployment of AI at the company level are the three main challenges confronting the Indian labour market. This chapter aims to discuss policy alternatives to address a rising need for health workers and provide an overview of changes to the healthcare sector's labour market.*

Methodology: *A review of the available literature was conducted to determine the causes of the widening skill gap despite a vibrant and prodigious young population. The background of the sustainable labour market is examined in this chapter, with a focus on workforce migration and mobility.*

Findings: *This chapter gives a comparative review of recent policy papers and evidence, as well as estimates of the health workforce and present Indian datasets. Furthermore, it highlights how important it is for all people concerned*

Contemporary Challenges in Social Science Management
Skills Gaps and Shortages in the Labour Market
Contemporary Studies in Economic and Financial Analysis, Volume 112A, 17–33
Copyright © 2024 by Swati Dwivedi and Ashulekha Gupta
Published under exclusive licence by Emerald Publishing Limited
ISSN: 1569-3759/doi:10.1108/S1569-37592024000112A015

to invest in today's workforce to close the skill gap and create better future opportunities.

Practical Implications: *This chapter's findings imply a severe shortage of human intellectual capital in India and a need to bridge this gap in the Indian labour market.*

Keywords: Skill gap; labour market; healthcare sector; young workforce; sustainability; workforce imbalance; COVID-19

1. INTRODUCTION

The term 'health workforce' describes 'the pool of all humans involved in protection, maintenance, or enhancement of population health' in the context of a healthcare system (Cometto & Campbell, 2016; Koopmans et al., 2018; Rao et al., 2016). The public health workforce encompasses a wide range of activities, including those aimed at reducing the prevalence of diseases, increasing the quality of life for citizens, and facilitating efficiency, which serves both the commercial and governmental sectors (Javanparast et al., 2018; Kangovi et al., 2018). India is a federation of states, each with its government, healthcare systems, and unique health challenges. Registered, official healthcare professionals and informal practitioners comprise India's health workforce, with the latter as the initial point of contact for a vast population (Ghosh et al., 2013). The National Health Workforce Alliance (NHWA) of 2018 reports that India has 5.76 million health professionals. This includes 1.16 million allopathic physicians, 2.34 million nurses and midwives, 1.20 million pharmacists, 0.27 million dentists, and 0.27 million traditional medical practitioners (see Fig. 2.1). According to NHWA, 8.8 doctors and 17.7 nurses/midwives are available for every 10,000 people (*Health workforce in India: Where to invest, how much and why?*, 2022; Karan et al., 2021). However, National Sample Survey Office (NSSO) estimates that the doctor and nurse/midwife density of actively working health professionals are 6.1 and 10.6, respectively. In light of the prerequisite requirements, the figures fall to 5.0 and 6.0, respectively. These numbers are far below the World Health Organization's (WHO) minimum requirement of 44.5 healthcare professionals per 10,000 people (Chotchoungchatchai et al., 2020). These are partly attributable to reduced funding for public health programmes and services. Health planners and policy makers have found it challenging to address the problem of health workforce imbalance due to the severe consequences it poses. It has repercussions on the efficiency and effectiveness of healthcare delivery, the responsiveness of emergency services, the availability of qualified personnel, and the contentment of providers and recipients.

This worldwide epidemic has had significant repercussions on the healthcare industry, among other harmful effects. The International Council of Nurses (ICN) reported on June 3, 2020 that because of their frequent contact

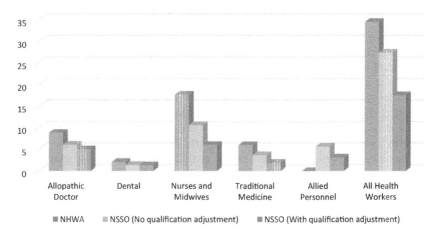

Fig. 2.1. Number of Healthcare Workers Per 10,000 People. *Sources*: Estimates from NHWA 2018 and NSSO 2017–2018 (*Health workforce in India: Where to invest, how much and why?*, 2022).

with infected patients, over 0.45 million health professionals had contracted COVID-19 worldwide by that date (Behera et al., 2020). This has resulted in the deaths of thousands. The United States, Italy, and other European countries have reported high COVID-19 infection and mortality rates among healthcare workers. Thousands of Indian healthcare professionals, including physicians, nurses, paramedics, and community health workers, have tested positive for COVID-19 since June 20, 2020. This includes over 2,000 health professionals in the nation's capital alone (Behera et al., 2020). The increasing number of COVID-19 patients placed a strain on healthcare workers in India that had never been seen before due to the country's chronic shortage of medical professionals.

Despite the apparent scarcity, the healthcare workforce is often believed to be unevenly distributed among the nation. To keep up with the growing demand, initiatives have been devoted to expanding the healthcare workforce. Several factors have undermined these initiatives, including rising populations, decreasing community healthcare purchasing capacity, increasing life expectancies, and the emergence of non-communicable diseases and other chronic conditions. The absence of reliable disaggregated data at the national and state levels has meant that evidence for this claim has been scant up to this point. If the current health workforce succumbs to sickness and death, recruiting and training new candidates will take time. As the number of healthcare professionals infected with COVID-19 rises, countries like India must take precautions to prevent the spread of the virus inside their borders. The purpose of this chapter is to examine the evolution of the Indian healthcare labour market and to propose potential governmental responses to the growing demand for medical professionals.

2. METHODOLOGY

The Web of Science, Scopus, PubMed, and Google Scholar were among the data-bases searched as criteria for including and excluding the study. The search was conducted using key terms related to the skill gap and imbalances in the health workforce in India. The 'AND' and 'OR' Boolean operators were also used to construct relevant words. After data source evaluation, all filtered sources were collected and checked for duplication using Mendeley Desktop Version 2.61.1. Titles and abstracts served as the primary criteria for screening. The full-text screening was also applied to the remaining articles. Studies evaluating incomplete publications (In press) and papers on the auxiliary subject were disregarded. We also excluded correspondence, discussions, editorials, books, systematic reviews, book chapters, conference abstracts, doctoral dissertations, and brief communi-cations. This study included papers that discussed the skill gap and imbalances in the health workforce in India, along with the policy response. Additionally, all relevant and referenced documents from the research and included reviews were searched.

3. INDICATORS OF IMBALANCES

Imbalances come in many forms, and their severity may be gauged using sev-eral different metrics. An economic skill imbalance exists when workers lack the competence their company requires. However, from a normative viewpoint, the fundamental gap is a need for more personnel compared to established stand-ards. Subcategories also include dynamic and static imbalances, with dynamic imbalances including self-resolving imbalances. The five different kinds of imbal-ances in terms of the typology are: Disparities in the healthcare industry may occur across different fields or even within a single field, such as when specific expertise is in limited supply. Disparities between urban and rural regions, as well as between poor and wealthy communities, are examples of what are known as 'geographic imbalances' (Ariste, 2019; Wang et al., 2020). There is also a divide between the public and private sectors and a disconnect between institutions and the services they provide. Disparities between the sexes in the healthcare work-force are also widespread (Boniol et al., 2019; Montañez-Hernández et al., 2020; Yassine et al., 2022).

The WHO uses various measuring indicators, including openings, staff growth, typical population-based metrics such as the number of physicians, nurses, and activity indicators such as overtime pay. One problem is that private practitioners cannot participate in the measurement process, despite their usage, prevalence, and application being positive in any healthcare system. Furthermore, the limi-tations on available funds tend to mask the actual severity of the situation. In actuality, health service delivery is primarily unequal and inequitable since there are significant discrepancies in health worker type, skill, distribution, and gender mix. This unequal distribution is caused by several factors, including unique geo-graphical restrictions like rugged terrains, migration of health workers, a lack of domestic training capacity, an inadequate mix of skills, underutilisation of skilled staff, variations in staffing patterns depending on situation-specific variables like income potential, job satisfaction, working conditions, demographic imbalances, and unacceptably low compensation. A nation's success in organising and providing health services, such as vaccine coverage, primary care outreach, newborn and child survival, maternal health, and a host of others, is directly correlated with the size and quality of its health workforce. Primary health care (PHC) aims to improve people's health overall, so ensuring that these workers are happy in their jobs and that new one is preserved is crucial.

The Bhore Committee of 1946 introduced comprehensive health care to India (Jha et al., 2022; Patel et al., 2022). Still, it was not until 1978 that the idea of primary health care was developed, and this was the critical first step towards achieving Health for All by the year 2000. India signed the Alma-Ata Declaration in 1978, which called for universal primary healthcare accessible to all people, particularly those living in underserved and rural areas (Park, 2011). PHC centres were set up in each community as part of a new, three-tiered healthcare structure. It was designed to be the public's first contact with the national healthcare delivery system. The Indian Public Health Standards (IPHS) have been developed with distinct criteria for human resources, physical assets, pharmaceuticals, and physical facilities. For example, regular preventative, promotive, and curative services are considered essential, whereas services, where an ideally high level is to be obtained are considered desirable. Human resources in health staff the facility as a hub for referring patients from four to six outlying subcentres to more specialised state hospitals. In addition to routine, emergency, and recreational services, they administer current and newly released initiatives. Without sufficient numbers of qualified health professionals, it was argued that achieving the Millennium Development Goals (MDGs) would be an impossible dream.

The lack of properly qualified and motivated health professionals is a major barrier to implementing health interventions to improve mother and child health and combat diseases. Constraints such as inadequate facilities, medication and supply networks, and data collection and analysis mechanisms all contribute to the failure to attain the desired health outcomes. Health workers and health outcomes have been proven to have a favourable link in several ecological studies spanning several countries (Baturina & Simakov, 2023; Juliana et al., 2022; Sood et al., 2022).

4. INDIA'S HEALTH POLICY AND ORGANISATIONAL FRAMEWORK

The public and private ownership models and various medical practices make up India's healthcare system unlike any other in the world (Roy, 2019). Human resources for health (HRH) policy in India has been developed according to the advice of numerous expert committees throughout the course of the last few decades. Because of the widespread shortages and inequalities in India's healthcare workforce, most of these panels pushed for a significant increase in productivity, a suitable skill mix among health professionals, and a minimum standard of physical infrastructure across the board. Unfortunately, HRH shortages and unequal distribution persisted in India despite these suggestions. The commercial sector has surpassed the public health system in service provision and hiring health personnel due to the latter's inability to rely on reliable financing sources (Mackintosh et al., 2016). There have been several changes in the healthcare system since 2005, when the National Rural Health Mission (NRHM) was launched, with the explicit purpose of raising the ratio of doctors to patients (Gopalakrishnan & Immanuel, 2017; Rather, 2022). In 2019, the Indian government announced three plans to expand the availability of human resources for health care (Karan et al., 2019), which includes:

1. creating new institutions to produce a better health workforce;
2. increasing the number of students accepted into existing medical schools; and
3. elevating existing current health centres to university-level medical centres.

At the same time, the government loosened regulations for the private establishment of medical schools and nursing universities. All of these factors point to an imminently increased supply of health personnel.

Professionals in India's healthcare sector come from various medical and healthcare backgrounds. According to data on the supply side, doctors and nurses come from a wide range of educational experiences and are registered with multiple boards and organisations (Karan et al., 2019).

Regarding the skill-mix ratio, NHWA stock data indicates a nurse-to-doctor ratio of 2.02:1 throughout India (see Fig. 2.2), with wide variances among states ranging from a high of 9.9:1 in Haryana and 10.7:1 in Himachal Pradesh to a low of 0.4:1 in Bihar and 0.6:1 in Uttarakhand. Based on NSSO data, however, it is estimated that the nurse-to-doctor ratio in India as a whole is 1.7:1, with the

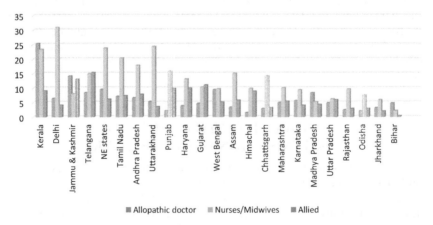

Fig. 2.2. Health Workers/Professionals' Ratio in States. *Sources*: Estimates from NSSO 2017–2018 (*Health workforce in India: Where to invest, how much and why?*, 2022).

highest ratios being found in the states of Punjab (7.1:1) and Delhi (4.8:1). From the present projection of 1.77 million, a trained health workforce of 2.65 million will be needed by 2030. However, the skilled health worker density will remain the same; in 2030, it is projected to be at 17.5 per 10,000 people. Reaching 22.8 trained health professionals per 10,000 people will need an additional 1.13 million employees. However, the number of nurses will increase by 200% by 2030. In that case, the overall number of trained health workers will rise to 3.45 million, with 2.02 million nurses (*Health workforce in India: Where to invest, how much and why?*, 2022; Karan et al., 2021).

5. WHO'S POLICY RESPONSE TO ENSURE A LONG-TERM HEALTH WORKFORCE

This section outlines the primary policy choices for every nation contemplating solution strategies for increasing healthcare workers' numbers and productivity. The WHO Global Strategy and Global Code of Practice on International Recruitment stress the need for nations to analyse the best methods for achieving 'sustainability' in their national health workforces (Buchan et al., 2019). The focus should be on nations stepping up to the plate to provide for their health workforce needs, initially and over time. This will allow them to manage their labour markets better and avoid harming nations with fewer resources by engaging in high levels of active international recruiting over the long run.

Despite the lack of a universally agreed-upon technical definition of 'sustainability', the WHO Handbook on Health Workforce Data suggests that the degree to which a country is 'self-sufficient' in its healthcare workforce can be gauged by the number of its members who received their education at home (Por et al., 2009). Using this metric, the dependence on foreign physicians in the Organization for Economic Cooperation and Development (OECD) and similar nations presently ranges from 2% to 60%, with an average of 6%. Sustainability does not imply that a nation can or should depend only on its educated workforce. Hence it is crucial that the existing contribution of foreign-trained employees is considered and that any future modification of this level is made explicit. While this metric may be useful for gauging the state of the nation's healthcare workforce, three additional significant obstacles must be overcome before any country can hope to achieve true healthcare workforce sustainability (Chopra et al., 2008; Glinos et al., 2015).

- First, they must fix the inefficient distribution of healthcare workers caused by market flaws. Workers in the wrong location, in the 'wrong' speciality to optimise access to adequate treatment, or with a less-than-ideal skill set will all contribute to subpar results.
- Second, instead of concentrating just on the initial supply of new employees via training, governments should direct their policy and financing towards enhancing the retention of workers. This would improve the availability and accessibility of excellent care by decreasing expensive attrition and increasing worker stability. As the retirement age rises in many nations, legislative

solutions must be implemented to ensure the health and welfare of the health-care workforce. This is a crucial argument; too frequently, policy makers pay more attention to tracking and controlling outflows than fixing problems with keeping people in the system.

- Thirdly, nations must raise the productivity of their labour force. To achieve this, it is possible to better use existing abilities, enhance the skill mix, create new positions, implement appropriate incentives, create a supportive work environment, and integrate and work together. Health care will be better in every way as a result of these changes.

6. LABOUR MARKET FRAMEWORK IN THE IDENTIFICATION OF POLICY CHOICES

Government officials require a guide to help them determine where and how they may enhance the long-term viability of their workforce via various initiatives and how those efforts should be sequenced and bundled together for maximum effect. The WHO's Global Strategy is based partly on an analysis of the labour market. This highlights the fluidity of the healthcare personnel and situates the immediate workforce concerns of training, distribution, retention, recruiting, and productivity within the national policy framework. Policy makers in many nations and settings may apply this framework with slight modification. It helps pinpoint where various policies, or 'entry points', could be implemented and how they are likely to interact with one another (Buchan et al., 2019).

As the healthcare industry grows and evolves, policy makers must thoroughly understand the healthcare labour market. In addition, it stresses the need to concentrate on market performance and productivity while simultaneously considering market regulation, flows across sectors, nations, and employment statuses; optimal student enrolment, employee hiring, employee retention, and worker distribution; flows of students into and out of schools; flows of employees into and out of schools; etc.

7. EDUCATING AND TRAINING THE WORKFORCE

There has to be a congruence between public health goals and the education and training of health professionals. Corresponding changes have not matched the fast changes in population and disease in the education of health professionals. A disjointed, stagnant curriculum characterises it, and out of date that produces ill-equipped graduates (Frenk et al., 2015).

The WHO has subsequently released recommendations for expanding health education globally (Rosa et al., 2022). Increases in education may boost health workers' numbers, competence, and impact. To better prepare health professionals for better healthcare delivery, the report recommended more cooperation between the education, health, other governmental institutions, and the business sector (Calder et al., 2022; Janamian et al., 2022; Vera San Juan et al., 2022).

The OECD has called on its member countries to revamp their medical professionals' initial education and training courses (Lillo-Crespo, 2022; Lynch et al., 2022). Human capital waste (when people are over-qualified for occupations) and patient care quality are both possible outcomes of the study's findings that a mismatch exists between the training health professionals get and the abilities they require to perform their tasks (when they lack specific skills).

More than 70% of the medical professionals who participated in the OECD poll said they had experienced over-skilling. These regulations should encourage a more thorough application of people's abilities, by transferring specific responsibilities from high-skilled to intermediate- and lower-skilled labourers.

In addition, transformational education should emphasise preparing health professionals to work together on complex problems to address the existing gaps in the health workforce. They emphasise the need for Continued Professional Development (CPD) to maintain a competent and safe staff since CPD activities are often linked with re-licensing or re-registration mandates.

8. IMPROVING RETENTION AND DISTRIBUTION

Policies that aim to improve the distribution of healthcare professionals may vary widely in both their success and cost. This will vary from nation to country, health system to health system, worker to worker, and policy and programme to policy and programme. A thorough understanding of the drivers and interests of the intended audience is crucial for crafting effective policies that can have a long-term and meaningful effect.

To increase retention and distribution, the policy might focus on: incentives to migrate monetarily; assistance, both academically and personally; and recognising that healthcare providers should keep up with current trends in their field. According to a WHO literature evaluation, educational interventions offer the most significant evidence of success. Still, their effects will most likely be maintained via adopting a coordinated 'bundle' of policies (Buchan et al., 2019).

9. HARNESSING TECHNOLOGY

While digitalising health systems, implementing health information and communications systems, and other technological advancements and upgrades may be difficult and expensive, they may have long-term advantages in enhancing health services' efficacy (WHO, 2019).

Some examples of essential domains where we might make a big difference are:

- Genomics and precision medicine may tailor therapy strategies to particular patient subgroups, increasing efficacy and opening new therapeutic avenues.
- ICT-enabled remote care may expand patients' access to medical care and meet their immediate medical requirements.

- Self-management is aided by technology, which may help patients take charge of their health and better understand their illness.
- Connecting data with AI can unlock new analytic power for patient diagnosis, triage, and logistics.

These technological advancements are expected to alter the duties and responsibilities of the health staff concerning their training, location, and availability. This, in turn, has far-reaching effects on how people choose their careers and how they are educated, trained, developed, and continue learning throughout their lives.

The OECD has emphasised the increasing efforts to expand access to healthcare stemming from technology that uses the internet to connect patients and doctors regardless of distance. Numerous studies have demonstrated the many positive outcomes that can result from incorporating ICT into the healthcare industry (Aceto et al., 2020; Becker, 2019; Bibbins-Domingo, 2019; Davenport & Kalakota, 2019; Mousa & Othman, 2020), such as enhancing productivity, decreasing errors, fostering team-based care, facilitating the incorporation of best practices into routine care, encouraging patient participation, resulting in more cost-effective services as a result of the reorganisation of professional roles and responsibilities.

Technology like clinical decision-making aids and multimedia training programmes play an essential part in ICT's ability to aid in the transformational education of the workforce. High-quality simulation experiences might replace up to half the required clinical hours in all prelicensure nursing programmes. As a result, developing new norms and accrediting practices for various forms of continuing education training will be necessary. Healthcare providers may also need assistance in learning to use computers.

10. MIGRATION AND MOBILITY POLICY RESPONSES

This subsection delves further into the policies that affect the movement and relocation of healthcare professionals. An improved appreciation that not all migration trends among health professionals are unidirectional has resulted in a more nuanced understanding of this phenomenon. Various variables affect the motivations ('push and pull') that cause people to move freely and involuntarily and the directions (and destinations) they choose to go in. Policy makers can better target their efforts when they fully grasp the driving forces that motivate individuals and groups. Some medical professionals relocate for just a short time, while others move on to a third country fast. Others regularly make trips across international boundaries to go to and from work.

Effectual policy measures on international labour market interactions necessitate that decision-makers account for the individual rights to move and their reasons for doing so, which may extend beyond mass immigration and also include, for example, fears for one's safety, seeking refugee status for political reasons, or a lack of employment, career, or educational opportunities in the country of origin. Gender and equality concerns in the decisions and experiences of emigrant health professionals are also acknowledged but not fully addressed.

11. ETHICAL RECRUITMENT

When the World Health Assembly convened in 2010, all member nations unanimously approved the WHO Code. It is the primary international framework for health worker migration and mobility, providing governments with direction and structure as they craft and execute their policies. The WHO Code's (Buchan et al., 2019) primary goals are to:

- Respect the rights, duties, and expectations of source nations, host countries, and migrant health workers.
- Set up and promote voluntary guidelines for the ethical recruitment of health professionals across international borders.
- Promote global dialogue and collaboration on issues related to the ethical recruitment of health professionals abroad.
- Provide a model for developing or enhancing the requisite institutional and legal framework for the international recruitment of health workers in member nations.

According to the Code, all signatory nations should address their domestic health workforces' retention, distribution, and productivity, and improve their workforce planning. As mentioned, the ultimate purpose is to message that member states should strengthen their local labour markets to lessen the need for aggressive foreign recruiting. This will reduce the burden on the nations of the final destination and lessen the 'pull' forces in the countries of origin that are driving away their citizens.

According to reports, the Code has helped certain nations initiate longer-term national health policy discourse. This has involved communicating with other branches of government and non-governmental stakeholders, such as civil society organisations, labour unions, regulating bodies, and professional associations.

In light of these cases, the Code may serve as a springboard for nations to either increase their attention on labour policy and planning at the national level or to enhance their existing processes in this area. They also serve as a helpful reminder that health worker migration is not only a problem that should be addressed by health ministers, regulators, and business leaders in the health industry. Updated knowledge of relevant policy activities and better mobility data definition and analysis have resulted from the WHO Code's requirement that member states report on its implementation regularly.

12. DISCUSSION

There has been a lot of focus on human resource investment to boost the availability of the health workforce in recent years (Cometto & Campbell, 2016). Investments of this kind may also increase the number of women in the workforce and encourage women to enter the formal labour market in India. The COVID-19 pandemic has elevated the importance of these debates on increasing investment and governmental attention to concerns about the health workforce.

In this research, we discussed the many facets of the skill gap and imbalance among healthcare workers in India and the current and future obstacles to a more robust healthcare workforce in both the federal and state spheres. These issues stem from a sizeable fraction of India's registered health professionals with various councils and organisations who are not active members of the country's healthcare workforce. The outflow of trained physicians and nurses from India to the West has been cited as a contributing factor (Kaushik et al., 2008; Mullan, 2006; OECD, 2019).

In this chapter, we found that many women with medical degrees are not participating in the labour force. These individuals are either unemployed but open to new job opportunities or have chosen to stay in the labour force. The gap between the number of nurses and midwives registered and actually working is especially wide for this group.

One key measure of health worker availability is the ratio of the number of health professionals per 1,000 people. Based on the current research results, it is obvious that additional investments in increasing the active health workforce are the most pressing issue that requires governmental attention in India. Additionally, we discover a less-than-ideal combination of medical doctors, registered nurses, medical doctors, and allied health professionals.

However, there are only two nurses for every medical doctor. Most OECD nations have a ratio of 3–4 registered nurses to one medical doctor (OECD, 2019). Even though the entire population of nurses in the nation is around three times the number of physicians, we discover that a sizeable fraction of nurses is not participating in the labour market. Facilitating nurses' access to stable job opportunities is another potential policy area for boosting nurses' numbers in the active health workforce. To improve access to healthcare workers and diversity of expertise, balancing doctor and nurse densities is essential. Equally problematic is the meagre ratio of doctors to other medical workers. A sufficient number of allied health professionals should be produced via enhanced training and educational infrastructure, as was underlined in the Global Strategy study and other comparable studies.

Another issue that needs governmental attention is more urban to rural medical staffing. Almost two-thirds of India's healthcare personnel are based in metropolitan regions, meaning that the country's rural population is severely underserved or must travel long distances to get medical care. There is also a noticeable imbalance in the distribution of medical professionals among India's states. Most of India's less developed states need more medical professionals. A more in-depth and comprehensive investigation is necessary to unravel the causes of this uneven distribution between states and comprehend the regional intricacies.

When comparing the public and private sectors, it is essential to note that the private sector employs a disproportionate number of physicians, whereas the two sectors share nurses relatively evenly. The public sector is the only place where conventional medical professionals are employed. These imbalances in the distribution of health professionals contribute to a need for more trained health personnel in many states and rural regions and a lack of parity in the distribution of health workers' specialised knowledge and experience. These results are consistent with previous research (Rao et al., 2016).

The public sector needs more qualified candidates for open posts. Specialists at Community Health Centres are especially hard to come by, but shortages are glaring in all states. Barriers to recruiting, cases challenging the hiring process and early resignations, especially from temporary positions, are all possible causes of the current vacancies. Government policy must prioritise the filling of open positions.

If present growth rates are maintained, the predicted population of qualified health professionals per 10,000 people in 2030 is expected to stay the same. The healthcare workforce is expected to grow by 2030, although the concentration of this profession is still the same. The doctor-to-nurse ratio is expected to stay the same by 2030 at the current supply-side growth rate. By 2030, the doctor-to-nurse ratio will be 1:1.5, attributable to an almost 200% increase in the supply side of nurses. This necessitates expanding nursing programmes at a quick pace. There was talk of a 1:2:1 doctor-to-nurse-to-ANM ratio in India in a 2012 High-Level Expert Group report to the Planning Commission. Working on both the supply and demand sides of the market will be necessary to have these many nurses by 2030. There needs to be more focus on the duties and responsibilities of nurses.

13. CONCLUSION

Subsidising technical universities and graduate schools is necessary for India to meet its HRH goals of boosting the skill mix and expanding the pool of active health workers. Further training and skill development for already employed but insufficiently trained health personnel is also necessary for India.

This study's research suggests several issues for policy interests, including:

- Increasing the number of people who work in the healthcare industry in regions that suffer from a shortage of healthcare professionals should emphasise the growth of medical schools (including medical, nursing, dental, and other related programmes) and the recruitment of their graduates to fill local vacancies.
- Increasing the number of nurses in the workforce is an urgent issue. Developing alternative nursing infrastructure and institutions may require a more protracted time frame for change to occur. Additionally, work must be done to improve the quantity and quality of nurse training programmes already in existence.
- A sizeable talent pool is not used to recruit more educated people into active labour markets, especially women, since they have yet to enter the labour field. It is essential to devise plans to upskill these graduates and make them more marketable to employers.
- You are mixing and matching the abilities of physicians and fewer nurses. There has to be a national initiative developed to increase significantly the number of nurses already in the field.

- Acquiring and deploying personnel rapidly for use in public health institutions. Effective recruiting practices help bridge the human resource shortages plaguing public sector organisations, especially at the primary levels.
- Using modern means. The potential for e-health and m-health solutions to enhance care delivery, facilitate speedy and efficient communication, and expand access to medical treatment.
- Putting money into research and development of new tools and the education and training of workers may pay off handsomely in this sector.
- Skills improvement courses for medical staff with less experience should be worked out.

According to NSSO statistics, several sectors of the health profession have less-than-ideal levels of education and training. There has to be a national level discussion on this topic between the Councils and the Ministry of Health to determine what can be done to fix the problem. We do not advocate for their official incorporation into the workforce. Still, we suggest the government examine training programmes to improve their abilities to take in a broader range of caregiving and ancillary health duties. Bettering healthcare workforce Data Live national registers of health professionals are needed, along with regular/periodic updates and adjustments to the database to ensure accurate information about registered health professionals. With active registers in place, it will be possible to rely less on survey estimates and more on complex data when making decisions and preparing for the future of the workforce, all while aiding in the quality assurance of the enrolled professionals. Investing more heavily in India's healthcare personnel is essential to achieving the above goals and expanding economic opportunity for all Indians.

REFERENCES

Aceto, G., Persico, V., & Pescapé, A. (2020). Industry 4.0 and Health: Internet of Things, Big Data, and Cloud Computing for Healthcare 4.0. *Journal of Industrial Information Integration, 18*. https://doi.org/10.1016/j.jii.2020.100129

Ariste, R. (2019). Availability of health workforce in urban and rural areas in relation to Canadian seniors. *International Journal of Health Planning and Management, 34*(2), 510–520. https://doi.org/10.1002/HPM.2712

Baturina, L., & Simakov, A. (2023). Students' attitude towards e-learning in Russia after pandemic. *Education Science and Management, 1*(1), 1–6.

Becker, A. (2019). Artificial intelligence in medicine: What is it doing for us today? *Health Policy and Technology, 8*(2), 198–205. https://doi.org/10.1016/j.hlpt.2019.03.004

Behera, D., Praveen, D., & Behera, M. (2020). Protecting Indian health workforce during the COVID-19 pandemic. *Journal of Family Medicine and Primary Care, 9*(9), 4541. https://doi.org/10.4103/jfmpc.jfmpc_925_20

Bibbins-Domingo, K. (2019). Integrating social care into the delivery of health care. *Journal of the American Medical Association, 322*(18), 1763–1764. https://doi.org/10.1001/jama.2019.15603

Boniol, M., McIsaac, M., Xu, L., Wuliji, T., Diallo, K., & Campbell, J. (2019). Gender equity in the health workforce: Analysis of 104 countries. *World Health Organization, March*, 1–8. https://apps.who.int/iris/bitstream/handle/10665/311314/WHO-HIS-HWF-Gender-WP1-2019.1-eng.pdf

Buchan, J., Campbell, J., Dhillon, I., & Charlesworth, A. (2019). Labour market change and the international mobility of health workers. *Health Foundation Working Paper, 5*, 18.

Calder, S., Tomczyk, B., Cussen, M. E., Hansen, G. J., Hansen, T. J., Jensen, J., Mossin, P., Andersen, B., Rasmussen, C. O., & Schliemann, P. (2022). A framework for standardizing emergency nursing education and training across a regional health care system: Programming, planning, and development via international collaboration. *Journal of Emergency Nursing, 48*(1), 104–116. https://doi.org/10.1016/j.jen.2021.08.006

Chopra, M., Munro, S., Lavis, J. N., Vist, G., & Bennett, S. (2008). Effects of policy options for human resources for health: An analysis of systematic reviews. *The Lancet, 371*(9613), 668–674. https://doi.org/10.1016/S0140-6736(08)60305-0

Chotchoungchatchai, S., Marshall, A. I., Witthayapipopsakul, W., Panichkriangkrai, W., Patcharanarumol, W., & Tangcharoensathien, V. (2020). Primary health care and sustainable development goals. *Bulletin of the World Health Organization, 98*(11), 792. https://doi.org/10.2471/BLT.19.245613

Cometto, G., & Campbell, J. (2016). Investing in human resources for health: Beyond health outcomes. *Human Resources for Health, 14*(1), 51.

Davenport, T., & Kalakota, R. (2019). The potential for artificial intelligence in healthcare. *Future Healthcare Journal, 6*(2), 94–98. https://doi.org/10.7861/futurehosp.6-2-94

Frenk, J., Chen, L., Bhutta, Z. A., Cohen, J., Crisp, N., Evans, T., Fineberg, H., García, P. J., Ke, Y., Kelley, P., Kistnasamy, B., Meleis, A., Naylor, D., Pablos-Méndez, A., Reddy, S., Scrimshaw, S., Sepúlveda, J., Serwadda, D., & Zurayk, H. (2015). Health professionals for a new century: Transforming education to strengthen health systems in an interdependent world. *Educacion Medica, 16*(1), 9–16. https://doi.org/10.1016/j.edumed.2015.04.011

Ghosh, N., Chakrabarti, I., & Chakraborty, M. (2013). Imbalances in health workforce in a primary health centre (P.H.C.) of Darjeeling District, West Bengal, India. *IOSR Journal of Dental and Medical Sciences, 8*(6), 18–22. https://doi.org/10.9790/0853-0861822

Glinos, I. A., Wismar, M., Buchan, J., Rakovac, I., BAG, WHO, & European Health Observatory. (2015). How can countries address the efficiency and equity implications of health professional mobility in Europe? European Observatory on Health Systems and Policies Report, pp. 1–28. https://www.ncbi.nlm.nih.gov/books/NBK464503/

Gopalakrishnan, S., & Immanuel, A. (2017). Progress of health care in rural India: A critical review of National Rural Health Mission. *International Journal of Community Medicine and Public Health, 5*(1), 4. https://doi.org/10.18203/2394-6040.ijcmph20175758

Health workforce in India: Where to invest, how much and why? (2022). https://cdn.who.int/media/docs/default-source/searo/india/publications/health-workforce-in-india-where-to-invest-how-much-and-why.pdf?sfvrsn=8ae98d85_2

Janamian, T., True, A., Dawda, P., Wentzel, M., & Fraser, T. (2022). Co-creating education and training programs that build workforce capacity to support the implementation of integrated health care initiatives. *Medical Journal of Australia, 216*(S10), S9–S13. https://onlinelibrary.wiley.com/doi/abs/10.5694/mja2.51526

Javanparast, S., Windle, A., Freeman, T., & Baum, F. (2018). Community health worker programs to improve healthcare access and equity: Are they only relevant to low- and middle-income countries? *International Journal of Health Policy and Management, 7*(10), 943–954. https://doi.org/10.15171/ijhpm.2018.53

Jha, N., Jain, B., Bhati, R., Mehta, A., Dhinwa, M., Kishore, S., Aggarwal, P., & Job, S. (2022). Situation analysis of implementation of National Health Programmes in Primary Health Centres (PHCs) at Uttarakhand. *National Journal of Community Medicine, 11*(05), 201–205. https://doi.org/10.5455/njcm.20200515043037

Juliana, A. P., Lemy, D. M., Pramono, R., Djakasaputra, A., & Purwanto, A. (2022). Hotel performance in the digital era: Roles of digital marketing, perceived quality and trust. *Journal of Intelligent Management Decision, 1*(1), 36–45.

Kangovi, S., Mitra, N., Norton, L., Harte, R., Zhao, X., Carter, T., Grande, D., & Long, J. A. (2018). Effect of community health worker support on clinical outcomes of low-income patients across primary care facilities: A randomized clinical trial. *JAMA Internal Medicine, 178*(12), 1635–1643. https://doi.org/10.1001/jamainternmed.2018.4630

Karan, A., Negandhi, H., Hussain, S., Zapata, T., Mairembam, D., De Graeve, H., Buchan, J., & Zodpey, S. (2021). Size, composition and distribution of health workforce in India: Why, and where to invest? *Human Resources for Health, 19*(1), 1–14. https://doi.org/10.1186/S12960-021-00575-2/figures/6

Karan, A., Negandhi, H., Nair, R., Sharma, A., Tiwari, R., & Zodpey, S. (2019). Size, composition and distribution of human resource for health in India: New estimates using National Sample Survey and Registry data. *BMJ Open, 9*(4), e025979. https://pubmed.ncbi.nlm.nih.gov/31133622/

Kaushik, M., Jaiswal, A., Shah, N., & Mahal, A. (2008). High-end physician migration from India. *Bulletin World Health Organization, 86*(1), 40–45. https://www.scielosp.org/pdf/bwho/v86n1/13.pdf

Koopmans, L., Damen, N., & Wagner, C. (2018). Does diverse staff and skill mix of teams impact quality of care in long-term elderly health care? An exploratory case study. *BMC Health Services Research, 18*(1), 988. https://doi.org/10.1186/s12913-018-3812-4

Lillo-Crespo, M. (2022). *Lessons learned by health professionals and good practices in relation with population well-being across Europe* (pp. 151–175). Springer. https://doi.org/10.1007/978-3-031-14425-7_9

Lynch, M., Kodate, N., Hickey, C., & O'Leary, A. C. (2022). Bridging the gap between healthcare professions' regulation and practice: The "lived experience" of community pharmacists in Ireland following regulatory change. *Journal of Pharmaceutical Policy and Practice, 15*(1), 1–15. https://doi.org/10.1186/s40545-022-00465-5

Mackintosh, M., Channon, A., Karan, A., Selvaraj, S., Cavagnero, E., & Zhao, H. (2016). What is the private sector? Understanding private provision in the health systems of low-income and middle-income countries. *The Lancet, 388*(10044), 596–605. https://pubmed.ncbi.nlm.nih.gov/27358253/

Montañez-Hernández, J. C., Alcalde-Rabanal, J. E., Nigenda-López, G. H., Aristizábal-Hoyos, G. P., & Del Castillo, M. L. D. P. (2020). Gender inequality in the health workforce in the midst of achieving universal health coverage in Mexico. *Human Resources for Health, 18*(1). https://doi.org/10.1186/S12960-020-00481-Z

Mousa, S. K., & Othman, M. (2020). The impact of green human resource management practices on sustainable performance in healthcare organizations: A conceptual framework. *Journal of Cleaner Production, 243*. https://doi.org/10.1016/j.jclepro.2019.118595

Mullan, F. (2006). Doctors for the world: Indian physician emigration. *Health Affairs, 25*, 380. https://doi.org/10.1377/hlthaff.25.2.380

OECD. (2019). *Recent trends in international migration of doctors, nurses and medical students.* OECD Publishing. https://doi.org/10.1787/5571ef48-en

Park, K. (2011). *Park's textbook of preventive and social medicine.* https://scholar.google.com/scholar?hl=en&as_sdt=0%2C5&q=Park+K.+Park's+textbook+of+preventive+and+social+medicine.+In%3APark+K+%28ed%29.+Health+care+of+the+community.21st.+Edition.+M%2Fs+BanarasidasBhanot+publishers.+Jabalpur+2011.pp.+828&btnG=

Patel, V., Bhadada, S., Mazumdar-Shaw, K., Mukherji, A., Khanna, T., & Kang, G. (2022). A historic opportunity for universal health coverage in India. *The Lancet, 400*(10351), 475–477. https://doi.org/10.1016/S0140-6736(22)01395-2

Por, E., Dal Poz, M. R., Gupta, N., Quain, E., & Soucat, A. L. B. (2009). *Handbook on monitoring and evaluation of human resources for health: With special applications for low- and middle-income countries.* https://apps.who.int/iris/bitstream/handle/10665/44097/9789248547706_por.pdf

Rao, K. D., Shahrawat, R., & Bhatnagar, A. (2016). Composition and distribution of the health workforce in India: Estimates based on data from the National Sample Survey. *WHO South-East Asia Journal of Public Health, 5*(2), 133–140. https://doi.org/10.4103/2224-3151.206250

Rather, T. (2022). Impact of National Rural Health Mission: A Public Welfare Programme of the Government on Indian Health Sector. *SSRN Electronic Journal.* https://doi.org/10.2139/SSRN.4015268

Rosa, W. E., Parekh de Campos, A., Abedini, N. C., Gray, T. F., Huijer, H. A. S., Bhadelia, A., Boit, J. M. G., Byiringiro, S., Crisp, N., Dahlin, C., Davidson, P. M., Davis, S., De Lima, L., Farmer, P. E., Ferrell, B. R., Hategekimana, V., Karanja, V., Knaul, F. M., Kpoeh, J. D. N., Lusaka, J. (2022). Optimizing the global nursing workforce to ensure universal palliative care access and alleviate serious health-related suffering worldwide. *Journal of Pain and Symptom Management*, *63*(2), e224–e236. https://doi.org/10.1016/j.jpainsymman.2021.07.014

Roy, V. (2019). Integrating indigenous systems of medicines in the healthcare system in India: Need and way forward. In *Herbal medicine in India: Indigenous knowledge, practice, innovation and its value* (pp. 69–87). https://doi.org/10.1007/978-981-13-7248-3_6

Sood, K., Kaur, B., & Grima, S. (2022). Revamping Indian Non-Life Insurance Industry with a trusted network: Blockchain technology. In K. Sood, R. K. Dhanaraj, B. Balamurugan, S. Grima, & R. U. Maheshwari (Eds.), *Big Data: A game changer for insurance industry* (pp. 213–228). Emerald Publishing Limited.

Vera San Juan, N., Clark, S. E., Camilleri, M., Jeans, J. P., Monkhouse, A., Chisnall, G., & Vindrola-Padros, C. (2022). Training and redeployment of healthcare workers to intensive care units (ICUs) during the COVID-19 pandemic: A systematic review. *BMJ Open, 12*(1). https://doi.org/10.1136/bmjopen-2021-050038

Wang, Y., Li, Y., Qin, S., Kong, Y., Yu, X., Guo, K., & Meng, J. (2020). The disequilibrium in the distribution of the primary health workforce among eight economic regions and between rural and urban areas in China. *International Journal for Equity in Health, 19*(1). https://doi.org/10.1186/S12939-020-1139-3

World Health Organization. (2019, February 6–8). *Future of digital health systems: Report on the WHO symposium on the future of digital health systems in the European region.* https://apps.who.int/iris/handle/10665/329032

Yassine, B. B., Rojewski, J. W., & Ransom, M. M. N. (2022). Gender inequity in the public health workforce. *Journal of Public Health Management and Practice, 28*(2), E390–E396. https://doi.org/10.1097/PHH.0000000000001374

CHAPTER 3

WORK-BASED LEARNING: PERSPECTIVES OF UNIVERSITY STUDENTS AND EMPLOYERS IN MALTA

Anne Marie Thake

Department of Public Policy, University of Malta, Msida, Malta

ABSTRACT

Introduction: *Work-based learning (WBL) bridges the gap between academic theory and exposure to real-life situations where students' knowledge is filtered and applied to relevant workplace environments.*

Purpose: *This study aims to examine students' and employers' voices on their perspectives of WBL. It focuses on students reading for an undergraduate degree in Bachelor's in Commerce in two majors, with a specialisation in Public Policy at the University of Malta.*

Methodology: *Questionnaires were sent to students to obtain their views on the experience and benefits of WBL. This was followed by structured interviews conducted with employers and undergraduate students to provide an overview of their respective work-based experiences. WBL providers were asked to draw up reports on the students' performance. The feedback which emerged from the structured interviews on the nature of these experiences was analysed. These tools helped to calibrate and refine the nature of these practices.*

Contemporary Challenges in Social Science Management
Skills Gaps and Shortages in the Labour Market
Contemporary Studies in Economic and Financial Analysis, Volume 112A, 35–47
Copyright © 2024 by Anne Marie Thake
Published under exclusive licence by Emerald Publishing Limited
ISSN: 1569-3759/doi:10.1108/S1569-37592024000112A016

Findings: *The study's findings show that WBL experiences help students increase technical knowledge, improve their soft skills, and learn new tools, sought after by employers. Feedback emanating from employers' perspectives serves to temper the University course curriculum to ensure that it is relevant to the requirements of modern-day society.*

Keywords: Work-based learning; students; employees; work-based experience; Malta; higher education; knowledge application

INTRODUCTION

WBL seeks to bridge the gap between academia and the world of work. It consists of work carried out in an organisation that is relevant to the degree they are reading for. 'Such a work-based learning experience is a critical component of a University course as it offers students the opportunity to explore and expand theoretical concepts in a real-life context and application' (Thake, 2021, p. 1). It contributes to 'developing [students'] workplace skills sets, complementing academic learning and providing valuable exposure to the working environment' (Poulter & Smith, 2015, p. 2). Such experiences are viewed as improving students' employability after graduation.

Work experiences give students the opportunity to learn about an organisation and develop their generic skills in the process. The breadth and depth of knowledge and expertise demonstrated by students confirm the value of the work experience. 'Students who focus on their degree studies only without spending time in the workplace, are unlikely to develop the skills and interests, employers are looking for' (Coughlan, 2013). Today, employers give non-technical, social skills and attitudes, such as communication, teamwork, adaptability and resilience, and importance (Cunningham & Villaseñor, 2014).

On the other hand, student WBL experiences bring different perspectives and innovative ideas that can help organisations keep pace with a rapidly evolving market. It gives them the opportunity to observe potential employees before hiring and can contribute to creating a skilled workforce.

The aim of this study is to 'listen' to students' and employers' voices on their perspectives of WBL. The research focused on students reading for a Bachelor's in Commerce with a specialisation in Public Policy. This is a three-year undergraduate degree programme offered at the University of Malta. In their third and final year, students are to undergo 50-hour unpaid Public Policy WBL where they are required to contact any public, private, or not-for-profit organisation of their choice. This simulates the process of applying for a post if a vacancy exists.

Structured interviews were held with Public Policy students to obtain insights and lessons learnt from such experiences. Their providers were also interviewed to elicit their perspectives on Public Policy WBL. This served as a valuable tool to calibrate and refine the nature of these practices. The supervised WBL experiences complemented the findings and themes that emerged.

This chapter is organised as follows: the next section outlines the literature on experiential learning. The context of these WBL offerings is provided. This is followed by the methodology used. The findings are presented and analysed. This chapter concludes with a discussion on the different voices of Public Policy students and employers and their perspectives on WBL.

LITERATURE

Work-based learning is learning that occurs in a work environment, through participation in work practice and process, and is integral to [the students'] education and training. (Atkinson, 2016, p. 2)

Universities have traditionally been responsible for delivering education and training to students, but with the massification of higher education and the increasing demand for work-based learning, employers are potentially taking on some of the role of teaching students. In higher education, employers demand that graduates be more 'work ready'. (Atkinson, 2016, p. 9)

This includes technical skills related to the occupation as practised in a work setting as well as non-technical skills such as critical thinking and problem solving. It can be argued on academic grounds that 'learning by doing' reinforces understanding by contextualising knowledge and promoting the 'application' and 'reflection' stages of Kolb's cycle of learning (Kolb, 1984).

Learning and doing cannot be separated. To use knowledge fully, it must be implemented, performed, and enhanced as part of a synergy (Helyer, 2010, p. 21). The learning experiences offered need 'to align with students' lives and priorities and those of employers; the higher education experience should be a holistic one, embracing varying contexts in which knowledge is produced, gained, built upon, and used ...'. It is acknowledged that learning also occurs outside the classroom and students can see this for themselves when the University facilitates WBL opportunities. This type of learning can be evidenced and accredited through higher education. It offers a different method of learning. However, students cannot just 'experience' the workplace passively. They need to actively engage in order to learn. 'This requires skills to reflect on what they have learned from the experience, knowledge, and build upon this learning' (Helyer, 2011, p. 103). Reflection is a tool of enquiry. Work experience allows students to reflect on and put into practice what they have learned from formal study. The Department of Public Policy at the University of Malta facilitates this experience embedded in the curriculum, leading to experiential learning. Research suggests that WBL experiences 'are considered by academics as one of the best ways to embed experiential learning and enable individuals to develop transferable skills and understanding of the workplace prior to moving into the employment market' (Helyer & Lee, 2014, p. 353). For most employers who offer [work-based work] experiences, 'such schemes have become an integral part of recruiting new graduates' (High Fliers, 2014, p. 35). University WBL schemes can be instrumental in preparing students for future employment. In some sectors, 80% of positions are filled by graduates who had previously undertaken WBL with the organisations (Briggs & Daly, 2012).

Context of the Study

WBL is a requirement of the Public Policy undergraduate course at the University of Malta. WBL is embedded in the Public Policy curriculum. The compulsory 55-hour unpaid WBL is conducted during the third year of the Bachelor of Commerce degree in Public Policy and another major such as Economics or Marketing or Insurance and Risk Management or Banking and Finance or Business and Enterprise Management or Accountancy. The students approach an organisation of their choice, planning, and agreeing to the logistics. Prior to the WBL experience, the employers, University coordinator, and students meet to discuss the objectives of the workplan, establish academic links, and explain the WBL assessment. These conversations contribute to integrating WBL into the degree programme. Some of the objectives included policy and comparative analyses, research work on specific policies and processes and consultation exercises which were complemented by cross team working and skills development. The WBL objectives are further elaborated below.

METHOD

This research focuses on analysing the WBL perspectives of students reading for an undergraduate degree at the University of Malta and the employers who engaged them during 2022. A questionnaire, in-depth interviews and WBL reports were used to obtain data from students and their employers, respectively. These research tools were used to enable an investigation and examination of the interpretation of students and employers' perspectives on WBL during their social interactions (Silverman, 2013). The feedback obtained from the questionnaire, assessment reports, and interviews led to the triangulation of data.

A questionnaire was devised and consisted of 12 questions. It was divided into five sections, namely, (1) basic information about the employer; (2) questions related to the WBL experience; (3) suggestions for improvements to this scheme; (4) its relevance to the degree course; and (5) learning outcomes, tools, and skills acquired. Questionnaires can be administered in a cost-effective and time-efficient manner. This questionnaire was sent to 10 Public Policy students who consented to participate in this research. All data were stored, and password protected to ensure confidentiality. The responses were processed according to the University of Malta's ethical guidelines.

The 10 employers who engaged these undergraduate students were interviewed. An interview guide was devised. It comprised 10 questions which were divided into two sections. This guide consisted of questions related to the WBL experience and suggestions for improvements as well as recommendations to this scheme. The research took place in 2022. These WBL experiences were held in the public sector, ministries, private companies, banks, and EU-related institutions.

The 10 employers were asked to report on the students' performance during their WBL experience. The documents were submitted to the Department of Public Policy, University of Malta for academic assessment. The reports were analysed to triangulate the data obtained from the interviews with each employer and the feedback from the students' questionnaire.

The data were collated. A thematic analysis (Braun & Clarke, 2006) was carried out which identified, rigorously analysed, and elicited themes from the student questionnaires, in-depth interviews with employers and their WBL reports. Eight themes emerged that are discussed in the next section.

Limitations of the Study

The selection of a qualitative over a quantitative method was 'trading depth for breadth' (Patton, 2002, p. 227). The small sample included a cohort of 10 undergraduate students and 10 employers. They carried out WBL in one academic year. This means that the responses are indicative and set constraints of generalisability (McKenzie et al., 1997). Although questionnaires are an economical way of obtaining data from students, they may not capture uncomfortable experiences in writing. Such views can be drawn out through interviews.

Although in-depth interviews provide more detailed information than other data collection methods, the interviews may be prone to bias. In-depth interviews do not allow for generalisations, however, they provide valuable information. Interviews are time-intensive and careful planning to conduct interviews, transcribe them, and analyse the results were factored into the fieldwork time frame. Interviewing employers was conducted on an individual basis, giving them the opportunity to speak freely, openly, and confidentially. Another limitation of this research is that it is specific to Public Policy students in Malta.

RESULTS AND DISCUSSION

Eight themes emerged from the findings. These were: (1) the WBL objectives and deliverables; (2) the experience; (3) relevance; (4) improvements; (5) WBL providers' approach towards the students; (6) missing content in the University course; (7) learning outcomes; and (8) tools and skills.

There were 10 students who completed the questionnaire. These were the full complement of third-year students enrolled in the Bachelor of Commerce specialising in Public Policy. Section 1 focused on basic information about the employer. Table 3.1 lists the organisations and departments where the students carried out their WBL experiences.

Students' WBL took place in 2022. They agreed with the WBL providers when to report for work. This was dependent on the assigned tasks. Some providers preferred that the student reported for work on a weekly basis. Others wanted the students to carry out their work on consecutive days. This occurred when the students had an academic term recess. Flexibility was encouraged.

Students' Voices

Section 2 of the questionnaire included questions related to the objectives and deliverables of WBL, the experience, its relevance, how this scheme can be improved and any missing elements in the undergraduate course.

Table 3.1.   Organisations and Departments.

Organisation	Department
Malta Financial Services Authority (MFSA)	Financial Crime Compliance (FCC)
Environment Resources Authority (ERA)	Compliance and Enforcement Directorate
Gozo Regional Development Authority (GDRA)	Head office
Ministry for Finance and Employment (MFE)	Budget Affairs Division
Ministry for Agriculture, Fisheries and Animal Rights (MAFAR)	Malta Food Agency
Commission on Gender-Based Violence & Domestic Violence	The Commission
Deloitte	Human Resources
Ernst and Young (EY)	EU Consultancy Department
Central Bank of Malta	Corporate Strategic Planning Department
Malta's Permanent Representation to the EU	Political Reporting

Source: Author's compilation (2022).

Objectives and Deliverables

The objectives of WBL consisted of understanding the relevant legislation and frameworks, analysing national and EU policies, statistical data, and trends, developing strategies, conducting research, transcribing interviews, conducting data analysis, and attending high-level meetings to mention a few. 'My work-based learning provider trusted me with proper responsibility' (S2). 'I received helpful feedback from my supervisor on the work I carried out. My supervisor told me that the work I did would be used for internal training purposes' (S1). Students had to communicate and collaborate with employees and clients and contribute to the work team (where applicable). Critical analysis, research, writing, and presentation skills were put into practice. 'I was asked to deliver presentations to case officers on conditions related to development projects imposed by Environmental Resources Authority (ERA)' (S3).

The respondents' deliverables included drawing up reports, giving feedback, transcribing interviews, conducting research, updating standards of practice, and delivering presentations. 'I was asked to summarise the paternity and parental leave policy which broadened my knowledge on the topic' (S6).

WBL Experience

Respondents were asked to rate their experience (1 was the highest and 5 was the lowest). Eighty per cent of the respondents felt that the work-based experience was positive and fruitful. 'I actually felt I was contributing to a project while at the same time building a rapport and building connections with another Department'. On the other hand, 20% felt that the work 'was too technical in nature and delved into natural sciences which I am not accustomed to' (S4). One student felt like 'a second-class intern, with relevant work given to other interns who were engaged with the organization for a longer period' (S3).

Relevance

The respondents were questioned whether WBL was relevant to their academic learning. Ninety per cent of the respondents stated that this experience increased their knowledge and were able to apply the theory learnt during the lectures to life situations. It was encouraging to understand the initial stages of the policy process within a government setting (S1). 'The Authority's responsibility to consult with different stakeholders, ties into the policy formulation of the policy cycle' (S4). On the other hand, one student stated 'that the role and functions of the EU are not mentioned enough during the lectures' (S5). Eighty per cent of the students claimed that during their WBL experience, they were able to put academic skills into practice. 'Some tasks involved statistical research and report writing skills' (S4).

WBL Improvements

The respondents mentioned a few improvements to the scheme. It was suggested that WBL is also offered in the second year of the course. 'If work-based learning experiences were offered a year before, we would have had more time to apply the knowledge gained from our studies' (S8). It was suggested that 50 hours are increased to have more time to carry out tasks and deepen the knowledge and experience on the job. WBL documentation could be simplified. The students suggested that a meeting attended by the student, WBL provider, and the University coordinator is organised to establish clear objectives and create linkages (Baturina & Simakov, 2023; Juliana et al., 2022; Sood et al., 2022).

WBL Provider's Approach

Ninety per cent of the respondents stated that they were welcomed and warmly greeted. 'My supervisor's approach was open and friendly' (S9). Some of the students praised their organisation. 'It was a very heart-warming welcome. I was treated as one of them and was entrusted with confidential documents' (S2). On the other hand, 10% of the respondents stated that the WBL providers were not ready for them. 'I felt like they were not prepared for me' (S5).

Any Missing Content in the Undergraduate Course?

The respondents were questioned on any missing academic course content. It was suggested that the students should be exposed to more problem-solving assignments. One student's WBL experience consisted of having to extract statistical data from voluminous statistics and felt that this would have been beneficial if they were taught how to manage big data at the University. EU legislation and institutions should feature more in the course. It was also suggested that guest speakers should be invited to share their experiences in the political and managerial arenas.

The third section of the questionnaire consisted of questions related to how beneficial WBL was, the learning outcomes, the tools and skills learnt and acquired, and those that still need to be worked on.

The Benefits of WBL

The respondents expressed their views on the benefits of WBL and what was not helpful. 'The exposure to real life situations was valuable' (S6). 'I liked the hands-on experience' (S10). One respondent stated that it was beneficial to be given relevant work and useful to interact with work colleagues. It was stated that the short WBL experience was stressful in order to complete the assigned tasks.

Learning Outcomes

WBL gave the students the opportunity to be exposed to an organisation's mission, structure, culture, and tasks at hand. Besides learning new concepts and roles, it also cultivated connections.

Tools and Skills

Some respondents stated that they were able to apply theory and framework into practice. One student stated that he was pleased to have conducted research on a subject he liked. 'I am glad to have sharpened this tool' (S4). Another student stated that she worked efficiently and produced reports in a timely fashion. Others claimed that they learnt how to work under pressure and meet the deadlines.

WBL 'allowed me to further develop my analytical and research skills' (S2). An emphasis was made on writing skills. 'I feel like my report writing skills have improved. I can submit a succinct policy document without any missing essential information' (S7). Sixty per cent of the respondents claimed that they needed to manage their time more effectively. One student felt she needed to work on her self-confidence. 'I need to work on my self-confidence when delivering a presentation' (S1). S5 claimed that he needed to work on being 'more adaptable, confident and friendly in a new workplace environment'. In conclusion, it was stated that 'I need to adapt to different people's styles, organisations and build a more dynamic range of skills' (S8).

Employers' Voices

The perspectives of employers were sought by conducting in-depth interviews. The interview guide consisted of 10 questions which gave the structure and focus during the interviews. The guide was divided into two sections consisting of questions related to the following seven themes, namely, (1) experience; (2) students' performance; (3) length of WBL; (4) tools and skills; (5) improvements and recommendations; (6) engagement with the University; and (7) a proactive approach.

WBL Experience

All employers stated that students' WBL was a positive experience for their organisation. 'It was a positive experience. This was the first time I had a student. I felt at ease in terms of the tasks he carried out' (E10). E2 stated that 'it is rare that we ask for Public Policy students to carry out work-based learning with us'. His organisation is moving into areas where Public Policy may become an important discipline. It was stated by all the WBL providers that 'the student was a good fit' (E9).

The interviewees stressed that such WBL experiences are beneficial to their organisation. 'We try and link the student's course to what they are studying. This would be beneficial for them. The organisation benefits by junior staff having to mentor students in specific roles' (E3). One employer stated that the student used his academic knowledge to explain the issues at hand and suggest general recommendations. 'We found the student to be intuitive; he grasped the task easily and took it on board professionally. He produced a good piece of work which was beneficial to the organisation' (E5). One of the organisations was working on youth policy and a campaign and found the student's input valuable. 'It was important that we understand a youth's world from a minority's perspective' (E4). Overall, the employers were satisfied. 'We were happy with the deliverables and will take on a Public Policy student next year' (E7).

Students' Performance

The employers were asked if the student was well-equipped academically and professionally to manage the assigned tasks. Overall, the students have a good academic grounding in the subject matter. Sixty per cent of the employers stated that it would have been beneficial if the students had a background knowledge of the organisations before undergoing WBL. This knowledge would have assisted them in their work. One employer stated that the student had a positive approach and the right attitude. Another mentioned that she was happy with the student's research and reporting skills. Surprisingly, an employer stated that although the student collaborated well with the team, he was not tech-savvy as expected of University students. The criteria used for assessing the students' performance include leadership and technical capabilities. These include the ability of the student to critically analyse, write well, communicate effectively, be responsible, ethical and take initiative.

Length of WBL

The employers were questioned on how the WBL scheme could be improved. Seventy per cent of the employers claimed that the length of the WBL should be one hundred hours like other institutions and disciplines that organise such experiences. One organisation clearly stated that

> it depends on what we want to get out of it. If the outcome of work-based learning is for students to learn the basic functions or shadow a work-based learning provider, then 50 hours would be sufficient. A longer work-based experience would enable students to learn the technical jargon and terminology, familiarise themselves with certain processes which would help them be part of a project. (E1)

Tools and Skills

One employer suggested that the students should understand the dynamics between the political and administration pillars. Other important skills included project management and writing skills. E9 emphasised the importance of analytical skills. 'Students may be able to analyse a document but find difficulty in expressing themselves in writing' (E3). E8 stressed the importance of creating connections and being 'visible'. 'Her presence in the room needs to be felt. Sometimes you need to look around the room to know if she is there or not' (E8). On the other hand, one of the employers claimed that the student needed to structure his thoughts and carry out the task in small bites. 'A mind map would have helped him digest and distil the documentation related to the strategy' (E2). E1 stressed the importance of communication skills. 'Sometimes when students try to be assertive, they can come across as either rude or aggressive'. This organisation made a distinction between those who formed part of University student organisations and those who did not belong.

> You can tell the difference between students who have worked in these student bodies and others who have not. They almost market themselves. In our organisation, these students have advanced faster than others in the hierarchy when we employ them. (E8)

WBL Improvements and Recommendations

Eighty per cent of the WBL providers suggested that the University course should invite guest speakers from industry and public institutions to be able to share their experiences with students. The curriculum should encompass themes such as antimony laundering, compliance, and EU affairs. It was stated that students may know what the context and the policies are, but it is important that they are familiar with the key players who run the programmes related to specific policies. From an administrative point of view, one organisation recommended that students should not use the Europass CV template. CV Applications need to be more personal. 'No photo is better than an inappropriate one' (E7). The Human Resource Manager of this organisation continued by stating that 'it would be a hard sell on my part to give a student a chance to work with our organisation' (E7).

Engagement With the University

Employers were asked to rank whether they were in sync and engaged with the University of Malta in the development of courses. Seventy per cent of the employers stated that they have never been involved or asked their feedback on the curriculum. Although larger organisations may be more aware of University courses, many medium enterprises are unfamiliar with programme offerings. Twenty per cent of the organisations stated that they were engaged with the University when the research was required to be conducted by students. Most employers stated that although they wish to engage with the University, they do not know which door to knock on.

Proactive Approach

Suggestions were given on how the Department of Public Policy can be more proactive and engaged in reaching out to employers to better understand the students' skill sets that are required for potential career prospects within organisations. WBL providers should be informed of what the course curriculum is all about. Employers often ask what these students learn. A channel should be opened to communicate with employers. A meeting prior to the WBL experience should be organised to clarify objectives and manage students' expectations. 'Students join organisations with an attitude of not wanting to broaden their level of input' (E6). All organisations agreed that they would be willing to share their work experiences with students. The Department of Public Policy could assist students by creating an employers' list which organises WBL. 'The Department may want to prepare a "yellow" directory of potential employers so that students can tap into it' (E1). One employer suggested that feedback could be obtained from the Department's alumni. 'It may be possible to set up focus groups to obtain feedback from public policy graduates' (E9).

CONCLUSION

The perspectives of students and employers dovetail in several aspects as noted in the findings and discussion of this research. In the main, employers agree that offering WBL to students exposes them to the world of work where they 'gain valuable employability skills while still at university' (Higson, 2012). Students develop the subject-specific, generic, and personal skills that employers value, making them more employable. WBL and study are a means of knowledge acquisition and skill formation (Guile & Lahiff, 2013).

Employers have come 'to realise that they need an adaptable workforce to survive constant change and future challenges' (Helyer & Lee, 2014, p. 366). Due to economic challenges, organisations expect added value from each employee. By spending time in the workplace, students are expected to adapt and be flexible by multi-tasking, emphasising flexibility, adaptability, and the need for cross-cutting skills. 'The importance of gaining work experience at University has become a prerequisite for finding employment upon graduation' (Trought, 2012, p. 7). In fact, a third-year University student remarked that a compulsory module on WBL offerings was a pull factor for selecting Public Policy as one of their two undergraduate majors. WBL is not embedded in the major disciplines, namely, Accountancy, Insurance and Risk Management, Banking and Finance, Marketing, Business and Enterprise Management, and Economics curricula.

Student WBL experiences can be challenging for students as they may have to learn quickly which causes stress. However, such an experience demands effective time management skills in completing the assigned tasks. Problem-solving techniques are put into practice. WBL causes students to meet and interact with staff at all levels, building their self-confidence, verbal communication, and taking initiative.

Most students and employers agreed that WBL would be more useful if the duration was lengthened. The WBL experience begins with the student spending time getting to know the organisation, its set up, structure, legislation, and policies. Employers felt that more time was needed to complete all tasks. 'It would have served well if we could have got more out of the relationship' (E10).

Undoubtedly, employers wish to engage with the University of Malta by offering students WBL, cultivating collaborations, or forming partnerships. Students become graduates and serve as a talent pipeline for organisations. Employers recognise the value of WBL as it gives employers the opportunity to identify potential talent and 'test' students prior to recruiting them. Students bring different perspectives and modern ideas that can help employers keep pace with a rapidly evolving market. They have access to the latest ideas, technology, and research, which may bring in the latest information and methods. WBL may provide the opportunity for employees to supervise or train a student, thereby supporting their own professional development. Future graduates contribute to the creation of a skilled workforce. Successful WBL experiences earn an organisation's reputation as a suitable place to work. Partnerships can contribute to building a culture of learning within an organisation and establish relationships with the University leading to collaboration on research projects or other training opportunities.

Despite the benefits of WBL, there are barriers and constraints in engaging employers in WBL. There may be limited information on the opportunities and processes associated with WBL. WBL providers may not have the time to supervise and guide. To encourage greater employer engagement, the learning experience must be valuable to both the student and the employer. There may be differing expectations about the outcomes of WBL. Administrative demands, potential legal concerns such as industrial relations and intellectual property, and the size of the organisation may be factors that constrain WBL.

The Department of Public Policy at the University of Malta can be more proactive and engaged in reaching out to employers to better understand the skill sets that are required for potential career prospects with organisations. Employers can be invited to form focus groups to obtain feedback on the course curriculum, their requirements and foster collaborations or form partnerships in projects. Employers are unsure 'what is policy analyst's role?'. It is the Department's responsibility to demonstrate what Public Policy students learn and what roles they can assume in the labour market.

It could be argued that in today's highly competitive workplace, WBL is as important as the formal undergraduate course. It acts as a vehicle for providing theory and practice as students develop specialist and generic skill sets. This benefits both the students and employers.

NOTE

A short summary of this article has been included in the *Proceedings of the International Scientific and Professional Conference on Service-Learning Community-engaged University*, May 20, 2022, Split, Croatia (pp. 169–172): https://sea-eu.org/wp-content/uploads/2022/07/service-learning-Proceedings_compressed.pdf.

REFERENCES

Atkinson, G., (2016). *Work-based learning and work-integrated learning: Fostering engagement with employers* (pp. 2–9). Education Resources Information Center (ERIC), NCVER.

Baturina, L., & Simakov, A. (2023). Students' attitude towards e-learning in Russia after pandemic. *Education Science and Management*, 1(1), 1–6.

Braun, V., & Clarke, V. (2006). Using thematic analysis in psychology. *Qualitative Research in Psychology, 2*(2), 7–93.

Briggs, L., & Daly, R. (2012). Why internships and placements are a popular route to employment. *The Independent.* March 21. http://www.independent.co.uk/student/career-planning/why-intern-ships-and-placements-are-a-popular-route-to-employment-7579681.html

Coughlan, S. (2013). Job advantage for graduates with work experience survey. *BBC News,* June 13. http://www.bbc.co.uk/news/education-22875717

Cunningham, W., & Villaseñor, P. (2014). Employer voices, employer demands, and implications for public skills development policy connecting the labor and education sectors. OUP on behalf of the World Bank. https://openknowledge.worldbank.org/handle/10986/27700. License: CC BY-NC-ND 3.0 IGO.

Guile, D., & Lahiff, A. (2013). *Internship: Conventional wisdom, models & recommendations.* Institute of Education, University of London.

Helyer, R. (2010). *The work-based learning student handbook* (p. 21). Palgrave MacMillan.

Helyer, R. (2011). Aligning higher education with the world of work. *Higher Education, Skills, and Work-Based Learning, 1*(2), 103.

Helyer, R., & Lee, D. (2014). The role if work experience in the future employability of higher education graduates. *Higher Education Quarterly, 68*(3), 366.

High Fliers. (2014). *The graduate market in 2014—Annual review of graduate vacancies & starting salaries at Britain's Leading Employer.* http://www.highfliers.co.uk/download/GMReport14.pdf

Higson, H. (2012). *How to improve employability: Aston University's Placements Programme.* The Guardian Higher Education Network. http://www.theguardian.com/higher-education-network/blog/2012/feb/29/aston-university-student-placements

Juliana, A. P., Lemy, D. M., Pramono, R., Djakasaputra, A., & Purwanto, A. (2022). Hotel performance in the digital era: Roles of digital marketing, perceived quality and trust. *Journal of Intelligent Management Decision, 1*(1), 36–45.

Kolb, D. A. (1984). *Experiential learning: Experience as the source of learning and development* (p. 2). Prentice Hall. http://academic.regis.edu/ed205/Kolb.pdf

Mckenzie, G., Powell, J., & Usher, R. (Eds.). (1997). *Understanding social research: Perspectives on methodology and practice.* UK Falmer Press.

Patton, M. (2002). *Qualitative research and evaluation methods* (3rd ed., p. 227). Sage.

Poulter, E., & Smith, B. (2015). A work placement review from an undergraduate's perspective (pp. 43–45). [Online: December 15]. https://www.tandfonline.com/doi/full/10.11120/plan.2006.00160043?scroll=top&needAccess=true

Silverman, D. (2013). *A very short, fairly, interesting, and reasonably cheap book about qualitative research* (2nd ed.). Sage.

Sood, K., Kaur, B., & Grima, S. (2022). Revamping Indian non-life insurance industry with a trusted network: Blockchain technology. In K. Sood, R. K. Dhanaraj, B. Balamurugan, S. Grima, & R. U. Maheshwari (Eds.), *Big Data: A game changer for insurance industry* (pp. 213–228). Emerald Publishing Limited.

Thake, A. (2021). An evaluation of public policy student placements: Outcomes of a Malta-based study. *Higher Education, Skills and Work-Based Learning, 11*(5), 1192–1209. https://doi.org/10.1108/HESWBL-07-2020-0172

Trought, F. (2012). *Brilliant employability skills—How to stand out from the crowd in the graduates' job market* (p. 7). Prentice Hall.

CHAPTER 4

SKILL GAPS IN CASUAL WORKING BY WOMEN IN THE INDIAN HANDICRAFT SECTOR

Reetika Dadheech and Dhiraj Sharma

School of Management Studies, Punjabi University, Patiala, Punjab, India

ABSTRACT

Purpose: *Preserving a country's culture is crucial for its sustainability. Handicraft is a key draw for tourism destinations; it protects any civilisation's indigenous knowledge and culture by managing the historical, economic, and ecological ecosystems and perfectly aligns with sustainable development. It has a significant role in creating employment, especially in rural regions and is an essential contributor to the export economy, mainly in developing nations. The study focuses on the skills required and existing gaps in the handicraft industry, its development and prospects by considering women and their role in preserving and embodying the traditional art of making handicrafts.*

Approach: *A framework has been developed for mapping and analysing the skills required in the handicraft sector using econometric modelling; an enormous number of skills have been crowdsourced from the respondents, and machine learning techniques have been used.*

Findings: *The findings of the study revealed that employment in this area is dependent not only on general or specialised skills but also on complex matrix skills ranging from punctuality to working in unclean and unsafe environments, along with a set of personal qualities, such as taking initiatives and specific skills, for example polishing and colour coding.*

Contemporary Challenges in Social Science Management
Skills Gaps and Shortages in the Labour Market
Contemporary Studies in Economic and Financial Analysis, Volume 112A, 49–82
ISSN: 1569-3759/doi:10.1108/S1569-37592024000112A017

Implications: *The skills mapping technique utilised in this study is applicable globally, particularly for women indulged in casual work in developing nations' handicrafts industry. The sustainable development goals, tourism, and handicrafts are all interconnected. The research includes understanding skills mapping, which provides insights into efficient job matching by incorporating preferences and studying the demand side of casual working by women in the handicraft sector from a skills perspective.*

Keywords: Machine learning; women worker; handicrafts; casual sector; crowdsourcing; sustainable development; skills mapping; sustainable development goals

1. INTRODUCTION

Skill is the most essential factor underpinning economic success. Indeed, in impoverished countries, skills, labour, technology, and wealth are all valuable. Economic growth is generally stifled by a need for more expertise and a willingness to put resources to good use. As a result, one of the challenges in planning these nations' progress is recognising potentially skilled resources and assuring their effective engagement. Advances in the quantity and quality of a nation's skilled labour force have been associated with economic prosperity (Chattopadhyay, 1975). Skill may be used for various problems, such as unemployment, income creation, GDP growth, cultural variations, and geographical factors in industrial advances. Skill upgradation is the utmost requirement in the handicraft sector too. The combination of globalisation and expanding handicraft markets, particularly in Western nations such as the USA, Canada, and Europe, also opens several new prospects. The market for handmade goods is enormous, especially in the high-end sector. Due to the fast growth of the middle class, notably in China and India, it is anticipated that it will increase not just in Western markets but also in all other areas. This pattern shows that the prospects for artisans in emerging nations to produce goods for these markets are growing.

With expanding international travel, an emphasis on interior décor, and a response to the uniformity of mass-produced items, the demand for 'cultural goods' is expected to increase. However, as globalisation increases, handmade items become more and more commodity-like, putting artisan producers under increasing pressure from global manufacturers owing to which handicraft exporters face a significant problem in keeping up with rapidly shifting market trends. Many observers worry that globalisation has made life and employment even more unstable in artisan communities worldwide (Yadav et al., 2023).

The production of handicrafts is now dominated by China, India, and numerous other Asian nations and is expected to remain so for the foreseeable future. Their stance is supported mainly by low-priced, high-volume, western-designed customised products as per the market demand. Many customers and purchasers look for distinctive items. Consumers of all stripes want a wide range of product alternatives, the ability to change a design as needed, and trustworthy partners.

Large direct-import retailers frequently conduct their business in a way that hinders micro and small businesses. Their procurement orders sometimes specify detailed labelling, packaging, packing requirements, high production capacity, and deadlines. New prospects also present new challenges: considering greater price competition and rising customer expectations, handicraft manufacturers must be more proactive in adapting designs to client needs, offer prompt production and delivery, and boost quality and efficiency.

Developing countries are the pioneers in handicrafts; many Micro, Small, and Medium Enterprises (MSME) cater to this segment, incorporating destitute communities. The global handcraft industry is expected to be valued at $1,091.2 billion by 2024, growing at 11 per cent annual pace (World Bank 2020 report submitted to United Nations). Trade in Indian handicrafts has increased by more than 40 per cent in the last five years, with three-fourths of produced products exported. Indian handicrafts are heavily exported in over a hundred countries, with the USA alone accounting for about one-third of India's handicraft exports. The key exporting nations of handicrafts are China, India, Vietnam, South Africa, Mexico, Ghana, Colombia, and Peru. Among all these, China, India, Iran, and Vietnam are the leaders in exports of handicrafts. The major importing nations of handicrafts include the USA, the UK, Spain, France, Hong Kong, the Netherlands, and Japan (Brabar & Krivoshlykova, 2022).

Due to lower capital speculations, the market for handicrafts is increasing, especially in developing nations such as India and China. With the rise of online retail and different e-commerce channels, the availability of handcrafted items has become more convenient for buyers, which, in turn, has pushed the deals of handcrafted merchandise around the globe. Moreover, the move from ethnic to modern designs, coupled with the solid request from workplaces, homes, and lodgings, is expanding the request for handcrafted items. Moreover, handicrafts commerce is also a critical source of colossal trade and potential remote trade; in this way, they are likely to boost the global craft market soon. India is known to be the most significant exporter of handicrafts among all other developing countries. The craftsmanship industry of India has ensured openings to more than 6 million talented specialists, including females who can utilise their abilities to pick up a legitimate business (Yadav et al., 2022h). India highlights being among the most elevated and assessed socially affluent countries globally. The crafted works of India have been cherished and respected worldwide and have left everyone awestruck (Yadav et al., 2022q).

The Indian market size of handicrafts measured US$3,968.0 million in 2022 and is looking forward to reaching US$6,218.4 million by 2028, showing a development rate (CAGR) of 7.7 per cent amid 2023–2028 (IMARC, 2023). The Indian government has been eager in recent years to make significant investments to encourage inclusive growth through the Make in India project, which has generated massive momentum for skill development in India, particularly among the young (Joshin et al., 2015). The National Skill Development Corporation (NSDC) offers private sector projects with skill development money in the form of loans or equity, financial incentives, and tax breaks. The NSDC focuses on 21 high-priority industries, as well as the unorganised sector, for skill development. Handlooms and handicrafts have been added as sub-sectors within these 21 sectors to aid young people in gaining skills (Borghans et al., 2008).

The handicraft sector in India is one of the country's oldest and largest. It is a substantial contributor to the country's GDP and exports. Handicrafts are objects that are manufactured by hand. Many handcrafters embrace natural, even unique, materials, while others use new, non-traditional aspects and may even upcycle manufactured resources. According to handicraft export statistics, our country's indigenous handicraft goods have several chances in local and world-wide markets in this age of globalisation. In this regard, the arts and crafts of Punjab are known worldwide. Punjab is a culturally diverse state in Northern India. Punjabi Arts & Crafts include a wide variety of handworks.

Punjab's creative traditions synthesise several elements that have left their mark historically and geographically. From the time of Alexander, the Great, through the reign of the Great Maharaja Ranjit Singh, and even much later, the cultural milieu of Punjab has undergone tremendous and nuanced incorporations, adaptations, and adoptions of unusual cultural and artistic characteristics (Gale & Kaur, 2002). The peaceful presence of artists from many tribes, races, and beliefs has left an indelible mark on the region's art. Punjab is known for its colourful traditional handicrafts, such as Phulkari (embroidery) is used on winter blankets or dupattas (long scarf taken on the chest by a woman), Durries are used as a bed or floor spread, and Jutti are used as footwear. These were valued in pre-colonial periods because they related to the social construct. As a vital component of the trousseau, durrie encouraged women to spin yarn at home and frequently deliver it to a local weaver to produce a rug.

1.1. Various Handicrafts in Punjab

1.1.1. Durries
Durrie weaving is a favourite pastime among Punjabi women. Durries are cotton fabrics that are used as floor coverings or bedspreads. There are also significant themes like stripes, squares, and checks. Needlework, weaving, and embroidery are known by several names in Punjab because they relate to some of life's most attractive features and are skilfully created by beautiful rural females. Weaving and needlework, on the other hand, are part of rural women's everyday life in Punjab. These weaving and embroidery items are commonly seen at significant events and festivals. Some needlework is Phulkari, which means 'flower work' and Bagh, which means 'garden work'.

1.1.2. Phulkari
Phulkari is a traditional weaving design from Punjab. It has been popular among Punjabi girls since the 15th century. It is the most popular Punjabi art and craft in India and worldwide. The most well-known component of phulkari is floral

embroidery. Phulkari is most typically linked with the embroidery found on dupattas and shawls. The stitching is excellent. When the foundation cloth is completely covered, it is called a Bagh, which means 'flower garden'. The most crucial component is the stitching size. The numerous themes and motifs on a piece of cloth are created using embroidery. Phulkari is often used in bright colours such as red, orange, blue, green, and crimson.

1.1.3. Pidhis

The most comfortable, elegant, and attractively manufactured 'Pidhis of Punjab' are among the remarkable goods of Punjab's handicraft sector. Before the invention of the 'Modular Kitchen', Punjabi women sat on a four-legged, functional stool. In addition to Punjab, several states still employ 'Pidhis' or little stools. The little stools, which are tastefully produced by Punjabi artists, today fulfil various functions and are used for the user's convenience on various occasions.

The 'Pidhis' and other little stools are constructed of wood. To add to the stools' grandeur, the craftspeople use multicoloured threads to give them a regal aspect. Splendidly tiny, short stools are incredibly appealing, exhibiting the state's artistic ability and inventive ideas. The owners choose tastefully adorned seats to add a traditional and regal touch to the gorgeous houses. The beautiful growth of the state's traditional handicraft industry has created a significant market for Traditional Art and Crafts of Punjab both within and outside India.

1.1.4. Wood Works

Traditional Punjabi art and craft include wooden creations. Punjabi carpenters have a long history of making diverse wood products. Punjabi woodwork is well-known all around the world. Visitors to Punjab carry home a keepsake of Punjabi handicrafts. Carpenters in Punjab are skilled woodworkers. They have always been well-liked. Woodwork is a popular source of revenue in Punjabi villages. Carpenters are well-known for their ability to create beautiful beds with mirror-enhanced backrests. Pawas were the carved legs of these beds. Peeras and Persians are typical low chairs made by Punjabi carpenters. This type of furniture may be seen in nearly every village in Punjab.

1.1.5. Basketry

Basketry is a fascinating and distinct aspect of Punjabi Art & Craft. Women do most of the basketry in Punjab's villages. Some of Punjab's basketry designs are well-known worldwide. Basket weaving and other similar crafts have long been a Punjabi heritage. The Indians used basketry mainly for domestic purposes. However, recognising these handcrafted objects as showpieces or attractive items in metropolitan homes has been trendy in recent years.

Basketry is made by cutting grass straws into little straws. These straws make mats, rugs, carpets, curtains, and hand fans. These are 'Pakkhe' hand fans from Peshawari. Kundaldar Pakkhi refers to the smaller fans. These fans are small and delicate, with beautiful curl tips. The Punjab Traditional Art & Crafts Department has made weaving fans a popular tourist attraction in the province (Kaur, 2011). The Indian subcontinent has used the craft for millennia to embellish various significant human goods, such as fabrics for temples and dwellings, cow drapes, wall and floor ornamentation, and many more.

The handicraft industry contributes significantly to job creation and exports. However, drawbacks in the sector include workers' lack of knowledge, lack of exposure to new technologies, lack of market intelligence, and many others (Ranjan & Ranjan, 2007). Handicrafts are critical to sustaining the existing millions of artisans and the growing number of new entrants into craft activity. It employs many artisans in rural and semi-urban areas and generates significant foreign exchange while preserving India's cultural heritage.

2. AIM OF THE STUDY

The study aims to develop a framework for mapping and analysing the skills required in the handicraft sector. Handicraft creation is a prominent labour frame in many developing countries. It accounts for a significant share of the commerce economy in a few nations, particularly emerging countries. World Bank data shows that nearly 78 per cent of women are doing casual work in the manufacturing industry. This industry accounts for about 27.49 per cent of global GDP (World Bank 2020 report submitted to United Nations). The global commitment of women in the field of craftsmanship is 87 per cent. Home-based experts govern this category; independent artisans and subordinate artists use various learned skills and deliver things from within the residential premises. Nonetheless, there is a skill gap in leveraging machines to complete tasks like stitching, sewing, and others (Oridi et al., 2022).

Handmade works are intriguing interpretations of a particular culture or society through local crafts and materials. Fine handmade things' social worth in culture is determined by how they are treated and passed down from generation to generation. In any event, western nations, such as the UK, the USA, and Germany, among others, want craftsmanship things that are modern and personalised. With increased globalisation, commodities are becoming increasingly commoditised, and artisans find their products competing with products from all over the world. It is no longer possible to look at traditional artisan groups and their objects in isolation from global market dynamics and rivalry (Ghosal et al., 2020). As a result, skill development in response to global market demand is critical. Women have traditionally dominated the laborious work and preserving the culture. However, due to several societal and economic constraints, girls need access to opportunities for aptitude enhancement. Females are also dominating the casual handicraft sector in developing nations. However, studies have revealed that girls need opportunities for skill advancement due to several societal and economic constraints (Mohsin, 2022). Globalisation and the rapid increase of invention have resulted in changes in social structures and ways of life and a significant impact on culture, owing to a desire for new items. So, skill mapping as per market demand becomes very much evident.

Trading in imports and exports is the astuteness of a nation. It shows how well a province is paying significance to the country's legacy. Artisans have created lovely, down-to-earth, and socially noteworthy crafts worldwide for centuries. The leading handicraft exporter countries are India, Vietnam, China, Oman, Spain, Indonesia, and many other developing countries. As per Vietnam's Ministry of Culture, Sports and Tourism (2018), the primary categories of handicrafts in Vietnam are ceramic, lacquerware, stone design, pearl inlaying, bamboo, gems, and wooden items. Craftsmanship skills have been passed down from one generation to another. Morocco's calfskin leather treaters illustrate how expressions of the past can be kept in the modern world by keeping them since the 11th century. Tibet's knife makers are famous worldwide. However, they also battle to preserve their trade; with the Chinese government's support, these craftsmen continued in the international market. Pakistani calligraphy, decoration with pen/brush, is famous worldwide. Turkey is famous for its rugs. Unlike numerous other nations, the uniqueness of Turkish mats is their double knots, making them durable and solid (Yadav et al., 2022).

Regarding art and culture, India is considered the highest-appraised culturally wealthy nation. The crafted works in India have been adored and regarded worldwide and have provided opportunities to around 6 million skilled workers, including female craft workers utilising their abilities to earn a livelihood. As per IBEF (2022), India dominates the world's export of handicrafts. The USA and the UK are the biggest importers of Indian handicrafts and cover approximately 50 per cent of the total handicraft imports in the world from India only. Hence, India has been chosen for the study.

The cultural worth of delicate handcrafted objects in a society is determined by how they are treated and passed down from generation to generation. Historically, women have dominated the handicraft industry and played a significant role in preserving this tradition. These labourers encounter awful working conditions, much lower pay, and considerable barriers and exploitation (Devi & Rajamohan, 2022; Jena, 2010). Globalisation and the rapid rise of technology have caused changes in social structures and lifestyles and have significantly impacted culture, resulting in a thirst for new things. So, updating skills and innovations in crafts becomes extremely important. Numerous training courses have been launched by several state organisations, NABARD,[1] KVIC,[2] D.C. (Handicrafts),[3] others give with a stipend and financial help and provide a venue to market the created items (Lab, 2017).

3. RESEARCH QUESTIONS

According to the literature, there is a significant skill gap between market-required abilities and handicraft artists. The results of our study established approaches we

---

[1]National Bank for Agriculture and Rural Development.
[2]Khadi and Village Industries Commission.
[3]Development Commissioner (Handicrafts) is an initiative by the Ministry of Textiles, Government of India, to provide technical/marketing knowledge to Cluster Artisans across India to showcase their talents.

used to assess the extent to which a variety of abilities are related to financial well-being as evidenced by higher pay and significantly better employment opportunities. We mapped out the distribution of abilities and created individual capacities among unorganised female workers in the handicraft sector.

The government's engagement in giving expertise space may be an approach objective. Indeed, in case preparation is given, it is questionable if the different skill development programs will be of high quality or viability. Amid the requirement for a few programs to provide preparation, there is a need for talented trainers, low situation rates, powerless industry interfacing, deficient fund sources, the need to institutionalise VET frameworks, and numerous other issues. For the most part, partners do not work together well (Prasad et al., 2017). Millions of work searchers would still need help finding occupations that coordinated their abilities on the off-chance governments could suitably train them.

Some quality experts lean towards in-work candidates are multilingualism, common and information, and solid individual and social properties. These capacities have been distinguished and archived. It was to be examined to what extent self-reported capabilities influence work promotion outcomes, particularly pay level and consistency. To the finest of our data, ordinarily, one of the essential activities is to tentatively see how capacities inside the artistry fragment, checking non-cognitive capacities and character characteristics, the impact comes almost inside the work grandstand in a making nation.

This chapter's organisation is as follows: the setting for the skilling issue in India is discussed in Section 2. Section 3 burrows significantly into diagram arrangement, test procedures, and respondent socioeconomics. In Section 4, we examine our observational approach, which combines econometric and machine learning methodologies. The outcomes of our thinking are highlighted in Section 5. In Section 6, the task is outlined.

4. LITERATURE REVIEW

In 2022, the handicraft sector was valued at a whopping US$ 704.7 billion. It is evaluated that between the years 2023–2028, it will increase by 11.8 per cent and will reach up to US$ 1,376.12 billion (USAID, 2021) owing to expanded requests for fashion adornments, home accessories, and jewellery as an imperative source of gigantic trades and potential foreign trade. The market is separated into private and commercial segments based on end utilisation. The private segment accounted for the most extensive end-use section since the rising request for fashion, jewellery, and household items. The primary territorial markets for crafted works are North America, Asia Pacific, Europe, Latin America, Africa, and the Central East Asia.

Developing countries are the pioneers in handicrafts; many MSMEs cater to this segment, incorporating destitute communities. The major handicraft imports nations include the USA, the UK, Spain, France, Hong Kong, the Netherlands, and Japan. The key exporting nations of handicrafts are China, India, Vietnam, South Africa, Mexico, Ghana, Colombia, and Peru. The major exporters of handicrafts are China, India, and Vietnam.

According to Sohu (2021), the imagination and ideas of women in the handicraft industry in China are neglected and stereotyped, and feminised works and aesthetics have moreover been marginalised within the market. Articles that included weaving, rug-making, sewing, straightforward carpentry, and woodwork having a feminine touch are either derided or neglected by experts. Additionally, as per Liu (2022), the truth is that feminised works are understood as mediums to touch on a routinised way of life to make them unable to be recognised as highbrow craftsmanship displayed in a built-up exhibition setting. Such unequally male-dominated stylish structures have thus driven craftswomen's low certainty and faltering. Meanwhile, despite being self-doubtful, they have also induced themselves that what the market recognises is not fundamentally significant. It contends that this pushing back and forward in their mindsets has challenged the male-led tasteful conventions and can alter the standard benchmarks in pair with unused inclinations of ceramic societies. A general hopeful picture cannot be drawn as women's creativity and inputs into the creative world have still been marginalised. It appears paradoxical that, in one viewpoint, the journey of female ceramic work.

Handicrafts have the potential to sustain not just millions of seasoned artists but also a rising number of new craft sector entrants. The sector employs many artisans in rural and semi-urban regions, earns significant foreign currency for the country, and safeguards India's cultural heritage. However, the sector needs more organisations and capital. A weak institutional framework includes the inadequate ability to use machines to perform required functions (e.g. cutting machines, dyes, and others), insufficient ability to conduct quality control, insufficient knowledge of material treatment, insufficient ability to conduct market-required designs and development, and insufficient ability to polish stone, marble, wooden, and metal handicrafts (Mohapatra, 2011).

All act as obstacles to its growth. Shafi et al. (2022) emphasised the sustainability of the handicraft trade through innovation and training. They examined the most reasons for artisans not to actualise innovation, and the emerging technologies were due to the need for training and education in this field, the need for budgetary help and need of capital, the need for information about unused innovations, non-attendance of market insights, and need of organisation laws.

Essentially, Bettiol et al. (2022) displayed a study about North Italian SMEs' generation framework based on an organised survey. Discoveries uncovered that the selection of the developing innovations still needs to improve since of a social considering and strategic demeanour. Moreover, Ghazinoory et al. (2020), in their study based on interviews with vital on-screen characters within the Lalejin (Iran) ceramics and earthenware industry, highlighted vital boundaries to the execution of the rising innovations need for training and inquiry in ICTs, low innovation level, need of information, and culture of advancement forms.

From the planning point of view, supportability may be a pivotal action to develop and revitalise the culture and economy of neighbourhood communities. The government, originators, and neighbourhood experts contribute to the restoration and economic improvement of craftsmanship. The Vietnamese government set up a training base within the craftsmanship town, presented an Internet instructing demonstration, and ventured into crafted works' development and learning handle. At the same time, the government deliberately presented cutting-edge progressed innovation and paid consideration to the foundation of industry standards (Tang, 2019).

Japan utilised the 'machining movement' as a social development to revive the farmland, which positively impacted the change of scene and natural quality, the conservation of social legacy, the advancement of well-being and welfare, and biological assurance. Within the handling plan for destitution mitigation, emphasising cooperation and feasible operation can better advance the legacy and advancement of painstaking work (Li, 2020).

As per Boonlaor and Chuenrudeemol (2014), collaborative work is included in contemporary craft practice. In the Bangchaocha community in Thailand, architects coordinated all partners within the community to take part in learning, make an environment and incitement for skilled workers, and aid recover nearby social identities and social resources. Within the Chinese farmland, the key issue within the modern legacy of painstaking work lies in how conventional crafted works from the past can be coordinated into modern society.

Tune (Sage et al., 2020) proposed strategies for securing conventional crafted works from the perspective of social generation, emphasising both legacy and development, stressing both the most profound sense of being and common sense and economy. Zheng and Saho (2019) proposed setting up a checking and assessment framework for the assurance of conventional crafted works within the period of social and inventive businesses and set up a 'cultural early warning' component.

China is expanding the inquiry about and honing exercises on the legacy and improvement of conventional handicraft work nationwide. It is completely appropriate for the methods, techniques, developments, and models of the financial enhancement of the traditional laborious task to address an immediate emergency burdened with challenging and laborious tasks.

Crafts have long been important in Punjab for functional and aesthetic reasons. These products were either manufactured at home by women or by community craftspeople. These goods were highly valued in the pre-colonial centuries because they were related to society's cultural construct. Phulkari (flower embroidery) was designed for winter blankets (shawls) and dupatta,[4] durrie as a bed or floor spread, and Jutti[5] as footwear. Durrie, for example, encouraged women to spin yarn at home and then transport it to a local weaver to make a rug as part of their trousseau (Vatsyayan, 2010). Invasions, historic trade routes, migrations, and events such as India and Pakistan's division in history have all contributed to and created a craft history of vibrant colours and forms mixed with a diverse range of creative abilities and methods (Crill, 1999).

Commercialisation, as we all know, began with the introduction of trade routes. For example, crafting and embroidering for a living has altered the shape of traditional embroidered handicrafts made purely out of love by family and community

---

[4]South Asian females wear a length of cloth in two folds over the chest and thrown back across the shoulders, usually with a salwar kameez.
[5]Jutti (Punjabi) or Punjabi Jutti (Punjabi) is a type of footwear prevalent in Northern India, Pakistan, and neighbouring countries. They are traditionally made of leather.

members. According to Frater (2010), the magnitude of the transition from art to commodities cannot be emphasised. Before the independence of India, many Punjabi crafts were already dropped with the onset of industrialisation, the availability of mill-made bed linens, carpets, toys, and footwear at a lower price as well as their availability in a variety of colours and styles than handcrafted village products. Even artists leave their fields to pursue more lucrative opportunities (Singh, 2005).

The human mind changes as time and civilisation pass. Even the craftspeople evolved with time. Backache, headaches, and eye strain, as well as cervical discomfort, decreased eyesight, needle pricking, frequent cutter cuts on hands, and pain in the knees, neck, and legs, impede artisans from continuing to instruct their family members as a job (Solanki, 2008). Many artists, however, instruct their family members for them to contribute to the family income. Artisans who have received continuous orders for many years have established their enterprises and think Punjabi heritage is in high demand.

There is no talent scarcity in the handicraft industry; this industry contributes significantly to job creation and exports, and all required skills and talents (Tripathy, 2021). Handicraft workers have lower levels of education and less access to current technologies. The business also needs more market intelligence. According to a report on the evaluation of the Ministry of Micro, Small, and Medium Enterprises ongoing Assistance to Training Institutions Scheme (ATIS) by a government-appointed expert JPS Associates (2012), 'workers lack education, exposure to new technology, market information, and other factors all contribute to the industry's disadvantage'.

Calico is considered one of the foremost imperative crafted works due to its impacts on national capital and job creation (particularly within the tourism industry) in Isfahan, Iran. Calico is an industry through which flower material is created utilising woodblock printing. Printing uses specific stamps struck by skilled workers on the clothing surface. This printed clothing has valuable applications, particularly in conventional enhancements, such as window ornaments, bedcovers, and numerous more (Shakerian et al., 2023).

According to a study by Kapur and Mittar (2014), there is a talent shortage in producing leather juta and bags. Handicraft workers must gain technological leather cutting and stitching skills, possess poor design abilities, need help executing designed templates, and must understand market trends. The primary components utilised in the production of Jutti have altered. Previously, only buffalo, cow, sheep, calf, and sambar[6] skins were used; however, raxin, velvet, hardboard, sheet sole (rubber), and leather board are now commonly used because leather is scarce. Taiwan, Drammer, Milar, Marble, Crepe, Soft foam, Ice nappa, Leather nappa, Capsule foam, Wrinkles and Gumeri, foam, and other Raxin varieties are available, with Taiwan being the best.

Tie, dye, and embroidery artisans need to gain the knowledge to operate embroidery machines. However, 10 per cent of India's artisans are lost yearly because their livelihoods are no longer feasible (Khan & Amir, 2013). Skill gaps[7]

---

[6]The sambar (Rusa unicolour) is a large Indian and Southeast Asian deer.
[7]Chindi durries are often called rag rugs, made from recycled fabric scraps.

in Chindi durri and Galicha handicrafts include the inability to ensure waste control and quality control, complete final finishing, insufficient designing talents, and a lack of grasp of market trends and expectations.

This industry is the second most significant source of income after agriculture; it is a vital vehicle of Indian history, culture, and identity; it symbolises a wealth of knowledge and skills gathered through centuries (Mittal, 2015). However, handcrafted items are losing value in modern markets because they cannot compete with machine-made products, have a fragmented value chain and inadequate infrastructure, and are unappealing to younger generations as a source of income. If current trends continue, India will lose far more than a collection of beautiful artefacts.

Due to the unorganised and casual nature of India's handicrafts and carpet industries, the only way to improve employment is to support and promote export industries while empowering artisan clusters. As India promotes and extends its traditional crafts, demand for Indian handicrafts and carpets will rise. As a result of industrial modernity, artisans trained in traditional designs for centuries are confronted with new design interventions to revitalise traditional art by experimenting and treating both traditional and contemporary materials and computer equipment simultaneously (Joshi et al., 2015).

Through various regulations, initiatives, and organisations, such as HCSCC,[8] the government is imparting new design concepts for upskilling artisans, allowing artisans and weavers to engage in the global market and meet national and global demand in terms of design and technology. HCSSC also intends to improve technology access, skill development, and backward and forward networking. Concept creation, product and process design, innovation, and technology consultancy are among the services it provides to the handicrafts and carpet sectors, as well as craftsmen and entrepreneurs (HCSSC, 2018).

The Indian Institute of Technology (IIT) Kanpur makes metal and glass handicrafts, and the Birla Technical Training Institute Pilani, which produces wrought iron, woodwork, and embroidery handicrafts, are two well-known training institutes for specialised crafts. The Development Commissioner (handicrafts) created and implemented workers' welfare schemes and programmes like the Babasaheb Ambedkar Hastshilp Vikas Yojana (AHVY), design and technological upgrade schemes, marketing support and services schemes, handicrafts artisans, and an extensive welfare scheme (Knowledge and News Network, n.d.).

As a result of industrial modernity, artisans who have been schooled in traditional designs for centuries are being challenged with new designs. Design intervention is the practice of creating new products, restyling existing products with changes in shape, size, colour, surface manipulation, function, and utility, exploring new markets and reviving former markets, applying outdated skills to meet new occasions and encounters, and introducing new resources, manners, gears, and skills (Kapur & Mittal, 2018).

The Indian Institute of Carpet Technology in Bhadohi (Uttar Pradesh) also teaches computer and information technology applications and carpet production. In contrast, Kolkata's National Institute of Research on Jute and Allied Fibre

---

[8]Handicrafts & Carpet Sector Skill Council.

Technology teaches jute handicrafts. In Udaipur, students learn how to extract, stand-ardise, and produce natural dyes in powder form. At the Maharana Pratap University of Agriculture and Technology, they learn how to dye and print with natural colours. These upskilling programmes will allow young people to exhibit their abilities and build the skills required to pursue a career in this industry (JPS Associates, 2012).

5. METHODOLOGY

Observation data were collected through a two-stage overview (Circulars 1 and 2) of Punjab-based women utilised within the craft industry. Female workers' statistical information, work histories, their evaluations (individual qualities), and a set of fundamental abilities were accumulated. Questions were asked to the respondents, relating to occupational and statistical information. This followed a self-assessment on the utilised crowdsourced capacities.

We used the Snowball sampling method with semi-structured questionnaires to collect data from the Ludhiana district in Punjab for two rounds over three months. Decentralised home-based businesses dominate the handicraft indus-try. Women dominate the handicraft industry in Ludhiana, where they engage in various occupations like carpet weaving.[9] A local non-governmental organisation assisted us in reaching out to the female workers. These women connected us to other female workers, 500 female craftsmen. A pre-tested questionnaire was used after asking for the consent of the participants. The survey questions were asked in Punjabi, but if the respondent was a migrant or unfamiliar with the local lan-guage, then the questions were translated into Hindi. A total of 250 participants among 500 were covered for each round.

5.1. Survey Design

The main survey questions in Round 1 focused on demographic characteristics (age, gender, education, parents' education, social group, migration, family size, and so on), economic status (household assets, savings, and expenditure), employment his-tory (wage, experience, primary occupation, and others), and work seeking behaviour (including job search and training). Given the value of essential skills in a volatile eco-nomic climate (Murnane & Levy, 1996; Peter-Cookey & Janyam, 2017), respondents were also asked to rank 11 fundamental abilities (reading/writing/speaking Hindi, English, and Punjabi; elementary math; Internet use; and mobile phone use) and 11 character qualities (whether they consider themselves confident, driven, organised, friendly, garrulous, make modern companions effortlessly, come up with modern thoughts, handle stretch well, believe others effectively, and lean towards schedule work). Inquiries about individual characteristics and work showcase results propelled our choice of highlights (Krueger, 2009, chapter 4). Respondents were relegated a 1 in case they felt 'greatly comfortable', self-evaluating their centre capacities if they felt 'not at all comfortable', and a 0.5 on the off-chance that they felt 'to some degree

---

[9]Zari craftsmen, Phulkari, basket making, and many others. Zari (or jari) is a fine gold or silver thread used in traditional attire.

comfortable'. A 1 was given to respondents in case they distinguished with a particular identity highlight, and in case they did not, and a 0.5 in case they were vague or undecided. In conclusion, respondents were asked to supply numerous characteristics and points of interest that they thought would assist them in the work showcase.

In Round 1, members were asked to rate themselves regularly on the 100 characteristics conjured the foremost. Perusing and composing Punjabi and Hindi were included in the list of 100 capacities in Circular 2. The complete list of gifts is shown in Table 4.1. The capacity to communicate in Punjabi may be related to more choices for local people to discover low-paying work. In expansion, respondents' age, sex, instruction, parental instruction, social bunch, relocation, family measure, work status, encounter, essential action, compensation, and preparation were addressed.

6. DATA ANALYSIS

6.1. Respondent Characteristics

Concerning the dissemination of occupations, Fig. 4.1 depicts respondent characteristics from Circular 1 information. Fig. 4.2 depicts the strategies used by representatives to discover their later business.

Parts A and B independently incorporate outline information on the capacities and factors used within the experimental examination. Female employees are active in 27 per cent of Phulkari work and 12 per cent of Jutti manufacturing. Females' work in Jutti making could have been better, such as pasting, giving finishing to the final product, and some other less valued activities. Females were not observed undertaking designing or cutting work in Jutti manufacturing.

Durri-making was done by 22 per cent of females. Women are also indulged in wooden engraving though their percentage in it is meagre; only 8 per cent of females are into wooden handicrafts, and they mainly use inlay work for making wooden products. Twenty-one per cent of females have been put in another work

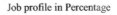

Job profile in Percentage

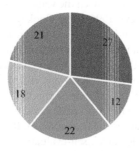

■ Phulkari workers   ■ Jutti making   ■ Durri or carpet making   ■ Wood engraving   ■ Others

Fig. 4.1. Percentage of Women Handicraft Workers Indulged in Various Handicrafts Making. *Source*: Authors' own compilation.

Medium of getting the work in percentage

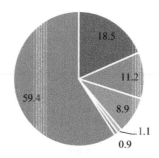

- Enquiring at job locations
- Self employed
- Job posters

- Labour contractors
- Online portals
- Refferals through friends and relatives

Fig. 4.2.   Percentage of Various Mediums Used by Handicraft Women Workers to
Successfully Obtain the Job. *Source*: Authors' own compilation.

category where there is no fixed work, and it is used in multiple handicrafts like
embroidery, basket-making finishing, dying, removing threads, and other knitting
and weaving work.

Almost two-thirds of the employment was secured through referrals from family
or friends who knew the business. This is an essential method in which casual work
done by women supplement official systems such as employment websites. Request
to work temporary workers at venture destinations have also been created as a fundamental hunt instrument. Reliance on web work entries is exceedingly low despite
accessibility to shrewd phones and direct self-rated aptitudes. This suggests that recognisable and physical–social systems prevail within the work search environment.

Almost two-thirds of the employment was secured through referrals from
family or friends who knew the business. Request to work temporary workers at
venture destinations have also been created as a fundamental hunt instrument.
Reliance on web work entries is exceedingly low despite accessibility to shrewd
phones and direct self-rated aptitudes. This suggests that recognisable and physical social systems prevail within the work search environment.

6.2. Empirical Strategy

Our exploratory approaches were facilitated by two fundamental goals: (a) making a layout of aptitudes among casual pros; and (b) finding which capacities
are related to better work comes about. In our consideration, we utilise a combination of Classic Econometric and Machine Learning procedures. Machine
learning approaches are significantly beneficial in applications requiring units of
charmed with many characteristics, such as self-assessments on a wide range of
competencies in Circular 2 data. Unsupervised learning procedures in machine
learning, such as k-means clustering and embeddings charts, shed light on the

basic structure in high-dimensional skill spaces, whereas coordinated learning
methodologies, such as insufficient backslide (e.g. Tie), can be utilised to select
properties that best anticipate.

6.3. Mapping the Skills Space

During mapping abilities, we are inquisitive about self-assessed aptitudes, the
co-occurrence, and the distributional pecking order of abilities.

6.3.1. k-Means Clustering

Utilising the regular k-means approach, we cluster the list of abilities from Circular 2
information. As the title infers, this strategy partitions the information into
k bunches centred on k central focuses. In our ponder, each of the examined abilities, s, is coupled with a vector of self-assessments, signified by the symbol $x(s)$.
Iteratively, the activity is rehashed, starting with developing k arbitrary cluster
centres. The symbol signifies the cluster middle where abilities are relegated $\mu(s)$.

Step 1: Clustering:

The computation's goal is to find k clusters by comparing cluster centres where
the aggregate of the squares of the interval expels between each capacity course
(line) $x(s)$, and the related centres $\mu(s)$ is as little as conceivable. It is related to
optimisation work.

Step 2: Updating cluster centres:

In the taking after stage, clusters k is upgraded by calculating the mean of
vectors in every Ck (clusters). Steps 1 and 2 are rehashed until joining or a fore-
ordained number of repetitions are accomplished. The overall number of clusters is essential to the k-means clustering calculation. This sum can be evaluated
utilising the 'gap statistic', as displayed. To calculate the ideal cluster number, we
utilised the clustering function kmeans() using the R package factoextra.

6.4. Determinants of Wages and Regular Work

We are interested in two labour market outcomes: the respondent's weekly income
and whether he or she receives a monthly payment consistently. The first is a
labour market performance evaluation industry standard. We are also concerned
about daily or weekly job stability because informal work carried out by women
is cyclical. As a substitute for job stability, we use regular monthly salary receipts.

6.4.1. Econometric Modelling

On Circular 1 information, we run different adaptations of the Mincerian wage
condition (Mincer, 1974) to explore the relationship between essential aptitudes
and compensation:

$$\log(\text{wages}) = \alpha_w + \beta_{edu}\text{Edu} + \beta_{exp}\text{Exp} + \beta_{exp2}\text{Exp}^2 + \sum_j \beta_{X_j}X_j$$
$$+ \sum_k \beta_{Sk}S_k + \beta_{imr}\text{IMR} + \varepsilon \tag{1}$$

The weekly incomes provided by respondents are referred to as salaries. Similarly, using Round 1 data, the following result equation has been used to assess the relationship between basic abilities and regular monthly wages:

$$\text{logit}(\text{Reg}) = \alpha + \beta_{\text{edu}}\text{Edu} + \beta_{\text{exp}}\text{Exp} + \beta_{\text{exp2}}\text{Exp}^2 + \sum_j \beta_{X_j} X_j$$
$$+ \sum_k \beta_{Sk} S_k + \beta_{\text{imr}}\text{IMR} + \varepsilon \tag{2}$$

Reg is a variable that relates to customary month-to-month income. Within the going before relapse conditions, Edu refers to the number of a long time of education, and Exp refers to the number of a long time of involvement. X_j could be a collection of controls that incorporates socially recognisable proof (sexual orientation, religion, and caste bunch) and history preparations. S_k means the respondent's self-evaluation of vital capacities and individual qualities ($k = 1$). Heckman's corrective term for minimising potential selection bias caused by improper outcome data from presently unemployed respondents is IMR (Heckman, 1979). Specifically, IMR $= \varphi$ (Emp d)/Φ (Emp d) is the inverse Mills ratio estimated from the selection equation:

$$\text{logit}(\text{Emp}) = \alpha_{\text{emp}} + \sum_m \beta_{Zm} Z \tag{3}$$

where Emp is an indicator variable for respondents currently employed, and Z_m ($m = 1, ..., M$) is a set of controls in the selection equation. We control for the mother's education, the father's education, the dependent ratio in the household, the asset index of the household, marital status, migrant status, whether schooling was in a Punjabi medium school and slum fixed effects. We also control for several years of experience, gender, caste, and religious community. Lastly, we control the proprietorship of a savvy phone and ownership of a bank account, demonstrating an essential level of money-related incorporation. In a few models, we, too, incorporate self-assessment of individual qualities in controls for the determination condition.

Each demonstration is expected to include four variants:

1. No checks for essential aptitudes or identity characteristics within the result condition or determination condition.
2. Checks for fundamental aptitudes within the result equation.
3. Checks for essential abilities within the result condition and controls for individual qualities within the determination condition.
4. Checks for fundamental abilities and individual qualities within the result condition and checks for individual qualities within the determination condition.

6.4.2. LASSO Regression
Although the affiliation between essential aptitudes and work showcase results is assessed utilising Mincerian wage condition determination, the number of

crowdsourced abilities for which respondents give self-assessment in Circular 2 is significantly more considerable at 106. In such cases, standard straight relapse models regularly create unsteady gauges with low exactness after issues counting multicollinearity. Inadequate relapse is one of the foremost well-known procedures within the machine learning writing fitting for such datasets, with the foremost well-known being the Tether method (Tibshirani, 1996).

Tether demonstrates determination and parameter estimation at the same time by including a punishment component to the standard direct relapse objective work.

By penalising large parameter estimate values, the additional term inhibits model overfitting. By minimising the objective function given $i = [1, 2, ..., N]$ observations of the dependent variable y_i and a collection of covariables $x_{i1}, x_{i2}, ..., x_{iK}$, the LASSO predicts parameter values for $\beta_1, \beta_2, ..., \beta_K$ by minimising the following objective function:

$$Q(\beta_1, \beta_2, ..., \beta_K) = {}^N\sum_{i=1}(y_i {}^K\sum_{k=1} x_{ik}\beta_k)^2 + \lambda {}^K\sum_{k=1}|\beta_k| \qquad (4)$$

The first term is the traditional linear regression scale parameter, while the second represents the overfitting cost. This cost term decreases a portion of the parametric values k to 0, thereby making it suitable for the issue of selecting the covariate given an extensive collection of possible covariates. The cost term's weight may be read as follows: when $\lambda = 0$, the predicted values are comparable to linear regression, when $\lambda = \infty$ the parameter estimates are equal to 0. In this case, the value of using a cross-validation approach is determined by its ability to reduce the remaining sum to the square's expansion by the total number of true coefficient values. Although LASSO was initially conceived for direct relapse, this demonstration has been extended to direct relapse models like calculated relapse. Given the semi-basis, routine centrality tests and certainty interims do not require Rope parameter estimations.

LASSO strategy has been utilised to analyse the affiliation between aptitudes and work advertise outcomes from the Circular 2 information. As some time recently, our results of intrigued are (1) log of the week-after-week compensation, log(wages); and (2) whether the respondent got standard month-to-month compensation, Emp. For both results, we consider three determinations. To begin with pattern determination, our covariates incorporate all aptitudes and statistic characteristics. Within the moment detail, we include the Heckman redress term, IMR, to the list of covariates where IMR is assessed as depicted in (4). Within the last determination, the IMR term itself is gotten by a LASSO detail of the Heckman condition that incorporates self-assessments of all abilities. We execute LASSO relapses in R utilising the bundle glmnet.[10]

---

[10]The command cv.glmnet has been used to predict $\hat{\lambda}$ via cross-validation and fit the derived LASSO model with the command glmnet.

7. RESULTS

We display two sets of outcomes in this chapter. The primary set is to outline the aptitudes space of respondents in our test. These give experiences into the conveyance of aptitudes inside the women's populace. We moreover show a mapping of how distinctive aptitudes are related to one another in terms of aptitude co-occurrence and aptitude pecking order. The moment set explains skill-based determinants of work results in specific compensation and standard month-to-month pay rates. This set focuses on sexual orientation aberrations as well as the relative benefits of skilling versus tutoring within the unorganised work market.

7.1. Skill Space Mapping

7.1.1. Basic Skill and Personality Trait Distribution

Fig. 4.3 portrays the mean appraisals of Circular 1 participants on fundamental capacities and individual qualities. Female answers were generally negative about each critical talent. It was found that female Internet usage was roughly 0.20. This is significantly less, and in today's era, the skill of using the Internet is necessary. As per Sharma (2017), the Internet has tremendously influenced how we interact and conduct business today. Because of the Internet, electronic commerce has grown, allowing businesses to communicate more effectively with their consumers and other enterprises within and beyond their sector. It is a global phenomenon that has rendered time and place irrelevant in many interactions.

The average grade for speaking Hindi is approximately 0.38, while the rating for reading and writing is around 0.18 and 0.2, respectively. Young women workers can understand basic English, but their speaking and writing could have been better. The highest mean evaluation grade of all necessary talents is for mobile phone use, which correlates to India's recent growth in mobile phone ownership. The affiliation chart shows that dialect gifts are associated with using mobile/cell phones and the web, as anticipated.

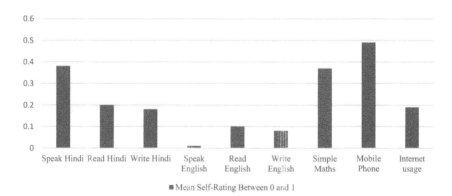

Fig. 4.3. Mean of Self-marked Ratings of Round 1 Responders on a Set of Basic Skills. *Source*: Authors' own compilation.

While respondents evaluated themselves poorly in vital abilities, most rated themselves relatively highly in personality traits, resulting in mean values of 0.8 or above in most categories (see Fig. 4.4). The attributes 'easy trusting' and 'organised' violate this criterion. The average female scores much lower in both regions. When respondents select a 'high exertion, more pay work' over a 'low exertion, less pay one', do they review themselves lower than 0.8 on regular?

The highest mean evaluation grade of all necessary talents is for mobile phone use, which correlates to India's recent growth in mobile phone ownership. The affiliation chart shows that dialect gifts are associated with using mobile/cell phones and the web, as anticipated.

7.1.2. Skill Distribution Through Crowdsourcing

We delivered a list of abilities and properties that respondents accepted were fundamental for the victory of Round 1. Respondents gave us an exhaustive scientific classification of the capacities, information, and characteristics that impacted their proficient victory. In and of itself, the sheer number of abilities stirred could be tremendous social progress.

The skills are essential skills and soft skills. Basic skills are the ability to write and speak languages, cash handling, document handling, self-defense, knowledge of colours, knowledge of mobile usage, following instructions, and others.

Several of these statements have been copied directly here such as some personal characteristics: 'stress-free, grinning face, making efforts', '(creating a reasonable) self-introduction, ability to express complex topics clearly, good behaviour with superiors, physical strength, time management, punctuality, teamwork, confidence, helpful, and many more'. The moment is a set of talents relating to specific work situations: 'ability to work in soiled settings, work alone at home, and others'.

Finally, our request was met with capacities such as sewing, colour schemes, planning capacity, and many others. We will allude to these critical inputs as

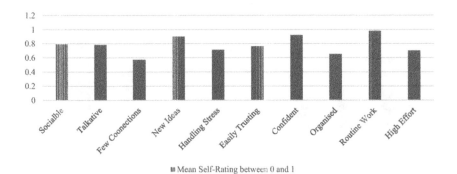

Fig. 4.4.   Mean of Self-marked Ratings of Round 1 Responders on a Set of Personality Attributes. *Source*: Authors' own compilation.

abilities, categorising them as 'linguistic', 'task', 'specialised', 'personal', and 'social'.

Talking, composing, and tuning abilities in Hindi, Punjabi, and broad 'task' capacities such as essential arithmetic and estimation are regularly the centre of standard instruction and have a long history of evaluation and assessment. Job-related assignment abilities are created through preparation and on-the-job involvement.

Individual qualities such as tidiness, promptness, genuineness, stretch adminis-tration, dressing sense, and 'social' capacities such as caring, invitingness, and the capacity to adjust one's temperament in a troublesome interaction are connected to a lifetime of familial instruction. This categorisation is critical for clarification since it recognises the tremendous extent of veritable characteristics that indi-viduals bring to long-term, fruitful work.

The bulk of our moment circular of overviews, in which respondents judged themselves on each capacity, went to the foremost frequently experienced these crowdsourced gifts. Table 4.1 delineates the respondent's cruel self-evaluation in Round 2 and the crowdsourced capacities. The abilities in each expertise region are shown in the expanding arrangement of self-assessment.

7.1.3. Crowdsourced Skills Co-occurrence

Utilising unsupervised learning techniques, ready to understand the conveyance, co-occurrence, and pecking order of abilities within the casual work showcase utilising our expansive dataset of nitty-gritty self-assessment information. Our primary strategy is k-means clustering (see Sections 7.1.1 and 7.1.2 for points of interest in the calculation). Table 4.2 presents the best seven clusters of the calculation in the climbing arrangement of the number of gifts in each cluster. Watching the aptitudes coexist interior a cluster is an appealing procedure for cluster investigation, mainly when dialect, errand, individual, and social capaci-ties are gathered nearby more particular calling abilities.

Clustering, too, gives a tremendous rational soundness check on the consist-ency and precision of respondent answers. Consider the aptitudes collocated inside Cluster 1 that includes pressing, administration, client benefit, deals, and imagination; Cluster 2 work in cutting cloth/leather and hand aptitudes; and Cluster 3 focuses on web utilisation, Punjabi tuning, Punjabi perusing, Punjabi composing, Hindi perusing, Hindi composing, and computer knowl-edge (Baturina & Simakov, 2023; Juliana et al., 2022; Sood et al., 2022; Zhang et al., 2021).

The remaining bunches are less particular, but they contain intriguing thoughts. Clusters 1 and 5 show up to be related to deals positions. They incorpo-rate capacities such as 'quality verification', 'inventory', 'packaging', 'customer service', and 'sales'. These clusters incorporate an assortment of imperative essential aptitudes, such as 'money administration', 'simple math', 'mobile phone utilisation', 'geographic awareness', and 'price monitoring'. These clusters, too, incorporate vital social aptitudes like 'administration', 'administering', and 'collaboration', as well as individual characteristics like 'dressing sense' and 'imagination'.

Table 4.1. The Average Self-evaluations of Skills from Round 2 Are Disclosed. Many Participants are Self-assured in Their 'Soft' Skills.

Skill Category	Skill Description	F	M	F − M
Basic Skills	Hindi writing	0.063	0.063	0.00
	Hindi reading	0.070	0.070	0.000
	Punjabi speaking	0.130	0.169	−0.039 ***
	Driving	0.013	0.016	−0.003 ***
	Punjabi reading	0.223	0.342	−0.119 ***
	Punjabi writing	0.242	0.351	−0.109 ***
	Internet usage	0.187	0.345	−0.158 ***
	Hindi speaking	0.296	0.311	−0.015 ***
	Hindi listening	0.346	0.463	−0.117 ***
	General knowledge	0.247	0.365	−0.118 ***
	Measurement	0.430	0.502	−0.072 ***
	Simple math	0.367	0.467	−0.100 ***
	Geographic knowledge	0.244	0.379	−0.135 ***
	Tracking prices	0.170	0.271	−0.101 ***
	Handling cash	0.178	0.201	−0.023 ***
	Mobile phone usage	0.669	0.767	−0.098 ***
	Colour knowledge	0.761	0.816	−0.055 ***
	Following instructions	0.798	0.801	−0.003
	Document handling	0.817	0.908	−0.0891***
	Self-defense	0.127	0.142	−0.015 ***
	Safety awareness	0.134	0.167	−0.033
Soft Skills	Management	0.189	0.251	−0.062 **
	Creativity	0.486	0.501	−0.015 ***
	Supervising	0.349	0.431	−0.082 ***
	Teamwork	0.595	0.637	−0.142 ***
	Confidence	0.657	0.579	0.042
	Adjusting attitude	0.862	0.862	0.000
	Active personality	0.761	0.799	−0.038 *
	Strong and loud voice	0.791	0.805	−0.014
	Punctuality	0.874	0.880	−0.006 ***
	Neatness	0.601	0.623	−0.022
	Time management	0.812	0.836	−0.024
	Politeness	0.823	0.858	−0.035 **
	Physical health	0.843	0.855	−0.012
	Smiling body language	0.847	0.855	−0.008
	Physical strength	0.753	0.766	−0.013
	Stress management	0.548	0.572	−0.024 **
	Relationship with owners	0.861	0.864	−0.003
	Hard work	0.943	0.878	−0.065 ***
	Helpful	0.773	0.769	0.004

Source: Authors' own compilation.

Table 4.2. The *k*-means Algorithm Generated Seven Optimal Clusters, Increasing in Ascending Order the Number of Skills Required.

Cluster 1	Packing, management, customer service, sales, and creativity
Cluster 2	Cutting cloth/leather and hand skills
Cluster 3	Internet usage, Punjabi listening, Punjabi reading, Punjabi writing, Hindi reading, Hindi writing, computer handling, English reading, speaking, and writing
Cluster 4	Measurement, general knowledge, working with tools, working in unclean areas, and knowledge of job
Cluster 5	Handling cash, simple math, mobile phone usage, geographic knowledge, tracking prices, colour knowledge, quality verification, inventory, supervising, and teamwork
Cluster 6	Designing skills, stitching, embroidery, working with flowers, working with cloth, working with wood, handling small tools, cutting, and delivery
Cluster 7	Safety awareness, working indoors, following instructions, self-defense, caring, smiling body language, communication, confidence, friendliness, helpful, neatness, patience, physical health, physical strength, hard work, positive attitude, punctuality, politeness, honesty, respectful, discipline, adjusting attitude, bold attitude, active personality, relationship with people, relationship with owners, speed of work, interest in work, stress management, time management, and work ethic

Source: Authors' own compilation.

Cluster 7 combines the bulk of individual and social abilities, most likely since respondents are less taught when rating themselves since they are related to cherished personalities, and the more significant part of respondents rate themselves emphatically. Clusters 4 and 6 include knowledge-related phonetic capacities and specialised information such as plan and apparatus utilisation.

7.2. Wage and Regular Work Determinants

7.2.1. Round 1: Fundamental Abilities and Personality Traits

Table 4.3 shows the Mincerian wage estimation result condition depicted in (2) from distinctive determinations utilising Circular 1 overview information. Table 4.4 shows the estimation discoveries for whether the respondent gets a customary monthly emolument, compared to (3). Table 4.4 shows the chance proportions of the coefficient gauges for ease of comprehension. Both sets join IMR terms to begin with and organise Heckman alteration condition.

The primary column in both columns signifies the determination in which neither one or the other of the choice conditions nor the result condition incorporates any controls for principal abilities and identity characteristics. The result condition determinations within the final three columns incorporate crucial aptitudes. The determination condition within the moment column does not include any identity characteristics. The third column includes identity characteristics in the determination condition determination. Finally, within the fourth column, identity characteristics are included in both choice and result conditions.

Identity characteristics are not considered within the determination condition for the moment column. The third column of the determination condition

Table 4.3. Results of the Equation Corresponding to (2) to the Mincerian Wage Equation Along With Heckman Adjustment from Various Specifications Using Round 1 Survey Data.

	Dependent Variable: Log of Weekly Wages			
Years of education	0.024*** (0.004)	0.008 (0.007)	0.007 (0.005)	0.006 (0.007)
Years of experience	0.118*** (0.007)	0.123*** (0.008)	0.130** (0.005)	0.131**(0.007)
(Years of experience)^2	0.00024*** (0.001)	1.0006*** (0.001)	−0.0004** (0.001)	0.0006*** (0.001)
Hindu	−0.068* (0.052)	0.003 (0.045)	0.007 (0.045)	0.038 (0.045)
Received some training	−0.032 (0.077)	0.136 (0.123)	0.181 (0.161)	0.107 (0.132)
Length of training	0.0001 (0.001)	−0.035 (0.051)	0.0.28 (0.041)	0.006 (0.041)
Hindi speaking		−0.067 (0.036)	−0.016 (0.081)	0.006 (0.072)
English speaking		0.00001 (0.0002)	0.00001 (0.0003)	0.00001 (0.0003)
Internet usage		0.066 (0.037)	1.505. (0.373)	0.089* (0.6)
Prefers routine work			0.071 (0.037)	0.707 (0.047)
Inverse Mills ratio	6.656 (8.400)	0.258 (0.260)	0.118* (3.057)	0.144** (0.060)
Constant	1.552 (0.690)	0.7.583*** (0.113)	−0.102 (0.057)	0.067 (0.037)
Outcome equation: Basic skills Controls	No	Yes	Yes	Yes
Outcome equation: Personality Trait Controls	No	No	No	Yes
Outcome equation: Other Demographic Controls	Yes	Yes	Yes	Yes
Selection equation: Personality Trait Controls	No	No	Yes	Yes
Observations	250	250	250	250
R^2	0.274	0.335	0.335	0.362
Adjusted R^2	0.261	0.313	0.313	0.331

Source: Authors' own compilation.
Note: $p < 0.1$; *$p < 0.05$; **$p < 0.01$; ***$p < 0.001$.

contains personality characteristics. Finally, within the fourth column, identity qualities are calculated into the determination and result conditions. The estimations within to begin with a column of Table 4.3 compared to the anticipated lines for the Mincerian wage condition: The week-after-week wage log increments in the coordinate extent to the number of a long time of instruction and involvement. The tiny negative coefficient on the square of involvement illustrates that involvement includes a concave influence. Female labourers begin with lower compensation and encounter taking after lower rates of pay increment. Each of these gauges is critical with 95 per cent certainty interim.

When vital skills are considered, the influence of schooling is diminished, as seen by the estimates in the final three columns. 'Internet usage' is the most potent

Table 4.4. The Estimate Determining Whether the Participant Receives Monthly wages with Heckman Correction Indent (3).

	Dependent Variable: Whether Regular Monthly Wage			
	(1)	(2)	(3)	(4)
Years of education	1.111*** (0.019)	1.014* (0.022)	1.047* (0.023)	1.061* (0.024)
Years of experience	0.839*** (0.026)	0.769*** (0.019)	0.866*** (0.028)	0.861*** (0.029)
(Years of experience)^2	1.002*** (0.011)	1.001*** (0.001)	1.003*** (0.001)	1.003*** (0.001)
Whether female	0.918 (0.236)	1.043 (0.431)	1.105 (0.460)	1.122 (0.485)
(Years of experience) (Whether female)	1.066*** (0.021)	1.063*** (0.011)	1.071*** (0.021)	1.076*** (0.022)
SC	1.201 (0.234)	1.247 (0.262)	1.288 (0.278)	1.213 (0.273)
ST	2.750 (1.604)	2.352 (1.461)	2.640 (1.673)	2.237 (1.419)
Hindu	0.469* (0.128)	0.467* (0.135)	0.569* (0.145)	0.593* (0.155)
Received some training	0.701 (0.210)	0.733 (0.331)	0.944 (0.361)	0.926 (0.364)
Length of training	0.889 (0.001)	0.987 (0.001)	0.998 (0.001)	0.998 (0.001)
Hindi speaking		0.500. (0.122)	0.562* (0.132)	0.537* (0.122)
English speaking		2.214** (0.561)	2.247** (0.476)	2.138* (0.535)
Internet usage		1.401 (0.362)	1.304 (0.273)	1.442* (0.326)
Prefers routine work				3.430*** (0.546)
Inverse Mills ratio	5.866 (8.500)	7.215 (11.681)	3.313 (2.039)	2.552 (1.769)
Constant	1.572 (0.590)	1.321 (0.617)	1.234 (0.871)	0.423 (0.456)
Outcome equation: Basic skills controls	No	Yes	Yes	Yes
Outcome equation: Personality trait Controls	No	No	No	Yes
Outcome equation: Other demographic Controls	Yes	Yes	Yes	Yes
Selection equation: Personality trait Controls	No	No	Yes	Yes
Observations	250	250	250	250
Log likelihood	−266.862	−348.137	−258.196	−248.085

Source: Authors' own compilation.
This table displays the likelihood of the coefficient estimates for the interpretation using round 1 data.
Note: $p < 0.1$; *$p < 0.05$; **$p < 0.01$; ***$p < 0.001$.

and significant fundamental ability connected with higher log pay. The following is the influence of 'Punjabi speaking'. Even when the signal is weak, 'Hindi speaking' is associated with higher compensation. Higher log profits have also been connected to personality attributes, including 'organisation', 'sociability', and 'trustworthiness'. Depending on the configuration, R^2 values range from 28 to 36 per cent. The fourth specification has the greatest adjusted R^2 value.

Table 4.4's first column estimations provide fascinating results: the chance of earning a stable monthly income drops with education and increases with age. In this case, an encounter is generally an intermediary for age and encompasses a positive relationship with compensation. Furthermore, it suggests that as female respondents' involvement develops, so do their chances of getting a steady paycheck. The cube of experience is positively related to regular earnings, suggesting that the odds of obtaining regular income rise with a certain number of years of job experience. The word 'Punjabi speaking' has a broad and lucrative connection (odds of regular salaries indicate an insignificant link with English speaking).

One of the most fundamental problems for casual work opted by women is a need for more access to larger opportunity structures, financial, technical, social, and political resources (Dadheech & Sharma, 2023). The fundamental reason for this lack of knowledge about the existing markets is linguistic problems (especially the English language for dealing with online national and international customers), which commonly impede craftworkers from conducting sustainable entrepreneurial firms (Paine, 1990).

'Punjabi Speaking' includes a sizeable and beneficial fan base. In differentiation, 'Hindi speaking' is related to a decreased chance of long-term work. Although having a web network boosts the chances of winning a steady salary, this flag is faint. A need for 'standard business', as said within the going before column, is related to an impressively higher plausibility of creating a consistent wage. Generally, the information from Circular 1 emphasises the significance of steady wage and encounter (or age) in foreseeing work showcase results.

The capacity to banter and utilise the web in Punjabi is also beneficial regarding financial soundness. The imperative abilities and identity characteristics questions in Circular 1 are fewer in number and were hand-picked by the journalists. The discoveries of Circular 2 of the survey are discharged at that point, in which respondents were asked to rate themselves on over 100 abilities crowdsourced from the Circular 1 study.

7.2.2. Round 2: Crowdsourced Skills
Table 4.5 outlines the aptitudes chosen to utilise LASSO relapse (alongside expected coefficient values) in an administered learning issue with log compensation as the anticipated result based on Round 2 information.

Table 4.6 portrays the gifts chosen as the required point through LASSO relapse (with evaluated chances proportions), resulting in monthly pay. The comes about of single organised Heckman choice show are appeared in both within the column, demonstrating that the IMR from a begin with arranged Heckman determination show is separate from the Rope assessment. The IMR is one of the Tether factors, agreeing to the discoveries within the moment and third columns.

The second column computes IMR utilising conventional Heckman relapse (without aptitudes), while the third utilises a LASSO demonstration with self-evaluations on all crowdsourced abilities. Peruses should remember that standard importance levels and certainty interim calculations are lost from the LASSO relapse discoveries. On

Table 4.5. Variables Chosen by LASSO Regression Using Round 2 Data, With Log Wages as Desired Outcome.

Variables Selected	Dependent Variables		
	Log of Weekly Wages		
	(1)	(2)	(3)
(A) Punjabi speaking	0.1946	0.1894	0.1323
Knowledge of embroidery	0.1206	0.1007	0.1058
Knowledge of colours	0.1449	0.1389	0.1400
Teamwork	0.0391	0.0095	0.0521
Data entry	0.0288	0.0253	0.0498
Knowledge of knitting	0.1742	0.1892	0.1599
Computer handling	0.0679	0.0443	0.0787
Supervising	0.1072	0.0899	0.1133
Geographic knowledge	0.0059	0.0053	0.0023
(B) Knowledge of mending	−0.0092		−0.0213
Knowledge of cutting	0.0131		0.0213
Bank			0.0004
Internet usage		0.0005	
Observations	250	250	250
Selection equation	No	Yes	Yes, LASSO

Source: Authors' own compilation.

the other hand, Rope relapses ought to be seen as a demonstrate choice approach in which the calculation chooses the finest indicators of the specified result.

Table 4.5 illustrates how distinctive suspicions lead to covering covariate choice, outlining the consistency of our discoveries. Two visit statistic information collection components are the number of extended times of instruction and encounter. In all three details, 'Punjabi tuning in (understanding)' could be an excellent compensation indicator, and the delicate aptitudes 'overseeing' and 'working in a team' are key pay indicators. On the other hand, the bulk of prescient capacity is tied to specific capacities, which are related to higher salaries. Pay increments are a great indicator of these gifts.

Table 4.6 illustrates how the various criteria result in overlapping covariate selection. In this case, 'experience' (a proxy for age) is related to a good chance of obtaining a consistent monthly income. They both concur with our Round 1 results. However, the number of school years is not specified in any Round 2 model specs. Regarding required aptitudes, 'Punjabi tuning in (understanding)' is chosen over criteria and related to the next plausibility of getting standard pay. Shockingly, several delicate gifts are related to a higher probability of getting a month-to-month compensation.

Possession linkages, on occasion, are related to a fourfold increment within the probability of getting a month-to-month salary. Promptness is another delicate expertise that more than copies the chances of a relentless wage. 'Following directions' and 'dressing sense' are related to a 50 per cent rise in the chance of having consistent pay. Many specialised abilities are also picked across criteria, implying more stable professions. Overall, Round 2 empirical

Table 4.6. Variables Chosen Using LASSO Regression Where the Desired Result Is Receiving Regular Monthly Wages.

Variables Selected	Dependent Variable		
	Whether a Regular Monthly Wage		
Embroidery work	1.5854	1.5597	1.6161
Weaving	1.8543	1.8641	1.8681
Carving	0.5201	0.5271	0.4873
Inlaying	0.8684	0.9222	0.8134
Years of experience	0.8762	0.9233	0.8024
Colouring	0.9564	0.9883	0.9436
Shading	0.9842	0.9841	0.9756
Stitching	1.0381	1.0122	1.0352
Punjabi speaking	1.1873	1.1831	1.1751
Knitting	1.2384	1.2451	1.2200
Computer handling	1.1493	1.1101	1.2296
Dressing sense	1.4492	1.4193	1.4836
Following instructions	1.3750	1.3255	1.4790
Data entry	1.4042	1.3796	1.5088
Punctuality	1.5852	1.5597	1.6161
Relationship with owners	1.8545	1.8650	1.8681
Using hands and small tools	1.9528	1.8913	2.1502
Inverse Mills ratio	2.9876	2.8141	2.5781
Confidence	1.9520	1.8913	2.1502
Time management	2.9874	2.8130	2.5481
Observations	250	250	250
Selection equation	No	Yes	Yes LASSO

Source: Authors' own compilation.
Notes: The first column represents a one-stage model. The second column contains the outcomes of a model with IMR computed using the conventional Heckman regression method (excluding skills). In the third column, IMR is calculated using a LASSO regression that includes all the skills.

findings confirm some of Round 1 findings, despite their labour being associated with lower pay.

Younger individuals are more likely to work in employment with a set monthly wage. Punjabi language proficiency is connected to both income level and consistency. The mix of crowdsourcing skills yields some interesting outcomes. The 'ownership link' is a strong predictor of long-term profitability. Other soft skills, such as 'punctuality', are essential predictors of consistent income. Finally, the pool of specialised talents revealed occupational wage disparities and inconsistency.

8. CONCLUSION

The study ponders the abilities possessed by women working within the craft division in Punjab. The essential information has been accumulated in two stages from add up to 500 women labourers working within the craft division. In Circular 1, the information was collected from 250 respondents' socioeconomics, work history, self-assessments on pre-specified questions, and abilities that respondents connect with moved forward. Work advertising comes about. In Circular 2, the information was collected from a limited run of statistics and employment-related questions from 250 modern respondents, as well as broad self-assessment information on the foremost commonly demonstrated gifts in Circular 1.

Utilising the information, ability contrasts, co-occurrence, progression, and factors impacting casual work showcase results can be inspected. The econometric and machine learning innovations have been utilised to better get and outline the gifts of casual labourers in one of the world's fastest developing rising economies. The think includes various modern components to the writing.

To begin with, despite the reality that an extraordinarily more significant part of Indian workers is utilised casually, quantitative investigations of India's casual work markets are rare. Although a few journalists utilise macroeconomic information to dissect casual work at the national level experimentally, a fair number of articles collect essential domestic-level information. Our investigation contributes to the writing by using primary data from casual females working within the craft industry in Punjab. At this stage, the article contributes to the body of proof on the effect of 'delicate' and standard assignment capacities in impacting work victory. The consideration of aptitudes has been picking up unmistakeable quality universally as a response to the developing 'gig' economy fuelled by the multiplication of online stages for work coordinating and expertise procurement. The paper contributes to this by highlighting an up-to-this-point unexplored populace of casual specialists in urban India.

Third, the consideration utilises standard econometric investigation, crowdsourcing, and machine learning strategies. This blended strategy approach permits the utilisation of the structure of standard social science overviews and the adaptability of a bottom-up approach towards analysing the significance of abilities in an urban casual setting. Subsequently, while the major share of connected machine learning inquiries about employment auxiliary information sources or essential information collected over gadgets and online, typically among the primary endeavours to gather and analyse essential information in a hands-on work setting with a see towards machine learning applications.

Using information from Circular 1, we assess female labourers' frail essential abilities. Mincerian wage estimation employing a Heckman redress is a connection between consistency of compensation, profit, and steady occupations. We, too, discover that involved or mature female workers are more likely to get normal compensation than more youthful and taught ones. The capacity to talk in Punjabi and utilise the web positively impacts both levels and consistency of compensation.

After controlling for centre gifts, the effect of instruction on wage levels is irrelevant. Crowdsourcing could be a pivotal component of our ponder in Circular 1 since it gives us a wealthy supply of information grounded in real-world situations. This procedure permits the revelation of abilities that respondents respect as vital but that quantitative analysts do not identify immediately. The most regularly happening crowdsourced capacities, such as individual and social properties, are trustworthiness, promptness, and interpersonal certainty, proposing the significance that responders put on these crucial angles.

Another subcategory of abilities is specialised, permitting us to select from a vast extent of occupation-specific work capabilities. A bottom-up approach may shed light on the gifts of underrepresented sub-populations in this region. Numerous non-traditional crowdsourcing abilities, such as 'geographic knowledge' and 'relationship with owners', demonstrated to be major indicators of work showcase comes about, positively anticipating week-after-week compensation and standard month-to-month pay.

Information from Circular 2 sheds encouraging data on aptitude gathering and pecking order, extending our understanding of the aptitudes space past ordinary econometric techniques. The inserting recommends that the foremost broadly watched capacities connected with casual work may be inconceivably cheap to obtain and supplant into or out. LASSO-assisted learning gives us a more disaggregated picture of the abilities connected with alluring career results.

The discoveries have a broad run of arrangement results. Concurring with the clustering information, the foremost stressing conclusion is the vast and impressive difference between common assignment and dialect aptitudes, which are progressively vital for self-sufficiency. Dialect capacities, such as English and Hindi, are required for portable phones, money-related administrations, and web information. A clear policy solution would be to form large-scale money-related and computer proficiency programs for female specialists.

A significant relationship exists between English dialect competence, computer/Internet proficiency capacities, and made strides in work results. In truth, when English and web utilisation skills are included, the interface between instruction and higher recompense vanishes. This information underpins a moment arrangement proposition that English and computer proficiency aptitudes be organised in schools. Computer abilities, as well as individual and social aptitudes, are emphasised in India's skilling programs, such as the Deen Dayal Upadhyaya Grameen Kaushalya Yojana (DDU-GKY), a large-scale rustic youth work arrangement (Kumar et al., 2021).

Moreover, the consideration illustrates the pertinence of interpersonal and social capacities within the advertised urban casual occupations; this has never been inquired about measurably in India. The massive number of crowdsourced reactions outlined the centrality of these aptitudes. Some attributes, such as 'punctuality' and 'dressing sense', are related to consistency within the month-to-month wage. The National Abilities Advancement Enterprise of India (NSDC) has set up a set of National Work Guidelines, void of interpersonal abilities, fundamentally concentrating on a broad set of essential assignment abilities required for work exercises (Shrivastav & Jatav, 2017).

The third vital conclusion, our discoveries unequivocally prescribe that 'delicate' interpersonal and social instruction and preparation ought to be joined into word-related necessities. Since these competencies have been troublesome to assess the same contemplations, it might also be challenging to give past the parental, societal, and common sense encounters that have already been utilised to secure them. However, their financial pertinence requires advanced investigation into these subjects. At long last, the inquiry underlines the significance of creating an unused worldview when targeting competencies for specialists within the casual craftsmanship industry. Analysts and policy makers have been exhorted to utilise the state 'untalented' to speak to casual craft labourers based on the gigantic assortment of personal abilities accumulated from respondents.

Because many of the described talents are highly specialised, the label 'low skill' is also deceptive. Nevertheless, the bulk of talents were found to be at similar levels in the hierarchy of skills, demonstrating good generalisability of the findings and mastering even highly specialised expertise. The results emphasise the importance of 'tacit and explicit knowledge' (Polyani, 1983) that can be incorporated into apprenticeship in addition to on-the-job experience training and cannot be isolated from the skills that workers value. Despite this, few studies and educational programmes are geared at defining, training, and acknowledging 'tacit' skills.

The author recommends a more advanced word for 'adaptable' and inheritable talents to characterise the capacities procured by artisans in this circumstance. The thought, too, highlights the noteworthiness of recognising competent abilities, tongue, interpersonal highlights, and their lively complementarities. There is not a little pile of 'fragile' capacities, instep a firmly decided zone of work, interpersonal, and societal characteristics that, on the off-chance that attempted fittingly and deliberately arranged, may empower for more practical planning and enrolling strategies and a scattered increment in social success.

There are a few imperfections within the thinking about as well. The essential limitation is that competency data is personality. Overview samplings are routinely utilised to gather statistics and financial information at the family level, but self-reporting on abilities can be the chaotic and inner voice. It was illustrated that respondents positively recognised their interpersonal and social characteristics. Interests, an impressive contrast in assessments, have been watched for most remaining abilities, meaning a vital flag within the information. The inquiry, in any case, does not consider the sex viewpoint.

Encourage thinking about objectives may incorporate investigating the demand/supply side of casual specialists within the craft industry and sex incongruities in competencies. Aptitude mapping may give extra knowledge into successful work coordination by counting request side inclinations. A randomised controlled ponder to survey the viability of required abilities intercessions proposed by the information is an inescapable step. Considering the unfathomability of the expertise set, one striking methodological progression is the utilisation of customised studies for competence mapping, which may be less inclined to steady loss. Besides, anticipating personalised ability securing paths rather than the one-size-fits-all preparing modules regularly utilised for aptitudes preparing within the Indian work advertise is a perfect inquiry in this industry.

Furthermore, along with the skills, the social security of handicraft workers should also be researched, and policies should be suggested. Government should also provide social insurance to these workers. As per Sood and Tandon (2012), the insurance industry has become increasingly global and inventive and is constantly reforming. Non-life insurance is becoming important in India. It is essential in the lives of all citizens and has grown on a massive scale, resulting in the emergence of several forms of insurance.

Indeed, almost any risk may now be subject to an insurance policy. Insurance is essential today because the risks that can be covered have increased in number and scope as the modern economic system has become more complex.

Government should take up plans to promote social insurance as per the needs of the handicraft workers. However, the Rajiv Gandhi Shilpi Swasthya Bima Yojana implemented by the Government of India intends to provide financial assistance to the artisans' community, including the craftsmen, their spouses and two children so that they may access the most outstanding healthcare services in the country (Dadheech, 2016; Gnot, 2011). However, these schemes are yet to be researched at the practical level of ground reality.

REFERENCES

Barber, T., & Krivoshlykova, M. (2022). *Global market assessment for handicrafts, 1*(1–57). United States Agency for International Development.

Baturina, L., & Simakov, A. (2023). Students' attitude towards e-learning in Russia after pandemic. *Education Science and Management, 1*(1), 1–6.

Bettiol, M., Capestro, M., Di Maria, E., & Grandinetti, R. (2023). Leveraging on intra- and inter-organizational collaboration in Industry 4.0 adoption for knowledge creation and innovation. *European Journal of Innovation Management, 26*(7), 328–352.

Becker, W. (2000). Teaching economics in the 21st century. *Journal of Economic Perspectives, 14*(1), 109–120.

Boonlaor, N., & Chuenrudeemol, W. (2014). Design promises: The case study of Bangchaocha bamboo basketry community. *Blucher Design Proceedings, 1*, 115–120.

Borghans, L., Duckworth, A. L., Heckman, J. J., & TerWeel, B. (2008). Estimating the technology of cognitive and noncognitive skill formation. *Journal of Human Resources, 43*(4), 972–1059.

Chattopadhyay, K. (1975). *Handicrafts of India*. Indian Council for Cultural Relations.

Crill, R. (1999). *Indian embroidery*. V&A Publications.

Dadheech, R. (2016). Women workers in unorganized manufacturing sector of Punjab. In 13th National conference on management, information technology and engineering. *Gian Jyoti E-Journal, 6*(3) 5–8.

Dadheech, R., & Sharma, D. (2023). Home-based work or non-home-based work? Factors influencing work choices of women in the informal sector. *International Journal of Sociology and Social Policy, 43*(1/2), 89–106.

Devi, E. S., & Rajamohan, S. (2022). Self-Employment creating opportunities for women in Fashion Items and Handicraft Designing in India – A study. *Asian Journal of Management*, 1–5.

Frater, J. (2010). In the artisan's mind: Concepts of design in traditional Rabari embroidery. In K. Vatsayana (Ed.), *Embroidery in Asia: Suidhaga: Crossing boundaries through needle and thread* (pp. 84–93). Wisdom Tree.

Gale, C., & Kaur, J. (2002). *The textile book*. Berg.

Ghazinoory, S., Sarkissian, A., Farhanchi, M., & Saghafi, F. (2020). Renewing a dysfunctional innovation ecosystem: The case of the Lalejin ceramics and pottery. *Technovation, 96*, 5–9.

Ghosal, I., Prasad, B., & Behera, M. P. (2020). Delineating the exchange environment of handicraft industry from market space to marketplace: An inclusive map for rurban development. *Paradigm, 24*(2), 133–148.

Gnot, M. (2011). *Working conditions laws database, Travail legal databases*. Retrieved December 9, 2022, from https://www.ilo.org/dyn/travail/travmain.home

Handicrafts and Carpet Sector Skill Council. (2018). *Participant handbook; Engraving/carving*. National Skill Development Corporation, Ministry of Skill Development & Entrepreneurship, Government of India.

Heckman, J. J. (1979). Sample selection bias as a specification error. *Econometrica: Journal of the Econometric Society, 47*, 153–161.

IBEF. (2022). India's handicraft craft: A sector gaining momentum. Retrieved May 30, 2022, from https://www.ibef.org/blogs/india-s-handicraft-craft-a-sector-gaining-momentum.

IMARC Group. (2023). *Global handicrafts market report and Forecast 2023–2028*. Handicrafts Market Size, Share, Analysis, Report 2023–2028. Retrieved April 8, 2023, from https://www.expert marketresearch.com/reports/handicrafts-market

Jena, P. K. (2010). Indian handicrafts in globalization times: An analysis of global-local dynamics. *Description Complex Systems, 8*(2), 119–137.

Joshi, M., Bahaduri, A., & Dixit, S. (2015). Skill development: Capitalizing resources and capabilities. *Yojana* ISSN 0971-8400 *special issue on Skill Development: Scaling New Heights October* 2015, 50–52.

Joshi, A., Kale, S., Chandel, S., & Pal, D. (2015). Likert Scale: Explored and explained. *British Journal of Applied Science & Technology, 7*(4), 396–403.

JPS Associates. (2012). *Report on evaluation of the Ongoing Scheme of Ministry of MSME – Assistance to training institutions.* Ministry of Micro, Small and Medium Enterprises.

Juliana, J., Aditi, B., Nagoya, R., Wisnalmawati, W., & Nurcholifah, I. (2022). Tourist visiting interests: The role of social media marketing and perceived value. *International Journal of Data and Network Science, 6*, 469–476.

Kapur, H., & Mittar, S. (2014). Design intervention & craft revival. *International Journal of Scientific and Research Publications, 4*(10), 1–5.

Kaur, P. (2011). Revival of Punjab's traditional handicraft: Phulkari. *Asian Journal of Management, 2*, 28–38.

Khan, W. A., & Amir, Z. (2013, February). Study of handicraft marketing strategies of artisans in Uttar Pradesh and its implications. *Research Journal of Management Sciences, 2*(2), 23–26.

Knowledge and News Network. (n.d.). *Handicraft sector suffers from skill shortages.* Retrieved December 7, 2022, from https://knnindia.co.in/news/newsdetails/sectors/handicraft-sector-suffers-from-skill-shortages

Krueger, N. F. (2009). The micro-foundations of entrepreneurial learning and education: The experiential essence of entrepreneurial cognition . In G. P. West, III, E. J. Gatewood, & K. G. Shaver (Eds.), *Handbook of university-wide entrepreneurship education* (pp. 35–59).

Kumar, D., Narwal, S., & Phogat, S. (2021). A review of rural development schemes in India. *Asian Journal of Sociological Research, 5*(4), 18–26.

Lab, T. H. (2017). *Lockwood Kipling: Arts & Crafts of Punjab and London.* The Heritage Lab. Retrieved December 7, 2022, from https://www.theheritagelab.in/lockwood-kipling/

Li, Q. S. (2020). Development modes and cases analysis of rural tourism in Japan. *Contemporary Economy of Japan, 2*, 72–80.

Liu, R. (2022). Drifting in China's porcelain capital: Self-realization and alternative-seeking of the self-employed craft workers in Jingdezhen. *Asian Anthropology, 21*(4), 263–282.

Mincer, J. (1974). *Schooling, experience, and earnings.* Human Behavior & Social Institutions No. 2.

Ministry of Information and Broadcasting. (1972). *Indian handicrafts.* Ministry of Information and Broadcasting.

Mittal, L. (2015). *Is India's handicraft industry in crisis?* The Lakshmi Mittal and Family South Asia Institute, Harvard University. Retrieved November 5, 2022, from https://mittalsouthasiainstitute.harvard.edu/2015/12/bridging-paradigms-for-livelihood-regeneration-handcrafted-aesthetic-goods-and-markets/

Mohsin, A., Retnanto, A. S., Afsha, Shaikh, I., & Pinontoan, D. (2022). *First-hand perspectives of the pro-female notion in the oil and gas industry in the gulf.* Paper presented at the SPE Annual Technical Conference and Exhibition, Houston, TX, United States.

Mohapatra, S. (2011). Problems associated with Artisans in making of handicrafts in Orissa, India. *Management Review: An International Journal, 6*(1), 12–19.

Murnane, R. J., & Levy, F. (1996). *Teaching the new basic skills: Principles for educating children to thrive in a changing economy.* Free Press.

Oridi, F. I., Uddin, M. S., Faisal-E-Alam, M., & Husain, T. (2022). Prevailing factors of rural women entrepreneurship in Bangladesh: Evidence from handicraft business. *Journal of Global Entrepreneurship Research, 12*(1), 305–318.

Paine, M. (1990). *Textile classics.* Mitchell Beazley Publishers.

Peter-Cookey, M. A., & Janyam, K. (2017). Reaping just what is sown: Low-skills and low-productivity of informal economy workers and the skill acquisition process in developing countries. *International Journal of Educational Development, 56*(56), 11–27.

Polyani, M. (1983). *The tacit dimension.* University of Chicago.

Prasad, S., et al. (2017). *Report of the Committee for rationalization & optimization of the functioning of the sector skill councils.* MSDE.

Ranjan, A., & Ranjan, M. P. (2007). *Handmade in India.* Council of Handicraft Development Corporations (COHANDS).

Sage, D., Vitry, C., & Dainty, A. (2020). Exploring the organizational proliferation of new technologies: An affective actor-network theory. *Organization Studies, 41*(3), 345–363.

Sharma, D. K. (2017). A study on innovation in banking and its impact on customer satisfaction. *Journal of Economics and Finance, 1*(1), 70–74.

Shafi, M. (2022). Geographical indications and sustainable development of handicraft communities in developing countries. *The Journal of World Intellectual Property, 25*(1), 122–142.

Shrivastav, R. K., & Jatav, A. (2017). An analysis of benefits and challenges of skilling India. In *9th International conference on science, technology, and management.* Indian Federation of United Nations Association, New Delhi. http://conferenceworld.in. ISBN: 9789386171719.

Singh, M. K. (2005). *Evolution in crafts: Negotiating the handmade and the machine made.* Craft Revival Trust.

Shakerian, M., Esmaeili, R., & Rismanchian, M. (2023). Association of ergonomics risk factors among Iranian calico crafts-men and musculoskeletal discomforts: A cross-sectional study. *BMC Musculoskeletal Disorders, 24*(1), 109.

Solanki, S. S. (2008). Sustainability of rural artisans. *Economic and Political Weekly*, pp. 24–27.

Sohu. (2021). *Every year, nearly 50,000 young people choose to be 'Jing Piao', and the post-90s generation who make ceramics in Jingdezhen has a monthly income of 30,000,* Sohu online. Retrieved April 6, 2023 from http://www.sohu.com/a/469136115_114778

Sood, K., Dhanaraj, R. K., Balusamy, B., Grima, S., & Uma Maheshwari, R. (2022). *Big data: A game changer for insurance industry* (Vol. 6). Emerald Publishing.

Sood, K., & Tandon, S. (2012). Developments in Indian Non-life Insurance Industry. *Indian Journal of Research, 1*(5), 16–27.

Tang, F. (2019). *Will Vietnam challenge China's manufacturing leadership in the electronics industry?* Counterpoint Research Technology Market. https://www.counterpointresearch.com/insights/will-vietnam-challenge-chinas-manufacturing-leadership-electronics-industry/

Tibshirani, R. (1996). Regression shrinkage and selection via the lasso. *Journal of the Royal Statistical Society: Series B (Methodological), 58*(1), 267–288.

Tripathy, P. (2021). *Will the handicraft sector enter a new era of skill development.* National Skills Network.

United States Agency for International Development. (2021). Thesaurus 2021 dataset | Development data library. https://data.usaid.gov/Information-and-Communications-Technology-Services/USAID-Thesaurus-2021-dataset/urw5-yqfi/data

Vatsyayan, K. (2010). *Introduction. Embroidery in Asia Sui dhaga: Crossing boundaries through needle and thread* (pp. 9–10). Wisdom Tree.

Yadav, U. S., Tripathi, R., Yadav, G. P., & Tripathi, M. A. (2022). Proposal of a global handicraft index for sustainable development: A visionary approach for small industry and developing strategies for handicraft (rural industry). *European Journal of Sustainable Development Research, 6*(2), 179–185.

Yadav, U. S., Tripathi, R., Tripathi, M. A., Shastri, R. K., Yadav, G. P., & Aliza. (2022h). Entrepreneurial development of artisan in ODOP in Uttar Pradesh to boost economy Strategies and New Approaches Towards Global Handicraft Index for Socio-Economic Welfare of Artisans. *Asian Journal of Management, Entrepreneurship, and Social Science, 2*(1), 1–17.

Yadav, U. S., Tripathi, R., & Tripathi, M. A. (2022q). Global handicraft index: A pioneering approach and developing strategies for promotion completion and Welfare of Artisan in the Digital. *World Bank Policy, 2*(1), 59–80.

Yadav, U. S., Sood, K., Tripathi, R., Grima, S., & Yadav, N. (2023). Entrepreneurship in India's handicraft industry with the support of digital technology and innovation during natural calamities. *International Journal of Sustainable Development and Planning, 18*(6), 1777–1791. https://doi.org/10.18280/ijsdp.180613

Zhang, J. Z., Srivastava, P. R., Sharma, D., & Eachempati, P. (2021). Big data analytics and machine learning: A retrospective overview and bibliometric analysis. *Expert Systems With Applications, 184*, 115561.

Zheng, B., & Shao, D. S. (2019). Three definitions of the concept of 'poverty alleviation by design.' *Art Life J, 2*, 18–22. Fuzhou University.

CHAPTER 5

A CONCEPTUAL MODEL FOR SKILL DEVELOPMENT: 'A KEY DRIVER FOR INCLUSIVE GROWTH AND SUSTAINABLE DEVELOPMENT'

P. S. Anuradha[a], L. Mynavathi[a] and M. Anand Shankar Raja[b]

[a]Department of Commerce, Christ University, Bangalore, India
[b]Department of Commerce, Kumaraguru College of Liberal Arts and Science, Coimbatore, TN, India

ABSTRACT

Purpose: *This chapter explores the two major schemes applicable to skill development in India: Skill Acquisition and Knowledge Awareness for Livelihood Promotion (SANKALP) and Pradhan Mantri Kaushal Vikas Yojana (PMKVY).*

Need for the Study: *The primary objective of this research is to check the role of these schemes in enhancing the skills of socio-economically stressed community members for their livelihoods. The secondary aim is to analyse the outcomes of these schemes through a qualitative inquiry.*

Methodology: *A survey was conducted, and the data was collected from trainees of the skill development programmes. Based on the responses, a qualitative*

Contemporary Challenges in Social Science Management
Skills Gaps and Shortages in the Labour Market
Contemporary Studies in Economic and Financial Analysis, Volume 112A, 83–100
Copyright © 2024 by P. S. Anuradha, L. Mynavathi and M. Anand Shankar Raja
Published under exclusive licence by Emerald Publishing Limited
ISSN: 1569-3759/doi:10.1108/S1569-37592024000112A018

content analysis was performed, which showed that most trainees have the thirst and urge to enhance their life skills for a minimalistic livelihood.

Findings: *The study concluded that though there are many schemes, only PMKVY is active. They focus on more than just youth communities. Instead, they consider individuals in different age categories.*

Practical Implications: *The Government of India (GOI) is progressing towards a healthy economy to compete with other countries. For this mission to be achieved, skill and labour development is paramount. Appropriate training must be provided and administrated through government schemes.*

Keywords: Skill Development Programmes; PMKVY; SANKALP; inclusive growth; sustainable development goal; community

INTRODUCTION

This chapter has a few abbreviations, which are essential to explain the concepts clearly. The abbreviations are presented in Table 5.1 to make readers understand different terminologies.

After 75 years of Independence and diversity, India is an eventful battle armed with economic liberalisation, with a motto to achieve inclusive growth and sustainable development by tapping the potential and skills of the population. India has gradually emerged as a learning-based economy because of its fit and qualified human capital glut. With the continuously rising impact of globalisation, India has a big chance to set up its precise position on the planet. However, it is essential to address the socio-economic conditions of underprivileged communities, which have the potential to contribute to achieving the sustainable development goals (SDGs). However, a majority of underprivileged communities have a massive collection of labour, suffering low minimum standards, sometimes even below the minimum standard levels (Chatterjee, 2016). The existing labour market has aged and cannot be considered for further training and development. Millennials who fall below the poverty line due to a lack of skill and exposure will remain at their levels. However, the youth born between 1996 and 2010 (Generation Z) will be the most potential and preferred cohorts. The youth's transition and will to leverage employment opportunities will also help achieve economic success (Okada, 2012). Today's youth will be the most preferred human capital and assets always.

First and foremost, it is essential to identify the potential labour force requirement and match it with the existing youth population by implementing comprehensive programmes for their skill development (Mitra & Verick, 2013). Instead of concentrating on everyone, finding the target population to be trained is essential. This focused empowerment through knowledge drives will leave a huge impact (Harmon et al., 2003).

There is a need to additionally create, engage and empower human capital to guarantee worldwide competitiveness. Today's Indian youth must undergo

Table 5.1. Abbreviations.

PMKVY	Pradhan Mantri Kaushal Vikas Yojana
SANKALP	Skill Acquisition and Knowledge Awareness for Livelihood Promotion
SDG	Sustainable Development Goal
GDP	Gross Domestic Product
GOI	Government of India
MSDE	Ministry of Skill Development and Entrepreneurship
NITI	National Institution for Transforming India
RPL	Recognition of Prior Learning
NSQF	National Skill Qualification Framework
SCs	Scheduled Castes
STs	Scheduled Tribes
OBCs	Other Backward Classes
NCVET	National Council for Vocational Education and Training
DLI	Disbursement-linked Indicators
STT	Short-term Training
PWMI	Persons With Mental Illness
GP	Gram Panchayat

special training to cope with world expectations and challenges. Through these efforts, the GOI has to strategically plan to achieve the SDGs, which are holistic and inclusive. These efforts should also effectively create sustainable jobs for the youth, enabling them to earn well and grow with moral values, discipline, creativity and good personality (FDRE, 2020). The dreams are significant for citizens to transform the nation into the world's number one economy with the most intellectual human resources.

Despite significant changes in education and training, there still needs to be a more skilled workforce to address various stakeholders' expectations and achieve sustainable development due to poor economic performance. India's current version is noteworthy in connection to the global economy. During 2010 and 2017, India's yearly actual national output (gross domestic product, GDP) development arrived at a midpoint of 6.7%, regardless of a generally shaky post-emergency worldwide economy that found the median value of just 2.7% yearly gains (India Skills Report 2020 1, 2020).

However, the country's economic progression is impacted by numerous deep-seated inadequacies that could undermine future development if not effectively addressed. We have witnessed strong economic growth in the last two decades, but job opportunities have averaged only around 2% in the formal sector. Statistics show that 80% of India's labour workforce exists in the informal economy (Akula et al., 2018). Nearly 12–15 million Indians enter the labour force every year. If these trends continue, the problems of the youth searching for employment will persist as a continual challenge. For those still looking for proper jobs, the only option is to work in the informal economy, resembling a low-productivity trap. India is therefore performing far below its true potential. The GOI proposes and implements policies and initiatives to challenge the current scenario, and one such initiative is skill building, one of the critical tools to improve the efficacy and efficiency of the labour force for improved economic productivity and sustainable livelihoods. Skill and knowledge development are the key drivers for an economy's inclusive growth and sustainability. The National Skill Development Mission (NSDM) was approved by the Union Cabinet on 01.07.2015 and officially launched by the Prime Minister on 15.07.2015, World Youth Skills Day (Ministry of Skill Development & Entrepreneurship, n.d.). The mission was developed to create convergence across sectors and states in skill training activities.

Further, to achieve the 'Skilled India' vision, the NSDM would consolidate and coordinate efforts and expedite decision making across sectors to achieve skilling at scale with speed and standards. The nation benefits from a demographic dividend, but there is a considerable challenge to tap this unprecedented opportunity unless there is a significant economic and social change. The present research aims to understand and comprehend the issues surrounding skill education and training to achieve sustainable inclusivity development.

RESEARCH DESIGN

The aim of this research is explained in four phases: The first phase deals with understanding the application of the PMKVY and SANKALP. A deep introspection into these two schemes will help to find the progression of schemes leading to various outcomes. Though there may be several, this research focuses on employment opportunities, awareness and consciousness, socio-economic advancement, skill enhancement and livelihood promotion. In addition, collecting primary data from the semi-urban population and understanding various perspectives, problems and challenges can help. It would establish a conceptual framework and development of a yardstick, which the government can consider to change the existing policies and schemes. This research also presents the roadmap to achieve the United Nations SDGs (Runde & Metzger, 2019). In addition, the conceptual models will help explain socio-economic conditions, their impact on skill levels and the impact of the training and development programmes.

INDIAN POPULATION AND CONTRIBUTIONS TOWARDS ECONOMIC GROWTH AND DEVELOPMENT

South Asian countries and their contributions to economic growth have been a significant challenge, especially in developing countries like India, where the resources are not utilised effectively. India can achieve better economic progress if it extends ample opportunities to the semi-urban population because her changing demographics and a strong demographic dividend are an asset for her growth and development. Apart from the semi-urban population, India should also give importance to youth development, which is vital to the nation's sustainable development. In contrast, much of the current working population should be given primary importance. The different communities, especially the semi-urban population, contribute to a rise in the GDP. Research (Navaneetham, 2002) mentions the structural age transition of young people to old ones. It has led to a decrease in the working youth and an increase in the working-age population. The shocking reality has triggered the alarm for economic reformers and policy makers.

India has immense wealth and resources; however, it must be utilised beneficially. The government has taken the initiative to invest in the youth because most face various challenges and issues related to skills and job opportunities. Tapping the youth to provide training and development programmes would motivate them to succeed more. When economies invest in people, it helps societies to drive economic benefits. However, effective talent management is crucial in achieving economic development goals. One of the major initiatives taken by the government is to implement the National Policy for Skill Development and Entrepreneurship for the youth, which constituted 28% of the total population of India and contributed 34% towards the national income as per the 2011 census (Kaur et al., 2022; Mehta et al., 2020). The youth is considered an asset to the nation's growth and sustainable development because innovative, talented, enthusiastic, trained and upskilled youth may reach greater heights (Davendra Verma, 2017). The Ministry of Skill Development and Entrepreneurship (MSDE) (earlier Department of Skill Development and Entrepreneurship) was introduced in early July 2014 on the government's initiative. The vision was to create a life-long learning environment.

A database has also been created to pool the data of skilled youth, which helps them seek job opportunities. India can enjoy an added advantage if the semi-urban youth is trained and provided with employment opportunities by the government, public and private organisations, as they would enable the nation to grow faster.

The semi-urban population contributes significantly to the nation's development in several ways. The literacy rate has improved among the semi-urban and urban female population. According to the 2011 Census, the national literacy rate is 72.98%. The literacy rate for females and males is 64.63% and 80.9%, respectively (Office of the Registrar General & Census Commissioner, India, 2011). The Indian semi-urban youth have no basic training programmes to enhance their skills. For example, through research by Rajendran and Paul (2020), it is mentioned that the northeastern states have a considerable unemployed youth population (57.37 per 1,000).

Moreover, these youths in the northeastern regions need unique training programmes. Thus, many state governments have come forward to provide opportunities for the semi-urban youth and train them to be skilful labourers. Youth communities can also be trained to be small-scale entrepreneurs involved in different business ventures, such as mushroom cultivation, handicrafts making and solar light assembling. Opportunities are plenty in India because of the unquenched demand from the growing consumer markets. Considering the advantages the youth can enjoy, the GOI has introduced a cascade of schemes that can facilitate and help the youth get different opportunities.

In India, there are six popular schemes, that is, Deen Dayal Upadhyaya Grameen Kaushalya Yojana, Pradhan Mantri Gramin Awaas Yojana, Gramin Bhandaran Yojana, Deen Dayal Upadhyaya Gram Jyoti Yojana, Mahatma Gandhi National Semi-Urban Employment Guarantee Act and Sampoorna Grameen Rozgar Yojana. They are exclusively for those who are not skilled or talented. There are a few other schemes for the skilled and unemployed, such as Kishore Vaigyanik Protsahan Yojana, National Service Scheme, Deen Dayal Antyodaya Yojana and PMKVY.

Though the government introduces separate schemes for the skilled and unskilled, there is a need to explore the unskilled, semi-urban youth population, which still needs to be explored and unexposed to them. There is a need to know whether they are aware of the schemes.

This research only analyses PMKVY and SANKALP for the semi-urban population. As an expected outcome, a conceptual model is proposed, which can be considered by the government to frame policies to achieve SDGs.

SCOPE OF THE STUDY

The USA is among the world's top countries regarding skilled labourers because the US Department of Labour provides training and development channelled under the public workforce system. The department is on par with the American job centre, which extends support for job seekers. Hence, the system is transparent and invites anyone who needs guidance and support (Office, 2019).

Another powerful nation prioritising skill development is China, which has planned based on market expectations for decades. It has encouraged those skills which will transform the economy. An article (McKinsey, 2021) mentions that China has set a new goal for 2023, focusing on the four levers for skill transformation, including digital transformation, collaborative ecosystem, enhanced vocational track and shift in mindset and incentives. Thus, it is well understood from the international markets that powerful nations provide training and development to transform existing skills, which would help economic progress. The vision and mission are well-framed, and the expected outcomes are pre-planned. However, this scope is not achieved in India, where the skill development schemes are only for a few counterparts, and support only reaches some.

Thus, the focus of this study is to understand how the two well-designed programmes, SANKALP and PMKVY, for developing the skills launched by the MSDE (Shahzad et al., 2021) produced an outcome. The emphasis is on the semi-urban population from different states, which can be a good source of human capital. According to a study by Chandrashekar and Shivanna (Study & Dist, 2020), the youth constitute 30% of the country's and the state's total population. The semi-urban population are the most vibrant, enthusiastic, creative and dynamic individuals, forming the most important sections of the population, who need to be given priority or a platform to contribute their individual goals for the overall mission of the nation. They have a strong passion and willpower to build the country. However, the necessary skills to capture their passion and willpower must be developed more.

These two schemes have been exclusively rolled down to develop the skills, upskill and reskill to meet the requirements of the contemporary situation. The scope lies in seeking to analyse the level of awareness about the SANKALP and PMKVY programmes among the semi-urban population from different states. The main agenda is to study the demographic factors of those who underwent skill training under the two schemes. In addition, the study explored the outcome of the skills and their impact in the pre- and post-training phases. The scope has been extended to study socio-economic conditions and their effects on achievements post the training programme.

PROBLEM STATEMENT

Indian youth can still not find suitable jobs to pull them out of poverty. The youth are trained in vocational education and have the basic skills but need to be provided with employment opportunities. The problem may be twofold, that is, either a child needs to receive quality training and technical education, or the youth today must have the potential to cope with the industry's demands and expectations. The drastic changes in lifestyle, behaviour, attitude and influence of socio-cultural factors would have been instrumental in distracting the youth from scaling their abilities. Nevertheless, semi-urban youth are exposed to technology and use the Internet frequently. They still need to gain the technical and soft skills that industrial firms expect. Problems are not just with unemployment. However, many youths from urban and semi-urban backgrounds still need to be made active. These issues make the young vulnerable and lazy, which might be a significant barrier for India to achieve SDGs. To tackle these issues, the government has introduced several schemes for skill development. The two popular methods, PMKVY and SANKALP, have been put into execution for the past five years (Patnaik et al., 2018; Selvaraj, 2019). However, few researchers have explored the schemes' level of awareness and reach to the Indian population. It has been concluded that many youngsters must be aware of the schemes and their benefits. Moreover, extensive research is needed on the schemes for achieving economic growth and sustainable development. Research can enable the government to find the problems, challenges and strategies to overcome them.

Henceforth, there is a solid need to intervene and analyse the outcomes of the schemes, which will help us to create a model that can explain the implementation process to a broad target audience benefitting the government, training units and other stakeholders. In addition, the primary aim of the scheme is to provide adequate training and development to the youth. However, there is a need to measure the effectiveness of the training and the skills of individuals in the pre-training and post-training phases to help youngsters obtain decent jobs. Talent cannot be acquired quickly; it must be practised and imbibed. So, the effectiveness of the skills gained through popular government schemes, PMKVY and SANKALP, remains questionable. A skill never remains static but changes occasionally based on industrial expectations. Thus, whether these two schemes help the youth thrive in the long run must be addressed.

PMKVY AND ITS INFLUENCE ON INDIA'S INCLUSIVE GROWTH AND SUSTAINABLE DEVELOPMENT

PMKVY is the flagship scheme of the MSDE. The study was performed in five states – namely, Assam, Bihar, Madhya Pradesh, Punjab and UP – to understand the scheme's impact on the lives of beneficiaries. Using the structured questionnaire method, about 717 respondents between 18 and 25 years from five states were interviewed to examine the employability and significant changes in income levels before and after training. The variables used to assess the impact include the quality of training, the trainer's efficiency and the infrastructure, recommendations by the trainees, post-training benefits and income pre- and post-training. The results showed that there had been significant improvements in the employability and incomes of the respondents. The desire to learn skills and get employed in various areas directed the respondents to enrol. The trainers were interviewed, and according to them, the government should continue efforts to improve skill development facets in the country. Some concerns included attendance issues, transport facilities, lack of placement opportunities post-training and collaboration with industry. The need for intervention by the private sector through Public Private Partnership (PPP) was crucial to enhance the skill development ecosystem and attain sustainability. The advent of the Industrial Revolution 4.0 emphasised the need to reinvent skills. A relook into skills for the future was also stressed.

An evaluation of the PMKVY programme concerning short-term training (STT) and recognition of prior learning (RPL) was made to assess if the certification impacted the employability and income of beneficiaries. A quasi-experimental matching design with a mixed approach was used, with a sample of 5004 and 1717 for STT and RPL, respectively. The sample covered both PMKVY and non-PMKVY respondents. Moreover, various stakeholders, such as employers, trained candidates and government representatives, were interviewed to understand the implementation and feedback process. Seeking employment opportunities, increase in income levels, start-ups, interest and time availability due to unemployment were suggested by friends as some of the reasons to get enrolled in the STT. The training programme enhanced trainees' self-confidence, technical knowledge and entrepreneurial attitude, while satisfaction with the placement opportunities was observed. The RPL programme was found to be relevant and contextual to the present needs required for seeking employment. About 35% of the respondents revealed that their income levels increased considerably after the certification programme.

To facilitate and accommodate Persons with Mental Illness (PWMI), many rehabilitation centres are run by NGOs. To avail of this benefit, the family must pay a minimal fee (Thekkumkara et al., 2021), NMHS recommends the intervention of the PMKVY scheme to assist and support PWMI in seeking employment through skill training, to combat the shortage of mental health professionals and rehabilitation facilities. PWMI may benefit from the process due to the activities and daily routines involved in the PMKVY programme. The involvement of mental health professionals will play a significant role in liaising with PMKVY concerning collecting required information related to the courses offered, duration of the training, process of enrolment and creation of microenterprises by skilled and successful PMKVY trainees, which has led to better bargaining power in wages. Mobile app-based employment opportunities, such as Urban Clap and House Joy, have paved the way for self-employment opportunities (Agrawal & Thakur, 2019). The PMKVY training centre of Gwalior was considered to study the impact of youth productivity. About 1,197 respondents were interviewed. The cause and effect of the training, productivity and performance were chosen as the independent and dependent variables to test the hypothesis. The study revealed that training is significant in exploring the potential and abilities of the trainees. Thus, productivity increased. The national skill policy facilitates and enables unemployed youth to explore different employment avenues, thereby contributing to the inclusive development of the nation.

SANKALP

SANKALP is a unique programme designed by the MSDE, collaborating with the World Bank and assisting with loans. It was launched on 19 January 2018 and has a tenure till 2023. The framework of the programme is such that the outcomes in the project are measured through the results, and Disbursement Linked Indicators agreed between MSDE and the World Bank (National Skill Network, 2020). The overall emphasis of this programme is skilling the ecosystem. The main aim of SANKALP is to implement the directive of the NSDM (Bureau, 2019). To boost the Skill India Mission, the Cabinet Committee in Economic Affairs approved two schemes in 2019: SANKALP and Skill Strengthening for Industrial Value Enhancements (STRIVE). The government identified skill indicators, including the number of districts with dedicated district skill development offices, submitting the skill development plans to their respective state skill development mission (SSDM). Management Information System is linked with the National level Portal, and a fraction of the skill development training is aligned with the National Skill Qualification Framework (NSQF).

The second remarkable step under SANKALP was creating awareness of a district-level skill planning database. It started with consolidating data related to various dimensions of resources in the district. The administrative officers utilised the Census, NSSO, Employment Exchange and other government agencies to conduct skill gap studies and other surveys for effective planning. The achievements are measured by completing the NSQF aligned with skill development. The percentage of graduates, who are wage or self-employed, within six months of completion, number of trainers and assessors trained/retained, translation of NSQF-aligned Qualification Packs (QPs) into model curriculum, trainers' guide and teaching–learning resource materials, strengthened the capacity of the District Skill Committee (DSC) and improved service delivery at the Gram Panchayat (GP) level for linking unemployed youth to local markets.

The key result areas are capacity building and amplifying the impact through decentralisation, enhancing market relevance and quality, boosting inclusion and improving access. The decentralisation in capacity building will take root from MSDE to the National Instruction Media Institute (NIMI), National Skill Development Corporation (NSDC), taken up by the DSC, and further below even the GPs. Capacity-building activities at the national level include supporting the National Council for Vocational Education and Training (NCVET), which provides vocational education and training. NIMI functions as a nodal agency to develop instructional materials, e-content, and question banks, train media developers and trainers, and enabling the translation of books into Hindi and other regional languages.

Capacity building at the SSDMs is supported with technical and financial resources and the State Incentive Grant (SIG) matrix, which is a list of indicators designed to measure the performance of states on three components: namely, strengthening institutions, market relevance and access to and completion of training by marginalised populations. The skill repository of all skill-related data across states and ministries, known as the Skill India Portal, was initiated to support the rapid scaling up of skill development. SANKALP is working towards enhancing the quality of Technical Vocational Education and Training (TVET), which is taking a market-driven approach to meet the requirements of the relevant markets.

Remodelling the Training of Trainers and Assessors programme provides a strong line of master trainers in partnership with the industry. According to the model, the training is based on the requirement. Boosting inclusion and improving access is another crucial area, focusing on providing opportunities to women, persons with disabilities and other marginalised sections. Under SANKALP, the mechanism to boost inclusion is achieved twofold: firstly, by understanding the challenges these sections face and developing pilot programmes to address them; and, secondly, by building a 'bottoms-up' approach, with the participation of the skill development machinery at the state and district levels.

SANKALP also aims to increase female participation. Gender Action Plan (GAP) provides a roadmap to translate this vision into strategy and focused initiatives for women's skill training on gender sensitisation and prevention of sexual harassment in the workplace. Besides these initiatives, SANKALP also designs and implements innovative skill development and entrepreneurial pilot programmes for persons with disabilities. The unique feature of this programme, SANKALP, is in skilling, upskilling and reskilling to meet the industry's requirements at the local, national and international levels.

Skill building is considered a powerful tool to empower people by enhancing their ability to contribute effectively to an organisation or to start their ventures. Developing skills for aspiring youth leads to employment opportunities and the creation of employment in case they are starting their experiences.

To promote their capabilities and initiate their business ideas, the SANKALP scheme has been approved, converging with effective governance, regulation and acting as a catalyst between the industry and skilled labour by providing vocational training with certification (Agarwal, 2018). A more significant number of graduates passing out of universities face a huge challenge to secure employment. This is mainly because the companies claim that the students lack the skills to meet the demands and that the acquired skills are insufficient to equip the students to meet the industry's demands. It is essential to make changes in the curriculum by embedding skill development, facilitating students with internship opportunities, building on leadership capabilities and developing the outcome-based course design with the course learning outcomes through which programme outcomes are achieved (Siddamal et al., 2020).

RESEARCH METHODOLOGY

This chapter follows a mixed research approach, employing quantitative and qualitative analysis (Johnson & Onwuegbuzie, 2007). After profoundly investigating the reviews about PMKVY and SANKALP, we took insights from secondary data. However, we have collected primary data from semi-urban Bengaluru, a city of mixed populations from different backgrounds. Half the people are migrants in search of jobs and career opportunities. Thus, the data collection from the city represents the Indian state. A questionnaire was constructed, considering a few primary elements, such as the level of awareness of the schemes, lacking skills, demographic questions, socio-economic factors, psychological factors and information on sustainable development of the nation. In addition, an interview schedule was also used to collect some data from respondents over the telephone. A majority of the respondents spoke Kannada, Tamil and English. Though they were not fluent in English, they could understand simple sentences and words, which helped the researchers to collect data. The information was coded in an Excel sheet in chronological order. Post-data arrangement in the Excel sheet had a content coding technique, which was used to pick out the most frequently used words, sentences and meanings (viewpoints). Through this content coding, it was helpful to identify the most commonly used verbs, further used to construct the conceptual model on skill development programmes, socio-economic conditions and the impact of skill levels attained. It was collected after a keen and transparent analysis of the responses. Thus, the data collection mechanism allowed the researchers to catch the clear views of the respondents.

The questionnaire had six major themes: levels of awareness of the schemes, lacking skills, demographic questions, socio-economic factors, psychological factors and information on sustainable development of the nation. Each question statement was constructed after a critical review and deep screening of the literature review. All the question statements were marked against Likert's 3-point scale with scaling options of disagree, neutral and agree. It was preferred to receive the exact responses from the youthful respondents. (When the spread of options increases, the respondents tend to pick up random options. Thus, to avoid it, the scaling options were limited to three.)

DISCUSSION

The researchers intended to understand the demographic factors of the respondents who underwent SANKALP and PMKVY schemes. The government has developed a pervasive initiative to extend employment opportunities for many individuals nationwide through a comprehensive training and development programme. First and foremost, to achieve the primary objective of this research, it is necessary to analyse the demographic factors. A majority of the respondents belonged to the Other Backward Caste (OBC) category, who were socially and educationally disadvantaged. The OBC category enjoys 27% reservations in education and job opportunities, and this is an initiative by the government to encourage them to reach a standard position in their lives and society. A majority of the respondents in this research were also OBCs. According to the Press Information Bureau, skill development programmes are extended to the marginalised community, which includes Scheduled Castes (SCs), Scheduled Tribes (STs) and OBCs. However, the majority of the trainees belonged to the OBC class. The other respondents, who occupied a minor portion, fell under the General Category (GEN).

The second most crucial demographic construct is gender. The majority of the respondents were female. While men and women occupy an equal position in urban localities, with equal rights and exposure to education, job opportunities and reservations, in the semi-urban landscape, there is still a taboo in which only men are educated and go out to look for jobs to run their families. Women are still considered a significant resource used only for household chores. Recently, women began to break away from this traditional myth and made efforts to explore, innovate, create, grow and sustain. Women with a motto to start small business units or work for other establishments search for skill development programmes. Hence, a majority of the respondents are female. These schemes will also motivate women of the same cluster and region to join the T and D programmes and make group efforts to start their small businesses.

The third crucial demographic factor is the nature of the job in which they are involved in post-skill training programmes. From the samples collected, it is understood that textile manufacturing units employ the majority. Most of them undertake sewing machine operating jobs in knit units, which may be because most women under this scheme already know the basics of sewing. However, they need a little more training to be professionals. It is also gleaned from the qualitative interviews that they have plans to start tailoring shops on more minor scales, which will help them to earn a stable income and develop gradually. It is also said that the 'knit' jobs give them a minimum monthly salary, but they have the habit of saving some of their salary with a keen motto to start a business.

A few women also intend to begin businesses in groups as partners. Regarding job opportunities and the present occupation, a few other respondents, who underwent training under SANKALP and PMKYC schemes, are in retail stores. They are working in stores, taking care of the merchandise arrangements, organising a retail store, providing essential information to customers and other aspects related to stocktaking and maintaining invoices. A few are into technical tasks, as most need to gain basic computer skills and are interested in technical skills. Though basic computer operating jobs are available, the youth are primarily disinterested because of the need for computer knowledge, which cannot be learnt during training.

In its programme, the GOI would provide orientation and basic training. However, the success of being employed in an organisation or a small-scale entrepreneur depends on the efforts invested by those who undergo training. SANKALP and PMKVY schemes would guide trainees, but further growth is needed. The other crucial demographic variable is educational qualifications. The analysis found that most are school dropouts, and only some have progressed beyond high school. A majority, who have enrolled under this scheme, are poor and are forced by their family to get involved in different occupations. In addition, they need more motivation to learn. Education should be given more importance and is always seen as a burden.

Moreover, only the male child in a family can explore, whereas females are restricted to only caring for the households. Most women respondents said they were interested in getting educated, reaching a good position and helping their families. Still, due to the restrictions among their relatives, they were asked not to attend school. Meanwhile, they developed a hatred towards education and did not make any efforts to get qualified.

Thus, analysing the demographic factors, it is understood that those undertaking SANKALP and PMKVY schemes are from a meagre socio-economic background, desperate to win in life and their careers, convinced that the training would change their lives.

However, they get only a basic orientation and training, which would help fetch them a minimal income and care for their day-to-day expenses. These schemes are not in-depth, nor can they upgrade the marginalised communities.

SOCIO-ECONOMIC CONDITIONS PRE AND POST THE TRAINING

A model known as 'ABC Classification' has been proposed regarding the socio-economic conditions. During the data collection process, questions related to socio-economic conditions were asked. Based on the response, a classification was developed for easy understanding and interpretation. In this ABC classification model, A denotes high impact, B denotes medium effect and C denotes no effect. This classification model was newly introduced in this research work to classify the qualitative data collected during the interview. The model helped in mapping the correct data under the right category. Thus, the outcome of the training was classified under these three categories.

Fig. 5.1 explains the ABC classification. All the models (Figs. 5.1 and 5.2) were created by authors after a detailed content coding based on the primary data received from the respondents. These figures were self-produced and not taken from any other sources.

Inference for Fig. 5.1

Fig. 5.1 clearly explains the three-tier classification (high impact, medium impact and low impact) of the skill development training on the socio-economic

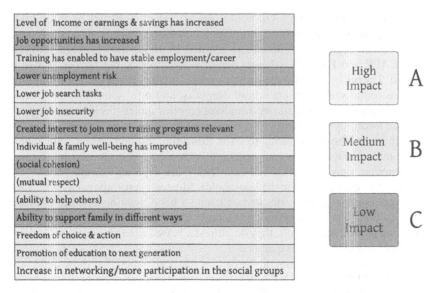

Level of Income or earnings & savings has increased	
Job opportunities has increased	
Training has enabled to have stable employment/career	
Lower unemployment risk	High Impact **A**
Lower job search tasks	
Lower job insecurity	
Created interest to join more training programs relevant	
Individual & family well-being has improved	Medium Impact **B**
(social cohesion)	
(mutual respect)	
(ability to help others)	
Ability to support family in different ways	Low Impact **C**
Freedom of choice & action	
Promotion of education to next generation	
Increase in networking/more participation in the social groups	

Fig. 5.1. ABC Classification Representing the Outcome of the Skill Development Programme on Socio-economic Conditions. *Source:* Compiled by authors.

conditions of the respondents who underwent training under SANKALP/ PMKVY scheme. Based on the replies, the respondents said that the training programme had undoubtedly helped them in a few aspects, but only partially. They enhanced their knowledge through continuous interaction with many allied social groups, which allowed them to understand the availability of job opportunities, exchange of ideas and motivation by peer social groups. They also said they were free from job insecurity due to their employment but feared their present jobs' validity. They were determined to undergo further training and development programmes through government schemes, to enhance their job positions and roles. The job they got after exposure to skill development training was temporary. Job insecurity was permanently embedded deeply in their subconscious, so they lived in fear. However, their jobs slightly improved their socio-economic conditions, as they improved their incomes, which helped them feed their families and get involved in savings. As their earning capacity was appreciated in their family circles and within their social groups, they felt respected. However, the training did not help them to occupy comfortable positions.

Inference for Fig. 5.2

Regarding the impact on skill attainment, based on the training undergone by the respondents, a new classification model has been suggested. Based on the qualitative response received during the interview, the levels are classified into four. The positive impact includes 'A lot more attained and a little more attained', whereas the negative impact includes 'No change and got worse'. Communication in the skill development programmes is more technical and creates confusion and

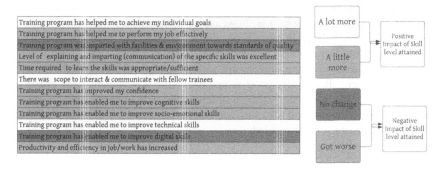

Fig. 5.2. Impact of Skill Levels Attained (During and After the Training Programme). *Source*: Compiled by authors.

frustration when the trainees need help to grasp and understand everything fully. Thus, the effectiveness of knowledge transfer could be better than expected. The trainers should use simple and less technical words to make the presentation more understandable.

Moreover, the training has nothing to do with socio-emotional skills. Indeed, when the family needs essential support to attend training under the scheme, there is no scope for improving empathetic skills. Most respondents said they have no support from family members to attend training because they feel it wastes time and energy. The orientation on emotional well-being is theoretical, so it may only positively impact if executed and practised. The training has improved their self-confidence and allowed them to learn something new. It is a positive sign of improvement, which most respondents mentioned. The trainees also got an opportunity to communicate with fellow members, who attended the training sessions, shared their issues, discussed and received feedback for personal development. Networking with fellow members, which would always be an additional value attained by an individual, is a positive outcome. It also provides a space to think, be creative and solve different issues. Hence, it has developed the trainees cognitively. These skill development schemes mainly focus on the nation's youth development, with a motto to improvise job opportunities and levels of literacy in India.

However, from the data, it is understood that the actual training is not exclusively provided to the youth but also to individuals in different age categories. Moreover, OBCs are given importance, while SC and ST members are not. SC and ST members enjoy certain privileges in employment exchanges through reservations. However, only the OBC category is selected. In that case, there may not be holistic development in extending training skill development, as only a tiny population of SC and ST members would be covered. The Indian government must provide skill development training to different categories and should not concentrate only on a group of people belonging to a specific cluster. Once the training programme is over, the attendees get decent job opportunities or become entrepreneurs at small-scale levels.

However, these are just assumptions, and there needs to be more evidence created by the government, which is showcased on government websites. The state must revamp the skill development programme, which would cater to the needs of different clusters. For example, women, young girls and boys, semi-urban youth, urban employees and senior citizens are various groups who need such training and development. Being very good in resources, the government must create a separate entrepreneurial ecosystem in different districts in every state to group and map all the women and men who can run their businesses. This handholding by the government is much needed.

CONCLUSION

Indian youth are the promising cohorts who would play a significant role in growth and prosperity. The world is now witnessing substantial challenges, which include economic, health and ecological crises. The only solution to energise everything is talented and skilled human forces. However, India has a vast, unorganised sector where most cohorts range between 18 and 35 years but need more skills and confidence. The government has taken a significant step to eradicate this skill crisis by introducing many schemes which will benefit them, especially the rural youth. These schemes benefit many rural and semi-urban youth. However, many need to be made aware of them. Moreover, there is no transparency in maintaining data about those who underwent the training. The data would be helpful for many researchers and other policy-making authorities.

Hence, PMKVY and SANKALP schemes enable the semi-urban population to undergo training to enhance their skills and potential. However, the skill development programmes must be modified to cater to the needs of the present market conditions and expectations. Such programmes should help people get decent jobs and measure the impact on growth and prosperity. Hence, skill development drives must focus on overall sustainability and goal achievements rather than concentrating on the development of only a few.

SCOPE FOR FUTURE RESEARCH

- There are still many areas that the government can identify to create a revolution. India has many rural and semi-urban populations who need more basic education facilities. Though there are a few government schools and colleges, the exposure to technology is considerably less. Thus, technical skill is zero among most rural, semi-rural and semi-urban populations. The training modules can concentrate on technical and technological skills and interpersonal development, through which expert committee members should create the teaching and learning modules.
- Private educational institutions, ranked high in various accreditations and titles and recognised in the country, must be allowed to train people in small batches. As there are faculty resources who are experts in multiple fields, the

training programmes would be more effective and become one of the best practices of an educational institution in social development.

- Apart from the above-stated group of educational institutions, many corporate organisations usually hold training and development programmes for their employees' growth and career. They arrange for the best experts and trainers from various fields. Hence, these corporate organisations can also allocate a small portion of the surplus to extend a knowledge-based service to the community. It would also help the government cover and benefit a considerable population spread in various ways. Moreover, after a contract, the trainees can be considered full-time employees after the training period according to the company's expectations.
- It is essential to understand the schemes given to members of the OBCs under the 'Welfare Measures' tag. The document published by the government in 2014 mentions several schemes, such as loans for education, overseas scholarships for education, qualification approvals, financial allowances and much more. However, there needs to be a caste-wise study to understand the in-depth impact of these schemes for socio-economic improvements. Though we declare that it is one nation with no-caste-wise distribution, there is a need to study various clusters of people to identify the niche needs and give them the best. Moreover, skills cannot be generalised but must be differentiated for multiple groups.

ACKNOWLEDGEMENTS

We thank all those who helped us write this chapter. Firstly, we are thankful to Christ University's management, who allowed us to work on this area of research.

REFERENCES

Agrawal, M., & Thakur, K. S. (2019). Impact of Pradhan Mantri Kaushal Vikas Yojana on the productivity of youth in Gwalior Region, India. *International Journal of Recent Technology and Engineering*, 8(4), 801–806. https://doi.org/10.35940/ijrte.d7385.118419

Akula, A., Rani, J., Lavanya, Y., & Scholars, R. (2018). Status of unorganised labour in Indian economy. *JETIR*, 5(10), 261–265.

Bureau, P. I. (2019). *Skill India's SANKALP scheme to focus on district level skilling ecosystem through seamless convergence and coordination*. https://pib.gov.in/newsite/PrintRelease.aspx?relid=192464

Chandrashekar. (2020, December). A sociological study of rural youth in Karnataka (Case Study of Hosadurga, Chitradurga Dist). *Pen Acclaims: A Multi-disciplinary National Journal*, 13, 1–16. http://www.penacclaims.com/

Chatterjee, S. (2016). Labourers of unorganised sectors and their problems. *International Journal of Emerging Trends in Science and Technology*, 4397–4405. https://doi.org/10.18535/ijetst/v3i07.18

Davendra Verma, P. D. (2017). *Central Statistics Office Ministry of Statistics and Programme Implementation Government of India* (pp. 1–86). Social Statistics Division. http://mospi.nic.in/sites/default/files/publication_reports/Youth_in_India-2017.pdf

FDRE. (2020). *Sustainable jobs for all: Plan of Action for Job Creation (2020–2025)*. Briefing document by Job Creation Commission Ethiopia. https://www.jobscommission.gov.et/wp-content/uploads/2019/11/National-Plan-for-Job-Creation-Brief.pdf

Government of India (Ministry of Skill Development & Entrepreneurship). (n.d.). *Government of India (Ministry of Skill Development & Entrepreneurship)* (pp. 4–32). https://www.msde.gov.in/sites/default/files/2019-09/National Skill Development Mission.pdf

Gupta, D., & Agarwal, S. (2018). Training prospects in power sector in India. *International Journal of Research in Engineering, IT and Social Sciences, 8*, 305–314.

Harmon, C., Oosterbeek, H., & Walker, I. (2003). The returns to education: Microeconomics. *Journal of Economic Surveys*. https://doi.org/10.1111/1467-6419.00191

India Skills Report 2020 1. (2020). (pp. 1–88). https://wheebox.com/assets/pdf/ISR_Report_2020.pdf

Kaur, S., Sehgal, J. K., & Grima, S. (2022). Virtual hiring: An effective green human resource management practice. *International Journal of Sustainable Development and Planning, 17*(6), 1699–1704. https://doi.org/10.18280/ijsdp.170602

McKinsey. (2021). *Reskilling China transforming the world's largest*. https://www.mckinsey.com/featured-insights/china/reskilling-china-transforming-the-worlds-largest-workforce-into-life-long-learners

Mehta, B. S., Mehta, S., & Kumar, A. (2020). International Youth Day, the rise of unemployed and idle youth in India. *Outlook India Magazine*. https://www.outlookindia.com/website/story/opinion-international-youth-day-2020-the-rise-of-unemployed-and-idle-youth-in-india/358529

Mitra, A., & Verick, S. (2013). *Youth employment and unemployment: An Indian perspective*. International Labour Organization.

National Skills Network. (2020). https://www.nationalskillsnetwork.in/national-education-policy-2020/

Navaneetham. (2002). *Age structural transition and economic growth: Evidence from South and Southeast Asia*. https://papers.ssrn.com/sol3/papers.cfm?abstract_id=1629748

NSDC. (2019, March). *Impact evaluation of Pradhan Mantri Kaushal Vikas Yojana (PMKVY) 2.0*. https://skillsip.nsdcindia.org/knowledge-products/pmkvy-20-impact-evaluation-report-executive-summary

Office, U. S. (2019). *Report to the Permanent Sub-committee on Investigations*. Committee on Homeland Security and Governmental Affairs, US Senate. https://www.hsgac.senate.gov/

Office of the Registrar General & Census Commissioner, India. (2011). https://www.censusindia.gov.in/

Okada, A. (2012). Skills development for youth in India: Challenges and opportunities. *Journal of International Cooperation in Education, 15*(2), 169–193.

Rajendran, V., & Paul, D. (2020). Skilling the semi-urban youth of the Northeast of India through rural technologies. *Asia-Pacific Journal of Rural Development, 30*(1–2) 195–202. https://doi.org/10.1177/1018529120946246

Runde, D. F., & Metzger, C. (2019, December). *Lessons for building creative economies*. https://csis-prod.s3.amazonaws.com/s3fs-public/publication/Runde_StrengtheningCreativeEconomies_v4_WEB.pdf

Schoonenboom, J., & Johnson, R. B. (2017). How to construct a mixed methods research design. *Kolner Z Soz Sozpsychol, 69*(Suppl 2), 107–131. doi: 10.1007/s11577-017-0454-1

Selvaraj, D. (2019). "Sankalp" – Innovative skill development in industrial knowledge. *Asian Journal of Multidimensional Research*. https://doi.org/10.5958/2278-4853.2019.00253.2

Shahzad, M. F., Khan, K. I., Saleem, S., & Rashid, T. (2021). What factors affect the entrepreneurial intention to start-ups? The role of entrepreneurial skills, propensity to take risks, and innovativeness in open business models. *J. Open Innov. Technol. Mark. Complex, 7*, 173. https://doi.org/10.3390/joitmc7030173

Siddamal, S. V., Shirol, S. B., Hiremath, S., & Iyer, N. C. (2020). Towards sustainable integrated model for skill development: A collaborative approach. *Procedia Computer Science, 172*, 460–467.

Suhagin, S., Patnaik, B.C.M., & Satpathy, I. (2018, September). ICT and Skill Development of the Workforce – A Review of Literature With Special Reference to PMKVY. *International Journal of Civil Engineering and Technology (IJCIET), 9*(9), 256–262.

Thekkumkara, S. N., Jagannathan, A., & Sivakumar, T. (2021). Pradhan Mantri Kaushal Vikas Yojana (PMKVY): Implications for skills training and employment of persons with mental illness. *Indian Journal of Psychological Medicine*, 1–4. https://doi.org/10.1177/0253717621997180

CHAPTER 6

THE DEVELOPMENT OF REMOTE WORK IN THE EUROPEAN UNION AND LATVIA

Sandra Jekabsone, Purmalis Karlis and Irina Skribane

Faculty of Business, Management and Economics, University of Latvia, Riga, Latvia

ABSTRACT

The need *for the study is justified by the fact that scientists and policy makers around the world are trying to identify the potential threat of digitalisation, looking for ways to adapt to new changes and take advantage of the opportunities offered by the information society and the knowledge economy and to mitigate risks. Digitalisation also changes the labour market – using information and communication technology (ICT) in the working process opens up new opportunities. Moving from a traditional office to another environment, combining work with private life and recreation more effectively, while remote work deals with costly jobs, spaces and congestion on the city streets. The* study *aims to assess the development of remote work in the European Union (EU) and Latvia, assessing its effectiveness and the possibilities for long-term use by analysing its impact on the transformational directions of the economy. During the analysis, the following* findings *were made: identified the potential and problems of the deployment of remote work in Latvia, determined the main challenges of remote work and policies to improve the situation. The analysis employs theoretical and empirical research* methods. *The theoretical method of analysis and deduction provides information on its impact on the economy from the scientific literature on remote work and its diverse aspects. The comparative method is widely used to identify aspects of remote work*

Contemporary Challenges in Social Science Management
Skills Gaps and Shortages in the Labour Market
Contemporary Studies in Economic and Financial Analysis, Volume 112A, 101–111
Copyright © 2024 by Sandra Jekabsone, Purmalis Karlis and Irina Skribane
Published under exclusive licence by Emerald Publishing Limited
ISSN: 1569-3759/doi:10.1108/S1569-37592024000112A019

distribution and economic development and their interaction. Practical implications *of research – to make recommendations on policy directions to improve
the situation, which would promote the further development of remote work.*

Keywords: Remote work; labour market; gig economy; new forms of
employment; structural changes; information and communication
technologies; digitisation; COVID-19 pandemic

1. INTRODUCTION

THE COVID-19 pandemic revealed the crucial role of remote work in maintaining economic activities and the economy's resilience to shock. For this reason, as
well as a significant increase in the number of new flexible forms of employment,
many national authorities have started to pay particular attention to their development and to identify the potential consequences that have been reflected in several
publications and studies (Bloom, 2020; Guatieri, 2020; Meunier, 2020; Neiman,
2020). Despite the increased interest in this topic in the last two years, the forms of
remote work, viability and impact on Latvia's economy have not been sufficiently
analysed. It should be noted that the topic of remote work is topical in today's society and has an interdisciplinary nature, particularly by assessing its impact on the
achievement of the objectives set out in the country's strategic planning documents,
such as reducing Latvia's regional disproportions, ensuring equal opportunities for
urban and rural residents to use ICT for personal and public purposes, including
education and retraining. It is also important that introducing new, flexible forms
of employment in the working process does not follow the legal framework.

This chapter aims to provide an assessment of the development of remote
work in the EU and Latvia, to assess its effectiveness and the possibilities for
long-term use, by analysing its impact on the transformational directions of the
economy. To achieve the objective, the study deals with the following challenges:
examining scientific publications on labour market developments towards flexible
forms of employment, analysing the possibilities for applying remote work and
limiting factors, analysing remote labour trends in Latvia and the EU and its
impact on the economy, highlighting the major challenges of remote work and
policies improving the situation, which would contribute to its future distribution.

Public statistical data from the Central Statistical Bureau (CSB), Eurostat, the
European Commission (EC), the Organization for Economic Cooperation and
Development (OECD), as well as scientific studies and surveys carried out, have
been used to analyses the problem.

2. THE DEVELOPMENT OF THE LABOUR MARKET
IN THE DIGITAL ERA

The labour market is experiencing the greatest tension in periods of economic
crises, particularly when crises are structural. In addition to structural factors,

technological development and digitisation strongly impact labour markets. The digital process is also affected by the rapid development of the *gig economy*, which covers different types of short-term employment (freelance, platform employment, self-employment, group employment, case work, etc.), which is rapidly spreading around the world, becoming a daily reality that transforms the labour market and employment (World Economic Forum, 2021). An essential feature of the giant economy is the use of digital platforms that enable employers to access the necessary employees and resources on request. As digital platforms grow, the number of employees employed and new forms of work organisation for these employees is increasing. As a result, many currently employed in traditional economic sectors and working full-time work face new challenges and challenges in the future; according to the authors, huge employment, including the use of platforms, will be comparable to traditional employment. EU countries identified flexicurity ('flexicurity') and the transition labour market ('transitional labour market') as the basic concept of labour market reform in Europe in light of the new challenges. At the EU level, this concept is integrated into the European Employment Strategy (1997). Flexibility is an important way to boost economic growth, as more flexible labour markets improve Europe's competitiveness, given the relatively low adjustment costs for businesses in an internationally very integrated economy to the new challenges.

The transformation and employment trends of the labour market today are largely driven by technological changes. One important factor influencing the labour market is technological progress, which constantly offers producers more advanced technologies and means of production. Thus, the future of the labour market for researchers is also linked to the fourth Industrial Revolution (*Industry 4.0*) and the digitalisation of the economy. Moreover, strong competition for market places and competition for consumers, as well as the desire to reduce production costs, inevitably lead to the fact that one of the victims of this fight of competition is human and, on a wider scale, labour markets, which are constantly changing both within their structure and in the number of workers forced to seek new jobs.

The authors would like to point out that researchers judge the impact of technological changes on labour markets on a very minor basis. So, for example, American researchers Atkinson and Wu (2017) view the technological threats as a 'false panic' and sharply criticise those who predict a decline in U.S. jobs by 80–90% over the next 10–15 years. In their view, such grim assessments result from flawed logic and empirical analysis. Statistics, however, show the opposite: job cuts in the USA are currently at historically low levels. Similar ideas regarding robots and the German industry have been expressed in a study assessing the impact of industrial robots on employment, wages and employment patterns in German labour markets between 1994 and 2014 (Dauth et al., 2018). Researchers believe that introducing industrial robots had little impact on employment in local labour markets, which specialise in industries with high levels of robot use. The use of robots has led to job declines in manufacturing, but was offset by gains in the business services industry. The study's authors also conclude that productivity is increasing in areas with a higher degree of automation, while the workforce's share in total added value is declining.

Consequently, there is no evidence that robots have been 'job killers', but they are squeezing the workforce out of Germany's manufacturing sector. In 2018, the European Research Group (Vermeulen et al., 2018) examined labour market development and employment problems widely. The peculiarity of their approach was that the expected employment impact of automation over the next decade was studied at both the macro level and the level of economic sectors, that is, taking into account multisectoral structural changes. They therefore proposed a concept of how the relocation of labour in the automation industries is offset by the compensatory effects of internal and intermediate sectors and, in particular, by newly created jobs in labour-intensive industries. They concluded that the loss of potential jobs in industries with high potential for manufacturing automation is balanced by job creation in those sectors where such technologies are created and in the service sectors. Therefore, when assessing the impact of technology on labour markets and employment, the issue of risk assessment for professions and tasks that will be automated in future decades due to artificial intelligence systems is also important. American researchers say 47% of jobs in the US are at risk of being automated 'someone indefinitely, possibly in the next ten or twenty years' (Frey & Osbourne, 2017). In the EU, on average 54% of jobs are threatened by comptroller (Bowles, 2014), according to the Bowles study. However, other researchers point out that these documents overestimate the risks of automation because they include professions, not work and job assignments, so they conclude that only 9% of jobs in the US can be automated (Arntz et al., 2016).

In summarising the results of the above studies, the manufacturing process of the application of new technologies, including the negative effects of robotisation and automation on employment, is more likely to occur in the US labour markets than in the EU. This can be partly explained by the level of liberalising the labour market, which is higher in the US than in Europe. At the same time, more active labour market policies in Europe could mitigate the impact of industrial robots, reducing the risk that people will get into long-term unemployment.

Together, the above factors create the conditions for creating alternative employment models. New forms of employment are a broad term to identify the most diverse forms of employment that arise or become more significant since 2000. New types of work are characterised by changing work patterns, contractual relations, places, working time and timetable, the wider use or combination of ICT. The *Eurofound* study identified new forms of employment in nine broad categories (Eurofound, 2015). The study points out that new forms of employment show growth trends and are explained by the transition of companies to more flexible business models, where a relatively large proportion of employment types are associated with the possibility of performing job tasks remotely.

In light of the above, the potential size of the labour market that can be involved in the economy of electronic platforms is large. Today's digitisation of technology and manufacturing processes can significantly impact employment and lead to significant changes not only in the labour market but also in the economy as a whole. In this context, the increased use of new forms of employment, including remote work, can reveal more opportunities to address employment problems for both workers and employers.

3. DEVELOPMENTS OF REMOTE WORK IN LATVIA AND THE EU

Technological development has allowed employees to become mobile and use wireless connectivity (*WiFi*) and various portable devices (laptops, tablets, and smartphones) to work independently of location. However, until 2020 (the COVID-19 pandemic), the remote working arrangements largely represented companies whose organisation provided higher mobility, better knowledge management for added value and the development of e-commerce. In 2019, an average of 14.4% of the total number of workers in the EU-27 worked entirely or partly in remote labour (Jekabsone et al., 2021). The COVID-19 pandemic has been a powerful factor contributing to the wider use of the teleworking regime. The restrictions introduced to combat the pandemic led to the search for the possibility of maintaining economic activities by providing adequate services. In 2020, the share of remote workers in total employment increased to 20.6%, reaching 24% in 2021 (Eurostat, 2022). However, it should be noted that the volume of remote work varies greatly between sectors and professions. In sectoral terms, remote working arrangements are most common in knowledge-intensive services, such as professional and ICT services, and the least widespread in manufacturing (industry), as well as knowledge in less intensive market services, such as trade, transport, catering, etc. (Dingel & Neiman, 2020). In Latvia, during the COVID-19 pandemic, 66% of workers in financial and insurance activities, 60% of employees in information and communication services, nearly 28% of employees in public administration and defence, as well as knowledge, administrative services and real estate operations, while the lowest percentage (9.3%) of employees working remotely was manufactured (Baranovs et al., 2021).

Similarly, the results on the potential for remote work in the sectoral section are also in the study *Teleworkability and the COVID-19 crisis: a new digital divide?* (Sostero et al., 2020). The authors of the study, based on labour force survey data in EU Member States, analysed the characteristics of individual professions, identified works that can or may not be carried out remotely, and assessed the proportion of staff employed in professions with high remote labour potential, including industry. According to their results, nearly all (93%) financial services workers can work remotely, and nearly four out of five employees in information and communication and about two-thirds of employees in real estate, professional, scientific and technical activity, education and public administration. Services sectors with a lower proportion of teleworking include health care (30%), retail (27%), and accommodation and catering (16%). However, in the primary sectors, as well as in the manufacturing and construction sectors, remote job opportunities are very limited to around 10–20% of the number of employees in the sector. By grouping professions by skill content, remote work is most common among highly skilled professionals, such as managers and professionals, showing that many professions currently working remotely need high cognitive and non-cognitive skills (Grundke et al., 2018). The potential for remote work is determined not only by the structure of professions and sectors in each particular economy but also by the availability of infrastructure that allows efficient work outside traditional offices or jobs. According to estimates by the ILO, nearly 18% of workers work in professions and live in countries with infrastructure that would allow efficient work from home (ILO, 2020).

However, detailed information that would allow an in-depth study of trends in remote work in different sections, such as sectoral and professional sections, is limited availability data. Overall, the EU's largest share of remote workers was in the Netherlands in 2021, 53.8% of all workers, but the lowest in Bulgaria and Romania (see Fig. 6.1).

Among the Baltic States, the majority of remote workers were in Estonia in 2021 (26.3%), which is almost two times more than in Latvia (13.6%) and Lithuania (14.3%). One of the factors explaining the different distribution of remote work in EU countries is the differences in the structure of the sectors. In Sweden, Luxembourg, Finland, the Netherlands, and Denmark, where the proportion of employees in high-tech and knowledge-intensive industries is increasing in total employment, remote work is also more widespread. Similarly, the application of remote work arrangements is also influenced by the model and culture of business management and job organisation.

The impact of COVID-19 on the increase in the number of remote workers in the EU Member States has also been very different. In 2020, compared to 2019, the largest increase in remote workers was in Luxembourg, Malta, and Ireland. Meanwhile, in 2021, the share of remote workers increased most in the Netherlands compared to 2022. The slowest growth in remote workers is for Poland, which in 2021 was only 0.9 percentage points higher than before the outbreak of the COVID-19 pandemic. In addition, it should be noted that, following an increase in the total number of workers working in remote work in 2020 (in wave 1 of the outbreak of the pandemic), the share of remote workers in Poland decreased in 2021 and was even at a lower level than in 2019. In the Baltic States, measures limiting the spread of the COVID-19 pandemic have contributed to an increase in the application of the remote labour regime, particularly in Latvia and Lithuania, where the proportion of remote workers was relatively low before the pandemic (see Fig. 6.2).

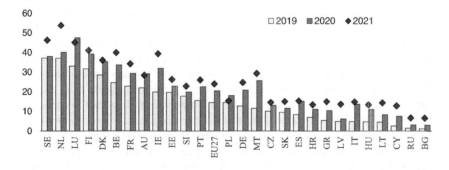

Fig. 6.1.   Remote Workers in EU Member States (% of Total Employment Aged 15–64).
Source: Created by authors using EUROSTAT data.

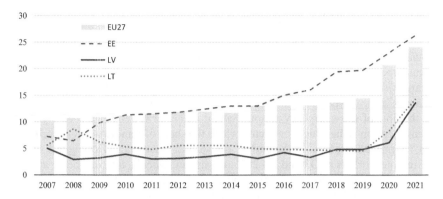

Fig. 6.2. The Dynamism of Remote Workers in the Baltic States and Average in the EU (% of Total Employment Aged 15–64). *Source*: Created by authors using EUROSTAT data.

In 2020, Latvia's share of remote workers increased to 6.1% in total employment but reached 13.6% in 2021. In Lithuania, the level of remote workers has also increased significantly in 2021 and represented 14.3% of total employment. However, the share of remote workers fluctuated in 2020 and 2021, reflecting the economic response to the waves of the COVID-19 pandemic, which can be seen in Table 6.1.

Table 6.1. Share of Remotely Employed Workers in Latvian Economic Sectors in the Period 2020–2021 in the Quarter (as a Percentage of the Number of Employees in the Sector).

	2020Q2	2020Q3	2020Q4	2021Q1	2021Q2	2021Q3	2021Q4
All in all	18.3	8.9	18	22.6	21.3	13.1	18.8
B–F Production sector	6.4	3.4	9.3	9.7	10.7	6.5	8.9
EU Trade, transport, accommodation and catering services	8.3	5.4	10.5	11.8	12.5	7.5	11.7
J Information and communication services	61.3	31.2	60.2	78.9	66.5	58.3	62.7
K Financial and Insurance Activities	64.2	49.2	65.5	73.6	62.8	56.9	81.6
L–N Scientific, administrative services; real estate operations	27.6	12.8	28.1	31.5	29.2	26.7	28.5
O Public administration and defense, compulsory social insurance	26.7	15	28.8	37.4	36.5	24.7	36.6
P Education	44.5	12.3	27.3	43.4	38	6.4	21.3
QS Health and social care, other types of economic activity	12.7	...	10.3	14.5	13.5	6.1	9.3

Eurostat (2022): https://ec.europa.eu/eurostat/data/database.

When assessing the quarter in Latvia in Q2 and Q4 2020, two-thirds of financial and insurance workers, three-fifths of information and communication services employees, nearly 28% of State administration and defense; compulsory social insurance workers, as well as scientific, administrative services and real estate operations (L–N) were carried out remotely in Latvia. The lowest (9.3%) share of remote workers was seen in the manufacturing sector (B–F). In 2021, the share of remote workers in all sectors was at a higher level than a year ago, both at the time of the emergency announcement and after the end of the emergency. The exception is the education sector, where the share of remote workers declined on 7 April 2021 following the end of the second emergency. The highest share of remote workers in Q3 and Q4 2021 remains in financial and insurance activities and the information and communication services sector. In general, it can be observed that in Latvia, in all sectors, remote work opportunities want to be used less actively, weakening social distancing restrictions. This shows that job calls and workers still prefer traditional work organisation models.

4. CHALLENGES AND FUTURE DEVELOPMENT OPPORTUNITIES FOR REMOTE WORK

The transition to a remote labour regime was one way of maintaining economic activities in the context of social dystopia and limiting the negative economic impact of the shock caused by the COVID-19 pandemic. Like any other type of work organisation, remote work has its strengths and weaknesses, on which sharp discussions have been taking place in recent years. The most important issues are the impact of remote labour on productivity, the reduction in greenhouse gas emissions, the flexibility of employment and the availability of labour, population inequalities, improvements in living conditions, etc. Remote work can increase workers' products vitality, reduce costs and get more free time, but this can lead to insulation and stress as the border between work and home runs out. Similarly, while working remotely, there may be increased uncertainty about income and uneven workload, since the employee must organise both the workplace and plan the amount of work. For example, Stanford University professor Bloom (2020) points out that full-time work at home is problematic for three reasons: (1) it is difficult to be creative from a distance; (2) to inspire and motivate themselves; and (3) without social interaction, the loyalty of employees is muted. From the employer's point of view, remote work can also create a series of new challenges. The employer should invest additional resources to supply staff with the necessary hardware and software, and consider training or technical support to ensure the best safety practice. It is also appropriate to adapt business processes to organise remote work and to carry out systematic monitoring and monitoring of employees. As noted in the OECD study, the work involved can both improve and hinder the business, and its overall effect depends significantly on the effectiveness, motivation and skilling of employees and on reducing labour and capital costs by releasing resources to boost productivity by promoting innovation and reorganisation (OECD, 2020). Remote work can also influence structural changes in real estate and labour markets, which benefit suburban homeowners and the level of labour participation, but hurts office owners, urban apartment residents and the finances of big cities. Increased deployment of remote work can also significantly impact recruitment and satisfaction, since teleworking can increase the number of employees, for example, by employing highly qualified workers who are linked to a particular place of residence for personal reasons. Similarly, remote work can have a positive impact on capital costs by reducing the company's required office space and equipment, reducing traffic congestion, carbon and particulate emissions, and lowering housing prices in particularly high-density cities (Baranovs et al., 2021).

In order to make efficient use of the opportunities afforded by remote work and to promote worker satisfaction, even after the end of the COVID-19 pandemic, policy makers have both to improve the legal framework and to encourage investment in the development of a more demanding infrastructure and training of employees (Jekabsone et al., 2021). Several issues require a more precise legal framework, such as workers' rights and obligations, whether firms can monitor remote jobs to assess their productivity, who is responsible for job security, etc. Policy makers should promote measures that require employers to provide workers with an appropriate working environment while working remotely, for example, with ICT equipment, and improve the regulation on covering workers' costs about work outside the office (OECD, 2020). One of the main policy lines should be to increase digital skills in society as a whole, focusing specifically on individual target groups (e.g. seniors, people with special needs, etc.). Another challenge to increasing remote work is to provide a social support infrastructure for workers, such as childcare facilities. Without the support of such a state or company, the burden on workers, particularly women, is increasing.

5. CONCLUSIONS AND PROPOSALS

1. Although most researchers link the future of the labour market to the fourth industrial revolution and the digitalisation of the economy, the range of factors affecting labour market changes is much wider. Changes in the global economy, technological progress, demographic change, a lack of resources, and the emergence of new economic models, including a gig economy, also significantly impact the labour market.
2. Remote work is one of the new employment models whose application, along with the COVID-19 pandemic in the EU, etc., has increased rapidly worldwide. The largest share of remote workers in EU Member States was in the Netherlands in 2021, where 53.8% of all workers worked remotely. Among the Baltic States, most remote workers were in Estonia (26.3%) in 2021, almost two times more than in Latvia and Lithuania, where 13.6% and 14.3% of all employees were remote.
3. The scientific literature for exploring the potential of remote work is dominated by Dingel's and Neiman's methodologies since it is based on a sufficiently

objective measurement to determine whether the work in question can be done remotely. Several studies have concluded that the potential for remote employment varies widely between sectors and professions. In sectoral terms, remote working arrangements are most commonly seen in knowledge-intensive services, such as professional and ICT services, the least widespread in manufacturing (industry), and knowledge in less intensive market services.

4. The increased use of information and telecommunications technologies can widen the range of occupations that could work remotely, but overall, the high proportion of remote workers in highly skilled occupations compared to moderate and low-skilled professions shows that teleworking could increase the gap between these groups and lead to structural changes in the labour market.

5. There needs to be more consensus in the scientific literature on the impact of remote work on the economy. The main issues discussed are the effects of remote labour on productivity, the reduction in greenhouse gas emissions, the flexibility of employment and the availability of labour, population inequalities and improvements in living conditions, etc.

6. Teleworking can increase workers' productivity, reduce costs, and provide more free time. Nevertheless, it can also lead to isolation and stress as the line between work and home blurs. Teleworking also increases income uncertainty and can lead to an uneven workload, as the employee has to organise both the workplace and the amount of work planned.

7. In the long run, teleworking can impact structural changes in real estate and the labour market, leading to changes in labour demand and supply across occupational groups, and regions. It can also increase labour force participation. However, several professions where teleworking opportunities are very limited, such as agriculture, trade, construction and industry, remain prevalent.

8. To ensure the effective use of the opportunities invested by teleworking and to increase employee satisfaction after the end of the COVID-19 pandemic, policy makers need to both the legal framework and encourage investment in appropriate infrastructure and staff training, as well as digital literacy in society as a whole, in particular targeting certain groups with insufficient skill levels.

REFERENCES

Arntz, M., Gregory, T., & Zierahn U. (2016). *The risk of automation for jobs in OECD countries: A comparative analysis.* OECD Social, Employment and Migration Working Papers No. 189. OECD Publishing.

Atkinson, R. D., & Wu, J. (2017). *FALSE Alarmism: Technological disruption and the U.S. labor market, 1850–2015.* WORK Series. Information Technology & Innovation Foundation.

Baranovs O., Salmins J., Skribane I. (2021). *Impact of teleworking on productivity and structural changes.* https://doi.org/10.22364/ltpepii.09

Bloom, N. (2020, June). *How working from home works out.* Stanford Institute for Economic Policy Rese arch (SIEPR). https://siepr.stanford.edu/research/publications/how-working-home-works-out

Bowles, J. (2014). The computerization of European jobs. *Bruegel Blogpost.* http://bruegel.org/2014/07/the-computerisation-of-european-jobs/

Dauth, W., Findeisenz, S., Suedekum, J., & Woessner, N. (2018). *Adjusting to Robots: Worker-level evidence*. Institute Working Paper 13. Opportunity and Inclusive Growth Institute, Federal Reserve Bank of Minneapolis.

Dingel, J., & Neiman, B. (2020). *How many jobs can be done at home?* Covid Economics: Weted and Real-Time Papers 1, April 3.

Eurofound. (2015). *New forms of employment*. https://www.eurofound.europa.eu/sites/default/files/ef_publication/field_ef_document/ef1461en.pdf

European Employment Strategy. (1997). https://ec.europa.eu/social/main.jsp?catId=101&langId=en

Eurostat. (2022). https://ec.europa.eu/eurostat/data/database

Frey, C. B., & Osbourne, M. A. (2017). The future of employment: How susceptible are jobs to computerisation? *Technological Forecasting and Social Change, 114*, 254–280.

Grundke, R., Marcolini, L., Nguyenii, T. L. B., & Squicciarini, M. (2018). *Which skills for the digital era?: Returns to skills analysis*. OECD Science, Technology and Industry Working Papers No. 2018/09. OECD Publishing, Paris. https://dx.doi.org/10.1787/9a9479b5-en

Guatieri, S. (2020). Will remotework change the economy remotely? https://economics.bmo.com/en/publications/detail/e5e9ccfa-a 20d-4 a 58-b 703-9 a 3 f 5 bde6d00/

ILO. (2020). *An employers' guide on working from home in response to the outbreak of COVID-19*. https://www.ilo.org/wcmsp5/groups/public/--ed_dialogue/--act_emp/documents/publication/wcms_745024.pdf

Jekabsone, S., Skribane, I., & Sproge, I. (2021). Opportunities of telework and its impact on the economy. *Economy, Finances, Management: Topical Issues of Science and Practical Activity, 4*(58), 23–37. http://efm.vsau.org/en/particles/opportunities-of-telework-and-its-impact-on-the-economy

Meunier, J. (2020). *Remote work: The future of work*. https://allwork.space/2020/09/what-does-working-remotely-mean/

Neiman, B. (2020). What a way to make a living. *The Economist*, September 12, p. 20.

OECD. (2020). *Productivity gains from teleworking in the post COVID-19 era: How can public policies make it happen?* https://read.oecd-ilibrary.org/view/?ref=135_135250-u 15 liwp4jd & title = Productivity-gains-from-teleworking-in-the-post-COVID-19-era

Sostero, M., Milasi, S., Hurley, J., Fernandez-Macias, E., & Bisello, M. (2020). *Teleworkability and the COVID-19 crisis: A new digital divide?* JRC Working Papers Series on Labour, Education and Technology. https://ec.europa.eu/jrc/sites/jrcsh/files/jrc121193.pdf

Vermeulen, B., Kesselhut, J., Pyka, A., & Saviotti, P. (2018). The impact of automation on employment: Just the usual structural change? *Sustainability, 10*, 1661. https://doi.org/10.3390/su10051661

World Economic Forum. (2021, May 26). *What is the gig economy and what's the deal for gig workers?* https://www.weforum.org/agenda/2021/05/what-gig-economy-workers/

CHAPTER 7

DETERMINING THE SKILLS NECESSARY FOR ONLINE SELLER–BUYER COMMUNICATION TO AVOID FRICTIONAL UNEMPLOYMENT DUE TO SKILL GAPS

Muthmainnah[a], Ahmad Al Yakin[b], Muhammad Massyat[c], Luís Cardoso[d] and Andi Asrifan[e]

[a]Teacher Training and Education Faculty, Indonesian Language Department, Universitas Al Asyariah Mandar, West Sulawesi, Indonesia
[b]Teacher Training and Education Faculty, Pancasila and Civic Education Department, Universitas Al Asyariah Mandar, West Sulawesi, Indonesia
[c]Faculty of Social Sciences and Governmental Sciences, Universitas Al Asyariah Mandar, West Sulawesi, Indonesia
[d]Polytechnic Institute of Portalegre and Centre for Comparative Studies of the University of Lisbon, Lisbon, Portugal
[e]Teacher Training and Education Faculty, English Language Department, Universitas Muhammadiyah Sidenreng Rappang, South Sulawesi, Indonesia

ABSTRACT

Purpose: *This study aims to identify communication speech acts and transaction terms in online stores (Olshop) during live streaming on Facebook amid the COVID-19 pandemic and to understand communication patterns between sellers and buyers when shopping on Facebook live streaming in Indonesia.*

Contemporary Challenges in Social Science Management
Skills Gaps and Shortages in the Labour Market
Contemporary Studies in Economic and Financial Analysis, Volume 112A, 113–135
Copyright © 2024 by Muthmainnah, Ahmad Al Yakin, Muhammad Massyat, Luís Cardoso and Andi Asrifan
Published under exclusive licence by Emerald Publishing Limited
ISSN: 1569-3759/doi:10.1108/S1569-37592024000112A020

The Need for Research: *This research is motivated by the skill gap arising from increasing buying and selling transactions through live streaming on Facebook. Cultural and demographic shifts, along with the widespread availability of modern technologies and marketing 2.0 have resulted in the global population adopting social media at rates far beyond our use of the Internet, making a compelling case by example and analogy that social media has the potential to level the playing field and is effective in reaching their target market.*

Methodology: *The type of research is descriptive-qualitative using corpus data instruments. The data collection technique in this study was carried out by reading and observing the data and listening to speeches about buying and selling women's equipment from various online stores on Facebook. Then select and sort the data designated as forms, strategies, and functions of speech acts in buying and selling transactions during live streaming on Facebook. The data analysis technique has three steps: (1) reducing the amount of data; (2) presenting the data; and (3) concluding.*

Findings: *The results show that there are four types of speech acts between sellers and buyers in the live-streaming online shop on Facebook, namely, assertive, directive, expressive, and commissive speech acts.*

Keywords: Communication patterns; live streaming; Facebook; online shopping; sellers; buyers; pragmatics

1. INTRODUCTION

The e-commerce industry is adopting several unique applications to increase customer engagement and boost overall business value (Huang & Benyoucef, 2013). According to Hilvert-Bruce et al. (2018), since 2011 live streaming's popularity has increased as an interactive multimedia platform for entertainment, social, and economic activities. Many sole proprietors and other small businesses have started using live-streaming platforms (like Facebook Live) to market their wares to customers directly. This chapter proposes a comprehensive framework to investigate the connections between consumers' valuation of live-streaming services, consumers' trust in those services, and consumers' active participation in those services, drawing on literature from retailing, adoption behaviour, and electronic commerce. It is found that trust in sellers has a direct and indirect effect on customer engagement, while trust in products and sellers has an indirect effect. Explaining how live broadcasting may boost business and customer devotion (Wongkitrungrueng & Assarut, 2020).

Einav and Lipson (2015) report that 47% of global live-streaming users spend more time viewing live streaming than a year ago, using data from the Interactive Advertising Bureau (IAB) in May 2018. Using live streaming provides a business with numerous possibilities for advertising, customer assistance, and sales. To compete, it is no surprise that in 2019, Wowza Media Systems partnered with large retailers like Amazon and QVC to run their live video shopping sites.

Even though the public's apprehension about online fraud and the Internet's ever-changing landscape may lead to a decline in e-commerce, online business has been on the rise. Facebook is one of Indonesia's many specialised social media; they use a communication approach to promote their online identity. Regarding social media users in Indonesia, Facebook, WhatsApp, and Instagram are in the second, third, and fourth positions, respectively, with a fairly large percentage. The same parent company, Facebook, Inc, owns all three social media platforms. It indirectly provides opportunities for business actors to use social media as a business tool to carry out marketing communication activities such as promotions and advertising, commonly referred to as 'social media marketing' (digital marketing or Internet marketing). It is called social media marketing because these activities utilise social media as a tool or medium to carry out marketing activities (Kotler et al., 2017).

Berger and Eisendle (2019), Wamuyu (2018), Berger and Thomas (2016), and Evans et al. (2022) argue that since the advent of Web 2.0, s-commerce has been adopted as a legitimate channel for conducting retail trade. Many studies have been conducted on the topic of customer engagement in e-commerce. Marketers and businesses alike now rely heavily on social media as the primary means of getting their message across to customers. It is also an important factor in shaping customer perspectives and decisions. Online stores, for example, often use customer-facing social media platforms to disseminate information about sales items, contests, promotions, and discounts, as well as to interact with customers and gather their opinions (Baturina & Simakov, 2023; Juliana et al., 2022; Sood et al., 2022).

Ngubelanga (2020) also argues that in recent years, especially with the advent of 5G network technology, video has penetrated every aspect of business and has become an important medium for disseminating ideas. There has been a recent increase in online retailers installing broadcast studios. During their live broadcasts, e-commerce streamers eat, play, and use the products they sell to viewers extensively. There is a conversation not only between the streamer and the viewer but also between the viewers themselves. Furthermore, studies have shown that customers have a greater impact on their peers' purchasing decisions. In terms of consumer engagement, new technologies (such as social media, mobile applications, augmented reality, and virtual reality) are fundamentally changing the nature of the network of interactions between customers, businesses, and other interested parties.

The term 'customer engagement' describes the enthusiasm and participation of customers in a company's products, services, or other endeavours (Wongkitrungrueng & Assarut, 2020). An interactive consumer experience is at the heart of customer engagement. Due to technological advances and the explosion of the Internet, computer-mediated marketing environments have emerged, resulting in these interactive consumer experiences. E-commerce has embraced live broadcasts to break the traditional static boundaries between multiple subjects in a single conversation. Before and after purchase, interactive features are very useful for building regular consumer engagement (Carlson et al., 2018; Vohra & Bhardwaj, 2019). In addition, Hu and Chaudhry (2020) found that social relationships involving interpersonal interactions positively increased consumer engagement and communication patterns, and they underlined the need for customer engagement in live-streaming e-commerce for operators to form partnerships. When it comes to live e-commerce streaming, how do communication patterns between sellers and buyers differ? Theoretical and empirical research by Chen and Lin (2018) both support the idea that live broadcasting is useful for e-commerce.

The precise operation of sellers' and buyers' communication patterns in encounters has been the subject of several empirical investigations. However, studies on the forms of communication between buyers and sellers of live streaming are still rarely investigated. In addition, the literature on attractive forms of communication between customers and sellers has prompted more research on communication patterns between sellers and buyers in online shopping when live streaming on Facebook. Several unique applications are being adopted by the e-commerce industry to increase customer engagement and boost overall business value (Huang & Benyoucef, 2013). According to Hilvert-Bruce et al. (2018), since 2011, live-streaming's popularity has increased as an interactive multimedia platform for entertainment, social, and economic activities. Many sole proprietors and other small businesses have started using live-streaming platforms (like Facebook Live) to market their wares to customers directly. This chapter proposes a comprehensive framework to investigate the connections between consumers' valuation of live-streaming services, consumers' trust in those services, and consumers' active participation in those services, drawing on literature from retailing, adoption behaviour, and electronic commerce. It is found that trust in sellers has a direct and indirect effect on customer engagement, while trust in products and sellers has an indirect effect. Explaining how live broadcasting may boost business and customer devotion (Wongkitrungrueng & Assarut, 2020).

Due to the absence of literature on engaging language communication patterns constructed in the context of live streaming, we need to pay special attention to this topic and understand better the skills required to address proactively changes in the training and education of future and current employees and employers.

2. LITERATURE REVIEW

2.1. Customer Communication in Online Shopping

Sun et al. (2019) note that because of the rapid development of Internet technology, text and images have long given way to multimedia presentations in online stores. There is only one way to conduct business online by incorporating social media. Moreover, some sellers on social commerce platforms have started using live streaming to engage in electronic commerce in Indonesia, thanks to the rising tide of this trend. Because of this, a new type of social commerce known as live-streaming commerce has emerged.

During live streaming, businesses communicate with customers in real time. Live streamers demonstrate product features and capabilities and provide a brief introduction. Customers may have questions about product costs, shipping options, and more. The response from a live broadcaster depends on what is happening in real time, which can influence the viewer's behaviour. To complete their purchase, the customer clicks on the embedded link provided by the vendor, like WhatsApp (Chen et al., 2017; Liu et al., 2021, p. 3075). There are three different types of live-streaming businesses:

1. Social networking sites that include live-streaming elements (such as Facebook Live) to simplify selling.
2. Live-streaming platforms that incorporate commercial activities (such as TikTok).
3. E-commerce sites, marketplaces (such as Shopee), or mobile applications that integrate live-streaming features.

Live-streaming commerce has many advantages over traditional e-commerce, including better product presentation, lower costs, a better shopping experience, and smarter sales logic (Li et al., 2021). Furthermore, live-streaming commerce is a new business strategy that brings sellers up front and in conversation with their customers.

The theoretical and practical effects of live-streaming commerce are attracting the attention of researchers. However, a sustainable commercial model for live streaming is only now taking shape. There are very few academic studies that cover the topic of the live-streaming business. Only in studies related to live streaming and social trading did we find a similar topic. Millennial generation customers (born between 1982 and 2000) who are accustomed to using social media for shopping (Yamawaki, 2017) find live-streaming commerce very useful. However, it centers on high-end products and the tastes of Brazilian and Italian consumers. This was proposed by Sun et al. (2022): visibility affordability, metavoicing affordability, and direction affordability all influence consumer tendencies to make purchases and are influenced by store convenience.

The purpose of this study was to examine the purchase intentions of IT professionals. According to Li et al. (2021), loyal users are important in building a successful live-streaming e-commerce platform. The researchers found that technological and social aspects positively influenced their emotional attachment to streamers and platforms. However, the product factor is ignored. Authenticity, similarity in attitude, and the ability to respond to consumer comments are all factors that Liu et al. (2021) found to increase viewers' sense of connection and investment in live streaming. For them, it all comes down to the live streamer. The existence of celebrity effects and lurker situations in the live-streaming business was established by Wu et al. (2021). According to Yin (2020), elements including perceived ease of use, situational influence, and social proof have a major influence on a consumer's propensity to purchase. The value that impacts the consumer's decision to buy is diminishing in their eyes. Hu and Chaudhry (2020) use several relational bonding, affective commitment, and customer engagement strategies to develop relationships with customers and inspire loyalty among them. They, directly and indirectly, found that social and structural ties increase customer engagement through emotional commitment. Live-streaming commerce is the next step in e-commerce because it incorporates social networks in real time. Cai and Wohn (2019) conduct e-commerce operations and transactions in a live-streaming environment.

This method uses a live-streaming platform, which combines live-streaming technology and infrastructure, to create a virtual space for real-time communication, entertainment, socialising, and even business. In this context, the live-streaming space generates a digital location to stream live, providing viewers with a path to observe and interact with the live stream. Most people who stream their lives online to a large audience have a sizeable following on one of these sites: Live-stream creators (Xu et al., 2020). Typically, live streams can demonstrate goods from multiple angles and encourage viewers to purchase while watching (Wongkitrungrueng & Assarut, 2020). Users are encouraged to participate actively in their communications and purchases thanks to the live-streaming trading environment's emphasis on interactivity (Kang et al., 2021).

When a business is conducted via live streaming, customers can see the products being sold in real time and talk to other streamers and customers in social settings like Wongkitrungrueng and Assarut (2020). Such experiences can help users form attachments more quickly (Li et al., 2021). The benefits of shopping while watching live broadcasts are well known. Hilvert-Bruce et al. (2018) note that live-streaming trading also helps viewers build virtual social relationships during real-time interactions, leading to feelings of intimacy and closeness with streamers, known as parasocial relationships.

According to Sjöblom and Hamari (2017), the live-stream trade paves the way for dynamic new relationships between media producers and viewers. By having positive experiences with products promoted by streamers, viewers are likelier to trust and like streamers, strengthening parasocial relationships. As a result, while watching a streamer's stream, viewers are naturally interested, amazed, and informed about the streamer's products and recommendations.

The audience felt present during (Chen & Lin, 2018) live presentation. Consumers become excited and happy with the site's interactive features, funny content, and new shopping opportunities. In this unusual situation, individuals are not only observers but also contributors to and shapers of events, giving them joy. Thus, the cognitive and emotional states that result from these qualities provide diverse user experiences, resulting in an increased desire to encourage consumption behaviours such as impulsive and hedonic consumption (Park & Zhao, 2016). In addition, the live broadcast itself, the audience's interaction with the streamer, the streamer's feelings, the product, etc., all become conversation starters among their peers. Also, viewers may want to talk about it with their friends and acquaintances in person or online (on sites like Facebook, Twitter, and YouTube).

This closeness is fostered by streamers' quick and courteous responses to viewers' comments and their consideration of viewers' viewing experiences and emotions (Hu et al., 2017). There is real-time interaction between the streamer and the viewer in live-streaming trading. Streamers, for example, offer advice tailored to the specific needs of their audience and often engage in impromptu performances, such as jokes or songs. Streamers can also choose to open up about their personal experiences in life and at work. Therefore, viewers intuitively feel the virtual connection and perceive a bond with the streamer. Baker et al. (1992) reviewed the literature on offline and online consumer research and found that social elements, such as the interpersonal skills of salespeople, were significant motivators. Live-streaming commerce gives viewers many ways to interact and talk to other streamers and viewers.

2.2. Pragmatics and Discourse Analysis Study

By 'live-streaming commerce', we mean transmitting monetary and other e-commerce-related activities through live-streaming media. To create a digital community, you need a place to go live and the tools and equipment to do so. An arrangement that facilitates seamless affordability cues for real-time engagement, entertainment, social activity, and commerce. The live-streaming room lets viewers watch and engage with streamers in real time. To learn about a product, shoppers using classic e-commerce platforms can only do so through one-way browsing and consumption of static product content (such as pre-recorded text, images, and videos). Spending time and energy searching for things, reading product information attentively, comparing alternative products, and making evaluations based on various types of information (such as, e.g., comments from other, unknown shoppers) are all part of the shopping process, according to Sjöblom and Hamari (2017).

Therefore, there are few opportunities for social interaction or pleasant experiences during this business transaction. Streaming trading has emerged recently and has proven promising potential as an innovative business model to combine dynamic real-time interactions between streamers and observers, provide correct information, and involve hedonistic aspects in attracting consumers to enjoy consumption activities. Live streaming allows viewers to get up-to-date details on various topics, connect with streamers on a personal level without ever seeing them in person, communicate with each other, and spend a few enjoyable hours communicating with the interesting people examined in this study.

Language plays an important role in the world of literature. This is because language influences the development of the literary world. After all, we can learn various other languages in it, as well as knowledge that can be used for language development. Language has an important meaning and role for humans when communicating with each other (Bracken & Oughton, 2006).

The process of communication in humans can occur through verbal and nonverbal communication. The function of language, in this case, is clear as a means of communication between humans, so the author relates this research to pragmatic studies. Pragmatics is a branch of linguistics that studies how linguistic units are communicated to express the meaning behind an utterance.

According to Cruz (2015), 'pragmatics and discourse analysis study the meaning of words in context, analysis of the parts of meaning that can be pragmatics and discourse analysis study the meaning of words in context, analysis of the parts of meaning that can be explained by knowledge of the physical and social world, and the socio-psychological factors influencing communication, as well as the knowledge of the time and place in which the worlds are spoken or written', which means pragmatics and discourse analysis is the science of the meaning of speech in its context, which analyses the parts of meaning that can be explained by physical knowledge and social science, not only social psychological factors that can affect the way of communication, but also the circumstances of the time and place in which the speech is spoken or written.

According to Bunt (2000) and Verschueren (2022), pragmatics is the study of the relationship between linguistic forms and the users of those forms. Through pragmatics, one can speak about the intended meaning, assumptions, goals, and types of action. Recanati (2004), Thomas (2014), and Cruse (2010) define *pragmatics* as the study of language in its context. This means that the study of pragmatics needs to involve interpreting what people mean in a particular context and how that context affects what is said. Pragmatics is the study of communicative acts in their social and cultural context.

As it has to do with the meaning of speech (utterance), pragmatics uses context-bound meaning. Treating language pragmatically means treating it by considering its context, namely, its use in communication events (Senft, 2014). According to Huang (2012), pragmatics is a branch of linguistics that studies language in terms of its use in communication. Speech acts as a form of communication. These are not events that occur by themselves but have a function, contain certain aims and objectives, and can influence or affect the speech partner.

In a speech act activity, humans play an important role in providing the information and the recipients of that information, called speakers or speech partners, and involving the speaker and two or more people who are his speech partners. An utterance is an utterance or utterance with a certain function in communication, meaning that the utterance or utterance contains a meaning. The actual speech intent must be identified by looking at the speech situation behind it. In examining the speech intent, a study situation that does not pay attention to the speech situation will lead to erroneous results.

Speech act events will not be separated from the context of the speech; the environment around the speech allows speech participants to interact in communication events and makes the linguistic forms used in the interaction understandable. Leech (2016), Warnke (2022), and Habermas (1994) explained that in speech events, speakers always consider the factors that play a role in speech events, called speech components. These speech components can be expressed as an abbreviation, speaking, each of which is the initial phoneme of one of the following factors: S: Setting and scene (background); P: Participant (participant); E: Ends (purpose); A: Act Sequences; K: Key; I: Instrument; N: Norms; and G: Genre. With the context of the speech, it can be easier to understand the intent of an utterance. This research focuses on speech acts closely related to language and literature.

According to Uoti (2022), speech acts are psychological symptoms, and their continuity is determined by the speaker's language ability in certain situations. The speech act is a pragmatic analysis, a branch of linguistics that studies language from the aspect of its actual use.

3. RESEARCH METHOD

This study used a qualitative research design. According to Merriam and Tisdell (2015), Tracy (2019), and Merriam and Tisdell (2015), qualitative research is research that intends to understand the phenomena of what is experienced by research subjects such as behaviour, perceptions, motivations, actions, and others holistically and using descriptions in the form of words and language in a special context that is natural and by utilising various scientific methods (Lune & Berg, 2017; Merriam & Grenier, 2019). The data in this study is in the form of speech segments in written form, which can be in the form of words, phrases, and sentences in conversations and their context in buying and selling transactions at online shops (olshop).

The speech segments taken are indicated to contain forms, strategies, and functions of speech acts during the transaction process. The data collection technique is used to obtain data that will be collected as research material. Techniques in a study must be carried out optimally to achieve research objectives. A data collection technique is needed in this study to achieve this goal. The data collection technique in this research is the documentation technique. Data analysis in this study is an interactive analysis technique. The interactive technique is a data analysis technique that involves conducting data analysis and data collection processes. This technique combines the implementation of data collection with data analysis so that both can be done together. The interactive analysis addresses speech segments indicated as forms, strategies, and action functions between sellers and buyers during live streaming on Facebook social media.

4. RESULTS AND DISCUSSION

The speech acts contained in online buying and selling on Facebook consist of four types of speech acts: assertive speech acts, directive acts, expressive speech acts, and commissive speech acts.

1. Assertive Speech

Assertiveness is a speech act that binds the speaker to the truth or proposition he expresses. Assertive speech acts are related to facts and aim to provide information. This speech act is related to knowledge, existing data, and what has happened and has not happened. In this study of speech acts in online buying and selling on Facebook, four kinds of sub-speech acts were found: stating, telling, showing, and mentioning.

a. State

Three data points show the speech act of 'state' in the study of online buying and selling speech acts on Facebook with contextual markers. The form of the assertive speech act of 'stating' in online buying and selling on Facebook can be seen in the following data:

Table 7.1 shows the speech act of 'state' in live streaming of online buying and selling on Facebook. According to the Cambridge Dictionary (2023a), means writing something, especially clearly and carefully. From this definition, it can be said that the assertive speech act 'states' is a speech act that is done to explain or explain something that aims to provide information related to facts. The information conveyed is based on events experienced or observed by the speaker and known to the speech partner. This can be seen in the context of a seller's speech contained in Table 7.1, the speech means its original Adidas. The seller states that the Adidas product he sells is original or genuine. Furthermore, in the speech of 10 NB, here for 8, 9, and 10 years old, it's big. The seller stated that the product information for NB was at the age of 8 or 9 years old, but in this speech, the size was 140 for 8 or 9 years old, this stated size for children aged 8 and 9 years old.

b. Tell

In the online buying and selling research on Facebook, there are four data included in the assertive speech act of 'tell'. The form of the speech act of 'telling' can be seen in the data below.

According to the Cambridge Dictionary (2023b), 'tell' means saying something to someone, often giving them information or instructions. The word 'informs' means to convey (news and so on) and means that it is known. The speech act of 'telling' is a speech act spoken by the speaker to convey something so that the hearer knows. This can be seen in the context of the speech at 1.59 minutes, when the seller conveys information about pants products. In the speech, those who want to request may well ... the seller informs the audience that he can request or choose and enter the order so that it is shown. In this speech, I give it for free, I give it away for free, and the seller tells me that there are free products. In the next speech, those who want to recap WhatsApp chat later. It means that the seller informs the buyer that the price recap is via WhatsApp chat.

c. Show

Assertive speech 'shows' in online buying and selling speech on Facebook. There are three data points with contextual markers. The form of the assertive speech act of 'showing' in the online buying and selling speech on Facebook can be seen in the following data:

According to the Cambridge Dictionary (2023c), how means to make it possible for something to be seen. It can also describe (1) to show; (2) to state; (3) to explain (with evidence, etc.); and (4) to signify (that ...). The assertive speech act 'show' means a speech act that is said by the speaker to show something or show something with evidence. This can be seen in this speech: the size is 140, fit for 7–8 years old, at 2.21 minutes while showing a yellow shirt to the buyer. In the story, the buyer mentions that this is for 8 or 9 year olds while pointing at the product's age of 8 or 9 years old. The next character, who can still walk, is an 8 or 9 year old, and the seller is tugging at the product to show the quality of the product she sells.

d. Mention

In the assertive speech act of 'mentioning' in the online buying and selling speech on Facebook, there are three data points with contextual markers. The form of the assertive speech act of 'mentioning' in online buying and selling on Facebook can be seen in the following data:

In the Cambridge Dictionary (2023d), the word mentioned means to speak about something quickly, giving little detail or using few words; this is described as: (1) to give a name to; declare the name of something; name: (2) pronounce the name (thing, person, etc.); call names. From this definition, it can be said that the assertive speech act of 'mentioning' is a speech act performed to pronounce the name of an object, person, and so on. This is from the speech that occurred at 1.09 minutes, when the seller called Mama Rafa. The name is commenting in the comment column. The next statement is from Yunikro; here the seller states the name of the product, namely Yunikro, then continues in the next minute from Yunikro.

2. Directive Speech Acts

Directive speech acts are the types of speech acts used by speakers to tell others to do something. Directive speech acts aim to influence or instruct the speech partner to produce an effect in the form of actions that are shown in the form of speech. In this study of speech acts in online buying and selling on Facebook, five kinds of directive speech acts were found, namely suggesting, asking, ordering, pleading, and ordering.

a. Recommend/Suggest

In the online buying and selling research on Facebook, there are four 'recommend' directive speech acts. To understand more clearly, the form of the directive speech act 'recommend' can be seen in the data below.

According to the Cambridge Dictionary (2023e), the meaning of the word 'recommend' is *to suggest that someone or something would be good or suitable for a particular job or purpose, or to suggest that a particular action should be taken, or* to give advice (recommendations and so on); recommend. The directive speech act of 'recommending' means an utterance spoken by a speaker whose function is to give advice or opinions to the speech partner for consideration. This can be

Table 7.1. *Assertive Speech Acts Data Corpus (1).*

No	Context	Speech	Minute
1	Seller express information about Adidas products	Here, Adidas, original	2.14
2	The seller declares information about the NB product	10 NB. Here 8- or 9-year-old mom. It's big	2.29
3	The seller declares information about the size of the clothes	This size is 140 for 8 or 9 years	3.20

Source: Adapted from Tamis-LeMonda et al. (2019).

seen in the context of the seller's speech when suggesting a Nike 20 shirt product. The Nike 20 shirt product is used as a comparison material with other products. This speech is bund. It's cute when the seller suggests a product to the buyer. Then, in the words 'Buy it' – that's what she said – the seller's virtual mother suggested that the product be bought as a result of another buyer's speech. Next, the speech should be continued. First, because 'I'm already sleepy', the seller suggested that if the giveaway was held, it should be continued.

b. Ask

The form of the directive speech act of asking was found in the research of online buying and selling speech acts on Facebook, namely:

To ask is to hope to be given or get something; to put a question to someone or to request an answer from someone (Cambridge Dictionary, 2023f). The speech act of asking is a speech act performed by the speaker to give or get something from the directive speech act of 'asking', namely, data with contextual markers. This can be seen in the context of the speech when the buyer makes comments to record the goods to be purchased, namely, green five. Furthermore, in the speech 'I want to give for free', the seller asks the buyer to wait until the giveaway is over to get a free product. In the words yes, it is. Just give it to Miss Nada, sorry. After all, one of the buyers asked the seller to give the product she bought to Miss

Table 7.2.   *Assertive Speech Act Data Corpus (2).*

No	Context	Speech	Minute
1	Seller provides information about pants products	pants, mom	1.59
2	The seller gives information that you can request	those who want to request, please	0.20
3	The seller gives information that there are free items	I give this for free. I love it for free	4.53
4	The seller gives information that can be recorded on WhatsApp	Those who want to recap later chat WhatsApp	8.41

Source: Adapted from Tamis-LeMonda et al. (2019).

Table 7.3.   *Assertive Speech Acts Data Corpus (3).*

No	Context	Speech	Minute
1	The seller shows the product size of the clothes		2.21
2	The seller shows the product size of the clothes	here, the size is 140 for seven or 8 year olds	2.33
3	The seller shows the size of the product that is suitable for traveling for a child of 8 or 9 years old	The one who can still walk is eight or 9 years old	2.47

Source: Adapted from Tamis-LeMonda et al. (2019).

Nada. The last is the speech. End moms (laughing), the seller asks the audience to end the live streaming.

c. Reign

In the directive speech act of 'governing' in the online buying and selling speech on Facebook, there are three data points with contextual markers. The form of the directive speech act of 'governing' in online buying and selling speech on Facebook can be seen in the following data:

To command, in the Cambridge Dictionary (2023g), means to be the king or queen of a country and give orders; to be ordered to do something. The directive speech act 'to command' means a speech act intended by the seeker to influence the speaker to take an action ordered by the speaker. This is shown in the context of the speech when the seller orders people to like, comment, and share so that there will be more viewers from the seller's live streaming. The context of this speech occurs at 0.48 minutes. Furthermore, in the speech help, like, comment, share, the seller ordered that the live stream be shared, which was continued in the next minute with the speech help, like, comment, and share. Comments come; 'mom helps comments come here'.

d. Begging

In the study of online buying and selling speech acts on Facebook, it was found that three data points were included in the directive speech act of the speech act 'beg' with the lingual marker of the foreign language, the word 'please'. The form of the directive speech act of 'begging' in the study of online buying and selling speech acts on Facebook is found in the following data.

To beg, in the Cambridge Dictionary (2023h), means if that is supposed to show the unique objectivity of utilitarianism, it fails by simply *begging* the question or asking respectfully. The directive speech act of 'begging' is a speech act that is said by the speaker to request something from the speech partner so that the speech partner does something that is ordered by the speaker. This is what the seller did at the last minute when she announced that he would stop broadcasting live while noting that she would be back live streaming tomorrow. Speech just bought … (laughs). It was already free; the buyer asked the seller to sell the item that was used as a giveaway prize. The last one is the speech: 'Well, mom, the seller begged the audience to allow him to end the live streaming'.

Table 7.4. *Assertive Speech Acts Data Corpus (4).*

No	Context	Speech	Minute
1	The seller says the buyer's name	Mommy Rafa	1.09
2	The seller mentions the name of the company or clothing production	From Yunikro here	3.40
3	The seller mentions the name of the company or clothing production	From Yunikro	4.00

Source: Adapted from Tamis-LeMonda et al. (2019).

e. Ordered

In the directive speech act of 'ordering' in the online buying and selling speech on Facebook, there is one data point with contextual markers. The data, which is the directive speech act 'to order', can be seen in the following data example.

In the Cambridge Dictionary (2023i), the meaning of the word 'order' is a request to make, supply, or deliver food or goods, or to command (to do something); order to go to (to do something); delegate. The directive speech act of 'ordering' is a speech act that is said by the speaker to the speech partner to order or do something. During the speech, 'I was already sleepy'. That's it. In the past, being sleepy was a rule that must be written in the comments column as a condition to get a pair of pants for free; this was done by the researcher without saying please comment, but the audience already understood the seller's intention.

3. Expressive Speech

The expressive speech act is a speech act that expresses the psychological attitude of the speaker towards the situation being experienced by the speech partner and third parties who are not directly involved in the speech. Expressive speech acts are contained in the online buying and selling speech act research on Facebook, namely thanking, apologizing, complaining, and praising.

Table 7.5. *Directive Speech Action Data Corpus (1).*

No	Context	Speech	Minute
1	The seller suggests that the buyer buy a Nike product no 20	If you want this, I'll give you a Nike product no 20	3.28
2	The seller suggests to the buyer a product	This one, mom. This is cute	5:40
3	The seller suggests to the buyer a product	Just buy it. That's what she said, Mom Maya	7.24
4	The seller suggests to the buyer a product	Should have continued It's been a while; I'm already sleepy. That's it (laughing)	6.35

Source: Adapted from Tamis-LeMonda et al. (2019).

Table 7.6. *Directive Speech Action Data Corpus (2).*

No	Context	Speech	Minute
1	The buyer asks the seller to note the items to be purchased, namely green clothes totalling 5	green 5	5.05
2	The seller asks the buyer to wait for the goods to be free	if you want this, I will give it for free	5:47
3	The buyer asks the seller to take the giveaway item for her	okay then. Just give Miss Nada, sorry	7.31
4	The seller asks the buyer to end the live-streaming	just end it (laughs) ...	8.59

Source: Adapted from Tamis-LeMonda et al. (2019).

a. Be thankful

In the study of online buying and selling speech acts on Facebook, it was found that four data were included in the expressive speech act of 'thank you'. The data that shows the expressive speech act of 'thank you' can be seen in the following sample data.

In the Cambridge Dictionary (2023j), the meaning of the word 'be thankful' is to be *happy* or *grateful* because of something, or to give thanks, give birth to gratitude, return a favour after receiving kindness, etc. The speech act of 'thank you' is done by the speaker to the speech partner because the speaker feels grateful or gets something good from the speech partner. This happened in the context of the speech when the seller thanked him for ordering the sale at 8.05 minutes. In the speech, it's already mom. Thank you, bud. The seller thanked the buyer and then continued at 8.48 and 9.09 minutes with the same speech.

b. Apologize

In the study of online buying and selling speech acts on Facebook, one piece of data shows the expressive speech act of 'apologizing'. The form of an expressive speech act 'apologizing' contained in the research on online buying and selling speech acts on Facebook can be seen in the following data.

According to the Cambridge Dictionary (2023k), the meaning of the word 'apologize' is to tell someone that you are sorry for having done something that has caused them problems or unhappiness, or to ask to be forgiven (forgivable). The expressive speech act of 'apologizing' is a form of speech act conveyed by the speaker with sorry words that have the aim of apologizing. Even though in the context of the corpus data, 4.11 does not mention an apology, it is a form of guilt that the seller wants to show because another audience member has mentioned a giveaway club held by the seller.

c. Praise

In the study of online buying and selling speech acts on Facebook, there are eight data included in expressive speech acts.

In the Cambridge Dictionary (2023l), the word 'praise' means to express admiration or approval of the achievements or characteristics of a person or thing, or to give birth to admiration and appreciation for something that is considered

Table 7.7. *Directive Speech Action Data Corpus (3).*

No	Context	Speech	Minute
1	The seller instructs the audience to like, comment, and share	help to like, comment, share, mom help like, comment, and share	0.48
2	The seller instructs the audience to like, comment, and share	help to like, comment, and share	0.56
3	The seller instructs the audience to like, comment, and share	help to test, comment, and share. comments come, mom help comments come	1.51

Source: Adapted from Tamis-LeMonda et al. (2019).

good, beautiful, brave, etc. Expressive speech acts 'Praise' is a speech act conveyed by speakers by giving birth to admiration and appreciation for something that is considered good, beautiful, dashing, and so on. This is what happens in the context of the speech when the seller says 'this is mom, this is cute' at 5.40 minutes.

d. Commissive Speech

A commissive speech act is a form of speech act that is understood by the speaker to bind himself to future actions. In the study of online buying and selling speech acts on Facebook, there are two types of commissive speech acts: promising and offering something.

e. Promise

In the commissive speech act of 'promise' in the online buying and selling speech on Facebook, there are data points, namely four data points with lingual and one data point with contextual markers. The following is data showing the comitative speech act of 'promise'.

The meaning of 'promise' (to tell someone that you will certainly do something; Cambridge Dictionary, 2023m) is to tell someone that you will certainly do something, or (1) to make a promise, stating that he is willing and able to do something (give, help, date, etc.); or (2) to be able to fulfil what has been said or has been agreed. The commissive speech act of 'promising' is conveyed by speakers to express their willingness and ability to do something for their interlocutor.

f. Offering something

In the study of online buying and selling speech acts on Facebook, it was found that nine data points were included in the commissive speech act of 'offering',

Table 7.8. *Directive Speech Action Data Corpus (4).*

No	Context	Speech	Minute
1	Seller begged to stop live streaming	tomorrow again mom. Insha Allah tomorrow	9.03
2	Buyers beg to buy items that are used as giveaways	just buy it (laughs). It's even been given for free earlier	7.12
3	Seller begged to stop live streaming	all right moms	8.19

Source: Adapted from Tamis-LeMonda et al. (2019).

Table 7.9. *Directive Speech Action Data Corpus (5).*

No	Context	Speech	Minute
1	The seller asked to mention if you could get the giveaway	already, already sleepy that's it already sleepy	5.52

Source: Adapted from Tamis-LeMonda et al. (2019).

namely seven data points with the lingual marker 'want' and two data points with contextual markers. To be able to understand the type of commissive speech act of offering something further, the following is data showing the commissive speech act of offering something.

To offer, in the Cambridge Dictionary (2023n), means to ask someone if they would like to have something or if they would like you to do something, or to propose something to someone (to be bought, used, contacted, etc.). The commissive speech act of 'offering something' is conveyed by the speaker to his interlocutor with the aim that the speech partner is willing to accept an offer from the speaker. Furthermore, in this story from Nike, well the seller also offers the products she sells. In the story of the 10 years, mom also includes an offer speech because the seller says it while displaying it to the buyer or audience. Furthermore, in this one speech, it's funny that the buyer again offers his product by praising her product.

g. Transactional conversation on WhatsApp

Researchers have tried to transact with online sellers who have been used as data in this study so that transactions via WhatsApp are summarised as research data. Below, a corpus of data has been created to make it easier for researchers to analyse.

Based on the corpus of data above, buyers and sellers use more assertive speech acts, namely questioning in WhatsApp conversations. According to the Cambridge Dictionary (2023o), the meaning of 'ask' is *to put a question to someone, to request an answer from someone, or* to ask something of someone, to inquire about something. It can be seen in Data 1, 2, 5 and 6, while Data 3 includes the type of speech act of informing, and data Table 7.7 is the type of speech act of state.

In Data 1, the context is a buyer asking questions about a clothing product, namely the price; in Data 2, the context is a seller asking questions about a size 8 or 9 shirt. In Data 3, the context that occurs is that the seller tells the buyer the total price of the product and states a discount to the buyer; in 4 context data, what happens is that a buyer states that he has shared a seller's lifestreaming post; in 5 context data, what happens is that a seller asks for a product to be taken by a

Table 7.10. *Corpus of Expressive Speech Acts (1).*

No	Context	Speech	Minute
1	The seller thanks the buyer	Thank you sist … (sister)	8.05
2	The seller thanks the buyer	It's done. Thanks, mom	8.28
3	The seller thanks the buyer	Thank you, all mommy. Thanks	8.48
4	The seller thanks the buyer	Thanks, mom	9.09

Source: Adapted from Leech (2016, pp. 36–40).

Table 7.11. *Corpus of Expressive Speech Acts (2).*

No	Context	Speech	Minute
1	The seller apologized to the buyer when he did the giveaway	Well … Maya mom, take it first	6.42

Source: Adapted from Leech (2016, pp. 36–40).

buyer, in 6 context data, what happens is that a seller asks how many products to buy and also the buyer asks how much discount he gets; while the contextual data that occurs is that the seller states the price for the deal.

4. DISCUSSION

Live streaming has recently become one of the most popular ways for self-employed sellers to make direct sales, as it gives customers a way to interact with them even though they can't see them. Existing research focuses on why and how people want to shop through live streaming. Still, not much is known about how sellers feel about it, as reflected in the communication between sellers and buyers and the existing communication forms. While anyone can take advantage of the possible advantages of live-streaming trading, sellers have varying degrees of success with this method. According to Parker et al. (2016), Lee et al. (2015), and Chaffey and Ellis-Chadwick (2019), data from live-stream sellers is used to determine the nature and scope of engagement metrics and to demonstrate how the live-stream sales process is dynamic and interactive through two-way communication between the seller and the seller and buyers in the live-streaming trade. This suggests that social commerce can be a strong marketplace when the economic utility from price incentives is strengthened and protected by the social utility from trust and sharing.

Table 7.12.   *Corpus of Expressive Speech Acts (2).*

No	Context	Speech	Minute
1	The seller praises the product she sells	This is cute, mom	5.40

Source: Adapted from Leech (2016, pp. 36–40).

Table 7.13.   *Corpus of Commissive Speech Acts (1).*

No	Context	Speech	Minute
1	The seller promises to return to do live broadcasts and also do give away	Later, God willing, if it's live again, I'll give another giveaway. In, if not in the middle, at the end …	8.31

Source: Adapted from Leech (2016, pp. 36–40).

Table 7.14.   *Corpus of Commissive Speech Acts (2).*

No	Context	Speech	Minute
1	The seller offers a yellow shirt product for 20,000	I want this yellow … yellow size 20	2.35
2	The seller offers a product from Nike	this is from Nike	3.03
3	The seller offers a 10-year-old product	ten years in here mom	3.38
4	The seller offers a product for children	it's so funny	4.43

Source: Adapted from Leech (2016, pp. 36–40).

Griffiths and McLean (2015) explore the impact of the adoption and use of social media on corporate communication and brand image as a form of discourse and textual analysis through social media brand communication, interactions with customers, and small-scale surveys with managers. While social media understands the importance of 'real' conversations with customers, only a minority adopt a 'human brand' approach. Even fewer seem to have a strategy for the characteristics of social media communication described by the four types of sub-speech acts found, namely, stating, telling, showing, and mentioning in Tables 7.1–7.4. The contradictory challenges of the immediacy and conversational tone expected of social media communication versus the need to manage brand image and control corporate communications are investigated in this chapter.

Therefore, talking about keeping the audience's interest and trust in the seller and the product is enhanced. In this way, the customer approach is preferred to achieve the commercial objectives in Tables 7.5–7.9. Wu et al. (2022) suggest that social trading can be a strong market when strategies such as intensively including short affirmatives in their turn-taking, such as 'correct' and right, for the skilful and frequent introduction of their partner's product reduce the uncertainty of consumers' online shopping regarding the product or company they work with in their live stream.

The results of this research are shown in Tables 7.10–7.15 ensuring that customers are happy is the most important thing in every sale or purchase. Customer satisfaction is a customer's overall opinion about a product or service based on their purchasing experience. Satisfaction or happiness can be compared to how well they think the product meets their expectations. When customers are happy with a product or service, they are likelier to tell others about it and continue buying or using it rather than switching to something else. This study related to Karim et al. (2022) findings that customer satisfaction and trust are very important, and

Table 7.15. *WhatsApp Conversation Action Data Corpus.*

No	Data	Types of Speech Acts
1	How much was the yellow Nike shirt?	Questioning
2	Size for 8 or 9 years old, mom?	Questioning
3	One hundred and thirteen thousand ladies, but we have a discount for those who enter our live stream, ladies, but must include proof of screenshots sharing the live streaming	Telling
4	Yes, I follow the live deck, I share it with the FB group instead	Stating
5	Ready mom, so want to take size for 8 or 9 years old, mom, the yellow one	Questioning
6	How many sheets ma'am? The dress?	Questioning
7	One hundred and seventy five thousand two mom. Sorry, we are slow to respond because we have a lot of customers at the moment	Stating

Source: Adapted from Leech (2016, pp. 36–40).

customer satisfaction with online shopping is directly related to factors such as security, delivery, availability of information, price, quality, and time.

5. CONCLUSION

Changes in how people act during the pandemic greatly affect how people shop online. Based on the results of this study, it was found that more people are using their Facebook accounts to shop online during the pandemic. People have come to accept that using technology to shop is a new way to do things. The results show four types of speech acts between sellers and buyers in the live-streaming online shop on Facebook: assertive speech acts, directive speech acts, expressive speech acts, and commissive speech acts. Assertive consists of four kinds of speech acts: stating with a total of three utterances, informing with a total of four utterances, showing with a total of three utterances, and mentioning with a total of three utterances. There are five kinds of directive speech acts:

1. Suggesting with a total of 4 utterances.
2. Asking for a total of 4 utterances.
3. Ordering with a total of 3 utterances.
4. Begging with a total of 3 utterances.
5. Ordering with a total of 1 utterance.

Expressive speech acts are thanking with four utterances, apologizing with one utterance, and praising with one utterance. Commissive speech acts include two sub-speech acts: promising with a total of one utterance and offering something with a total of four utterances.

Understanding the skills necessary for buying and selling transactions through live streaming on Facebook will help in addressing the frictional unemployment due to skill gaps that we are already facing and provide educators with the knowledge of curriculum needs to proactively address this gap. Moreover, these findings add value to the current limited literature on the subject and provides policymakers with insights of how to tackle frictional unemployment which may result from a lack of specific new skills.

REFERENCES

Baker, J., Levy, M., & Grewal, D. (1992). An experimental approach to making retail store environmental decisions. *Journal of Retailing, 68*(4), 445–460.

Baturina, L., & Simakov, A. (2023). Students' attitude towards e-learning in Russia after pandemic. *Education Science and Management, 1*(1), 1–6.

Berger, M., & Eisendle, D. (2019). Web 2.0 and the concept of 'data controller': Recent developments in EU Data Protection Law. *Indian Journal of Law and Technology, 15*, 20–39.

Berger, H., & Thomas, C. (2016). SMEs-social media marketing performance. *International Journal of Web Engineering and Technology, 11*(3), 215–232.

Bracken, L. J., & Oughton, E. A. (2006). 'What do you mean?' The importance of language in developing interdisciplinary research. *Transactions of the Institute of British Geographers, 31*(3), 371–382.

Bunt, H. (2000). Dialogue pragmatics and context specification. *Abduction, Belief and Context in Dialogue, 2*, 139–166.

Cai, J., & Wohn, D. Y. (2019). Live streaming commerce: Uses and gratifications approach to understanding consumers' motivations. In *Proceedings of the 52nd Hawaii international conference on system sciences* (pp. 2548–2557).

Cambridge Dictionary. (2023a). *Apologize*. Cambridge Dictionary. https://dictionary.cambridge.org/dictionary/english/apologize?q=Apologize

Cambridge Dictionary. (2023b). *Ask*. Cambridge Dictionary. https://dictionary.cambridge.org/dictionary/english/ask

Cambridge Dictionary. (2023c). *Begging*. Cambridge Dictionary. https://dictionary.cambridge.org/dictionary/english/begging

Cambridge Dictionary. (2023d). *Mention*. Cambridge Dictionary. https://dictionary.cambridge.org/dictionary/english/mention?q=Mention

Cambridge Dictionary. (2023e). *Offer*. Cambridge Dictionary. https://dictionary.cambridge.org/dictionary/english/offer

Cambridge Dictionary. (2023f). *Ordered*. Cambridge Dictionary. https://dictionary.cambridge.org/dictionary/english/ordered

Cambridge Dictionary. (2023g). *Praise*. Cambridge Dictionary. https://dictionary.cambridge.org/dictionary/english/praise?q=Praise

Cambridge Dictionary. (2023h). *Promise*. Cambridge Dictionary. https://dictionary.cambridge.org/dictionary/english/promise?q=Promise

Cambridge Dictionary. (2023i). *Recommend*. Cambridge Dictionary. https://dictionary.cambridge.org/dictionary/english/recommend?q=Recommend

Cambridge Dictionary. (2023j). *Reign*. Cambridge Dictionary. https://dictionary.cambridge.org/dictionary/english/reign?q=Reign

Cambridge Dictionary. (2023k). *Show*. Cambridge Dictionary. https://dictionary.cambridge.org/dictionary/english/show?q=Show

Cambridge Dictionary. (2023l). *Show*. Cambridge Dictionary. https://dictionary.cambridge.org/dictionary/english/show?q=Show

Cambridge Dictionary. (2023m). *Tell*. Cambridge Dictionary. https://dictionary.cambridge.org/dictionary/english/tell

Cambridge Dictionary. (2023n). *Thankful*. Cambridge Dictionary. https://dictionary.cambridge.org/dictionary/english/thankful

Cambridge Dictionary. (2023o). *Ask*. Cambridge Dictionary. https://dictionary.cambridge.org/dictionary/english/ask?q=Ask

Carlson, J., Rahman, M., Voola, R., & De Vries, N. (2018). Customer engagement behaviours in social media: Capturing innovation opportunities. *Journal of Services Marketing, 32*(1), 83–94.

Chaffey, D., & Ellis-Chadwick, F. (2019). *Digital marketing: Strategy, implementation and practice.* Pearson.

Chen, A., Lu, Y., & Wang, B. (2017). Customers' purchase decision-making process in social commerce: A social learning perspective. *International Journal of Information Management, 37*(6), 627–638.

Chen, C. C., & Lin, Y. C. (2018). What drives live-stream usage intention? The perspectives of flow, entertainment, social interaction, and endorsement. *Telematics and Informatics, 35*(1), 293–303.

Cruse, A. (2010). *Meaning in language: An introduction to semantics and pragmatics.* Oxford University Press.

Cruz, M. P. (2015). Pragmatics and discourse analysis. *The Encyclopedia of Applied Linguistics, 6*(5), 1–6.

Einav, G., & Lipson, N. (2015). The times they are a'changin'… from newspapers to TV, traditional shifts to digital. In *The new world of transitioned media* (pp. 81–101). Springer.

Evans, L., Frith, J., & Saker, M. (2022). Worlds of Commerce. In *From microverse to metaverse* (pp. 49–56). Emerald Publishing Limited.

Griffiths, M., & McLean, R. (2015). Unleashing corporate communications via social media: A UK study of brand management and conversations with customers. *Journal of Customer Behavior, 14*(2), 147–162.

Habermas, J. (1994). Actions, speech acts, linguistically mediated interactions and the lifeworld. In *Philosophical problems today* (pp. 45–74). Springer.

Hilvert-Bruce, Z., Neill, J. T., Sjöblom, M., & Hamari, J. (2018). Social motivations of live-streaming viewer engagement on Twitch. *Computers in Human Behavior, 84*, 58–67.

Hu, M., & Chaudhry, S. S. (2020). Enhancing consumer engagement in e-commerce livestreaming via relational bonds. *Internet Research, 30*(3), 1019–1041.

Hu, M., Zhang, M., & Wang, Y. (2017). Why do audiences choose to keep watching on live video streaming platforms? An explanation of dual identification framework. *Computers in Human Behavior, 75*, 594–606.

Huang, Y. (2012). *The Oxford Dictionary of pragmatics*. Oxford University Press.

Huang, Z., & Benyoucef, M. (2013). From e-commerce to social commerce: A close look at design features. *Electronic Commerce Research and Applications, 12*(4), 246–259.

Juliana, A. P., Lemy, D. M., Pramono, R., Djakasaputra, A., & Purwanto, A. (2022). Hotel performance in the digital era: Roles of digital marketing, perceived quality and trust. *Journal of Intelligent Management Decision, 1*(1), 36–45.

Kang, K., Lu, J., Guo, L., & Li, W. (2021). The dynamic effect of interactivity on customer engagement behavior through tie strength: Evidence from livestreaming commerce platforms. *International Journal of Information Management, 56*, 102251.

Karim, B. A., Setiawati, N., Halidin, A., Marannu, B., & Arsyad, Y. M. (2022). E-Commerce during Covid-19 pandemic: An analysis of Tokopedia use as a trade medium among members of Facebook Group. *Journal of Positive School Psychology*, 6124–6137.

Kotler, P., Kartajaya, H., & Setiawan, I. (2017). *Marketing 4.0: der Leitfaden für das Marketing der Zukunft*. Campus Verlag.

Lee, K., Lee, B., & Oh, W. (2015). Thumbs up, sales up? The contingent effect of Facebook likes on sales performance in social commerce. *Journal of Management Information Systems, 32*(4), 109–143.

Leech, G. N. (2016). *Principles of pragmatics*. Routledge.

Li, Y., Li, X., & Cai, J. (2021). How attachment affects user stickiness on livestreaming platforms: A socio-technical approach perspective. *Journal of Retailing and Consumer Services, 60*, 102478.

Liu, G. H., Sun, M., & Lee, N. C. A. (2021). *How can livestreamers enhance viewer engagement in eCommerce streaming?* Hawaii International Conference on System Sciences (pp. 3079–3089).

Lune, H., & Berg, B. L. (2017). *Qualitative research methods for the social sciences*. Pearson.

Merriam, S. B., & Grenier, R. S. (Eds.). (2019). *Qualitative research in practice: Examples for discussion and analysis*. John Wiley and Sons.

Merriam, S. B., & Tisdell, E. J. (2015). *Qualitative research: A guide to design and implementation*. John Wiley and Sons.

Ngubelanga, A. (2020). *Post-purchase experiences as antecedents to customer satisfaction within mobile commerce in Cape Town*. [Doctoral dissertation]. Cape Peninsula University of Technology.

Park, S. H., & Zhao, Z. (2016). *Alibaba Group: Fostering an E-Commerce Ecosystem*. China Europe International Business and Richard Ivey of Business Foundation.

Parker, G. G., Van Alstyne, M. W., & Choudary, S. P. (2016). *Platform revolution: How networked markets are transforming the economy and how to make them work for you*. WW Norton and Company.

Recanati, F. (2004). *Literal meaning*. Cambridge University Press.

Senft, G. (2014). *Understanding pragmatics*. Routledge.

Sjöblom, M., & Hamari, J. (2017). Why do people watch others play video games? An empirical study on the motivations of Twitch users. *Computers in Human Behavior, 75*, 985–996.

Sood, K., Kaur, B., & Grima, S. (2022). Revamping Indian non-life insurance industry with a trusted network: Blockchain technology. In K. Sood, R. K. Dhanaraj, B. Balamurugan, S. Grima, & R. Uma Maheshwari (Eds.), *Big Data: A game changer for insurance industry* (pp. 213–228). Emerald Publishing Limited.

Sun, J., Dushime, H., & Zhu, A. (2022). Beyond beauty: A qualitative exploration of authenticity and its impacts on Chinese consumers' purchase intention in live commerce. *Frontiers in Psychology, 5682*, 01–17.

Sun, Y., Shao, X., Li, X., Guo, Y., & Nie, K. (2019). How livestreaming influences purchase intentions in social commerce: An IT affordance perspective. *Electronic Commerce Research and Applications, 37*, 100886.

Tamis-LeMonda, C. S., Custode, S., Kuchirko, Y., Escobar, K., & Lo, T. (2019). Routine language: Speech directed to infants during home activities. *Child Development, 90*(6), 2135–2152.

Thomas, J. A. (2014). *Meaning in interaction: An introduction to pragmatics.* Routledge.

Tracy, S. J. (2019). *Qualitative research methods: Collecting evidence, crafting analysis, communicating impact.* John Wiley and Sons.

Uoti, K. (2022). *Apology as a Speech Act Set: Apology strategies of social media influencers in the context of the Covid-19 pandemic.* [Master's thesis]. University of Turku, UTUPub.

Verschueren, J., Östman, J. O. (Ed.) (2022). Contrastive pragmatics. In *Handbook of pragmatics: Manual.* John Benjamins Publishing Company. (p. 349).

Vohra, A., & Bhardwaj, N. (2019). From active participation to engagement in online communities: Analysing the mediating role of trust and commitment. *Journal of Marketing Communications, 25*(1), 89–114.

Wamuyu, P. K. (2018). Leveraging Web 2.0 technologies to foster collective civic environmental initiatives among low-income urban communities. *Computers in Human Behavior, 85*, 1–14.

Warnke, L. (2022). *Speech Act prediction across turn boundaries in conversation.* [Doctoral dissertation]. Tufts University.

Wongkitrungrueng, A., & Assarut, N. (2020). The role of livestreaming in building consumer trust and engagement with social commerce sellers. *Journal of Business Research, 117*, 543–556.

Wu, C. C., Chen, C. J., & Chiang, T. W. (2021, January). Forming the strategy for livestreaming e-Commerce: An action research. In *Proceedings of the 54th Hawaii international conference on system sciences* (pp. 2770–2779).

Wu, K. J., Xu, I. L., & Yan, A. H. (2022). Conversation in livestreaming sales: A case study in China. *International Journal of Linguistics, Literature and Translation, 5*(10), 11–17.

Xu, X., Wu, J. H., & Li, Q. (2020). What drives consumer shopping behavior in livestreaming commerce? *Journal of Electronic Commerce Research, 21*(3), 144–167.

Yamawaki, M. A. C. (2017). *The millennials luxury brand engagement on social media: A comparative study of brazilians and italians* [Doctoral dissertation]. FGV –EAESP, São Paulo.

Yin, S. (2020, July). A Study on the influence of E-commerce livestreaming on consumer's purchase intentions in mobile internet. In *International conference on human-computer interaction.* Springer (pp. 720–732).

CHAPTER 8

A BIBLIOMETRIC ANALYSIS OF EMPLOYEE ENGAGEMENT IN HIGHER EDUCATION BASED ON THE SCOPUS PLATFORM

Simranjeet Kaur[a], Rupali Arora[a] and Ercan Özen[b]

[a]*University School of Business (USB), Chandigarh University, Punjab, India*
[b]*Faculty of Applied Sciences, Department of Finance and Banking, University of Uşak, Uşak, Turkey*

ABSTRACT

Introduction: *The growing body of research on employee engagement (EE) has resulted in a new human resource management paradigm. Human resource management researchers are investigating how EE can help with employee retention in higher education.*

Purpose: *The purpose of this chapter was to determine the quantity, growth trend, global distribution, top journals and authors, dominant countries, and dominant subject areas in EE in the higher education sector.*

Methodology: *The researcher employed a bibliometric analysis technique using VOS viewer software on one of the worldwide used databases, Scopus. Four combinations of the words were combined in this work using the logical operators TITLE-ABS-KEY ('Employee engagement' AND 'Higher education' OR 'Higher educational institutions' OR 'universities'), thereby broadening the scope. This bibliometric analysis analysed 139 documents on EE scholarship.*

Contemporary Challenges in Social Science Management
Skills Gaps and Shortages in the Labour Market
Contemporary Studies in Economic and Financial Analysis, Volume 112A, 137–149
Copyright © 2024 by Simranjeet Kaur, Rupali Arora and Ercan Özen
Published under exclusive licence by Emerald Publishing Limited
ISSN: 1569-3759/doi:10.1108/S1569-37592024000112A021

Findings/Practical Implications: *EE in higher education is still a developing phenomenon; this review aims to educate and inform contemporary researchers by providing an overview of the field's current state.*

Keywords: Employee engagement; higher education sector; bibliometric analysis; employee retention; Scopus; VOS viewer; Human resource management

1. INTRODUCTION

The word 'Employee engagement' (EE) has been interpreted in various situations since its initial use in 2002 (Luthans & Peterson, 2002). EE has become a major topic of discussion in academic and business circles over the last two decades, with evidence indicating that engaged employees are more productive and enjoy a higher level of well-being both in and out of the workplace (Harter et al., 2013). EE has become a leading concern because employees continually change jobs, resulting in high attrition rates. An engaged workforce produces results, stays in one job for an extended period, and most importantly, is a constant ambassador for the organisation (Chandani et al., 2016). According to Saks (2006) EE is critical for attaining individual and organisational goals like job satisfaction, well-being, and a good attitude about work. The first scholarly paper on EE was published by William Kahn (1990). A closer review of the various definitions supplied by scholars across time reveals three dimensions/aspects of engagement: cognitive, emotional, and behavioural.

The cognitive dimension reflects an employee's perceptions and beliefs about his or her supervisor, the work environment, and the broader organisational culture. The emotional dimension reflects the employee's attitude towards the supervisor and the organization. The behavioural dimension is manifested in the employee's efforts at work and relationships with co-workers. Academic researchers define EE as changing over representative potential into worker execution and business achievements (Saks, 2006).

1.1 Engagement of Skilled Employees

Engagement is a state of emotional and intellectual organisational commitment or group that results in behaviour that assists the organisation in fulfilling its customer promises – and thus improves business results (Vance, 2006). Employees interested in their work and devoted to their organisations provide critical competitive benefits to their employers, including increased productivity and less employee turnover (Vance, 2006). Many empirical studies have shown that highly competent and qualified staff retention becomes more challenging (Ngobeni & Bezuidenhout, 2011). According to Manuel (2002), around one-fourth and half of teachers who chose teaching as a career leave their employment and the teaching profession entirely during the first 3–5 years. According to the Society of

Human Resource Management Foundation's standards on retaining employees, replacing an employee might reach up to 50–60% of the individual's annual salary. Indian educational institutions have recently faced a severe retention crisis. Due to a lack of experienced and dedicated academicians, both the cost of retention and the rate of turnover have risen (Kaur, 2021; Ventura, 2021).

In light of the growing importance of EE, by posing the following research questions, this bibliometric analysis intends to shed light on the evolution of the literature specifically related to EE in higher education.

RQ1: What is the total number of papers published on EE in higher education, the increasing trend, and the global distribution of developing and developed countries?

RQ2: Finding the publications on EE that received the highest citations?

RQ3: Who are the pioneer authors with the most citations and the most publications on the subject of EE?

RQ4: What are the associated keywords in EE?

RQ5: What are the most popular areas of EE research?

2. RESEARCH METHODOLOGY

In recent years, bibliometric evaluation has gained prominence due to its ability to provide in-depth information on certain themes (Ellegaard & Wallin, 2015). Garfield introduced this valuable method in 1955, stating that it combines a range of statistical techniques to examine and scan documents, such as articles, review papers, and books. It is a process in which analytical methods are used to explain a scientific research problem and to bring attention to disciplinary tendencies. This method is novel and original in comparison to traditional framework construction. As a result, bibliometric analyses inform the reader about the topic's historical trends, shed light on its advancements, and pave the way for future research.

2.1 Selecting a Database and Search Criteria

The first stage of bibliometric assessment is to discover databases that are relevant to the research topic. As a result, sources of information must be credible as well as acceptable to conduct analysis and develop sound judgements (Rueda et al., 2007). All three databases, Google Scholar, Web of Sciences, and Scopus, are reputable and up-to-date. Our analysis examined the Scopus Index, one of the most widely used databases by scholars worldwide.

The search for articles solely about EE was conducted using four distinct combinations of logical operators, TITLE-ABS-KEY ('Employee engagement' AND 'Higher education' OR 'Higher educational institutions' OR 'universities'). When this sting was entered, the system displayed 154 documents about EE in higher education. Following this phase, we meticulously examined all publications and discarded documents categorised as conference papers, and the final count came to 139.

2.2 Measurement

The VOS viewer software was chosen for analysis as it examines the relationships among the most cited authors, collaborative projects between multiple authors, collaboration between nations, organisations, keywords, and pertinent knowledge about the subject (Jan van Eck & Waltman, n.d.). Additionally, this application is utilised for cluster analysis, which entails the visualisation of geographic network maps with the aid of a structure indicating clusters of co-authorship and co-occurrence.

3. DATA ANALYSIS

3.1 The Total Number of Publications in the Field of EE in Higher Education,
Their Growth Trend, and Their Global Distribution

Between 2005 and 2021, the Scopus database contained 139 documents relating to EE in higher education. This included 118 articles, 10 review papers, 6 book chapters, and 5 additional sources. The EE scholarship's trajectory is depicted in Fig. 8.1.

The number of papers varied between 2005 and 2021, however, the concept has gained too much traction in the eyes of researchers in 2018, 2019, and 2020. These years saw the publication of 67 papers out of 139. This upward trend in the graph indicates that EE is still a contemporary phenomenon in higher education, as demonstrated by the rapid spike in the body of literature.

According to the heat map in Fig. 8.2, the United States (45), Malaysia (17), India (13), and South Africa (11) dominate generation of expertise in the context of EE, followed by Pakistan (9), the United Kingdom (8), Australia, Indonesia, Nigeria, and Thailand all of which have 6 documents, Canada and China both have 4 documents, the Netherlands and Vietnam has 3, Germany, Saudi Arabia, and the United Arab Emirates has 2. Malaysia is the leading producer of documents in developing countries, with 17, followed by India (13), South Africa (11), Pakistan (9), Indonesia (6), Nigeria (6), Thailand (6), China (4), Vietnam (3), Saudi Arabia (2), and Brunei Darussalam, Hungary, Iraq, Jordan, Lithuania, Namibia, Oman, Panama, Philippines, Poland, Portugal, Spain, Uganda, and Trinidad and Tobago produced 1 document each. Fig. 8.3 shows countries with bigger dots (like the United States, Malaysia, United Kingdom, Canada, and Vietnam) have a higher number of publications in the domain.

The developing countries produced 91 documents, accounting for 65% of the total. Thus, while developing countries produce more literature on EE in higher education, the number of documents per developing country needs to be higher.

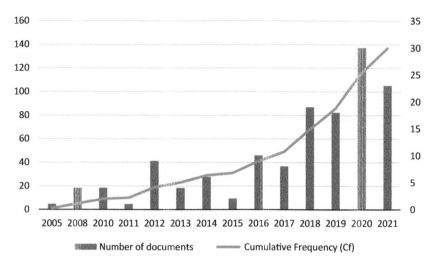

Fig. 8.1. The Number of Papers Published Annually and Cumulatively From 2005 Until 2021. *Source*: Authors' compilation.

Fig. 8.2. Worldwide Publication Distribution in Developed and Developing Countries, Scopus Database. *Source*: Authors' compilation.

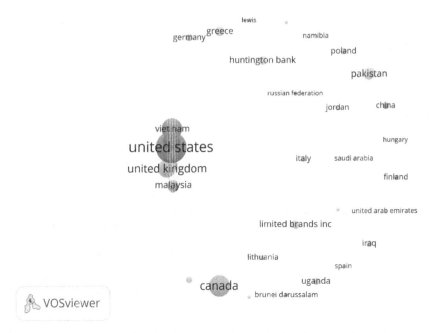

Fig. 8.3.   Country Citation Network. *Source*: Authors' compilation using
VOS viewer software.

3.2 Analyses of the Most Influential Journals With the Most Documents

The next objective was to identify the number of most cited journals and documents. There are top five journals, and the publication of documents in these
periodicals provided additional insight into the academic impact of EE in
higher education. The ranking of journals according to their number of documents is shown in Table 8.1. EE in higher education has numerous publications in various journals. While the majority of literature is published in the
field of business and management, the *Journal of Applied Research in Higher
Education* has the highest number of documents (5), *Problems and Perspectives
in Management* (4), *SA Journal of Human Resource Management* (4), *European
Journal of Training and Development* (3), and *Journal of Nursing Administration*
(3) indicating that the term employee engagement's central perspective is
employee retention. EE has also been discussed in journals such as decision
sciences, arts and humanities, and social sciences, demonstrating the EE's multifaceted nature. Table 8.2 summarises the top most cited journals in the field
of EE in higher education. Fig. 8.4 shows diagrammatic presentations of the
journals publishing on EE in higher education, bigger dots symbolise journal
with higher number of publications.

Table 8.1. Top Five Journals Publishing EE in Higher Education Scholarship.

Ranking Based on the Number of Documents				
Ranking	Journal Name	Domain	Documents	Scopus Citations
1	*Journal of Applied Research in Higher Education*	Social Sciences: Education	5	6
2	*SA Journal of Human Resource Management*	Social Sciences, Business, Management and Accounting	4	8
3	*Problems and Perspectives in Management*	Social Sciences: Demography Business, Management and Accounting: Organisational Behaviour and Human Resource Management	4	2
4	*Journal of Nursing Administration*	Business, Management and Accounting: Organisational Behaviour and Human Resource Management	3	30
5	*European Journal of Training and Development*	Nursing: Leadership and Management	3	1

Source: Authors' compilation.

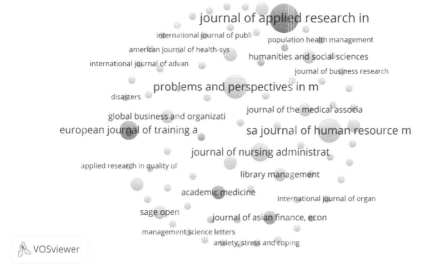

Fig. 8.4. Source Citation Network. *Source*: Authors' compilation.

Table 8.2. Top Five Journals Based on Scopus Citations.

Ranking	Journal Name	Documents	Scopus Citations
	Ranking of Journals on the Basis of Scopus Citations		
1	*Business Horizons*	2	129
2	*Human Relations*	1	125
3	*Employee Responsibilities and Rights Journal*	1	104
4	*South Asian Journal of Business Studies*	1	56
5	*Journal of Hospitality and Tourism Management*	1	45

Source: Authors' compilation.

3.3 Pioneering Authors in the Field of EE Scholarship

Additionally, bibliometric analysis provides information about the most eminent authors in a particular field (White & McCain, 1998). Between 2005 and 2021, the most prolific contributors to the field of EE in terms of Scopus documents are M. S. Abdullahi and K. Raman, each with 4, followed by S. A. Solarin (3), A. Bhana (2), N. Chaiear (2), S. H. Juan (2), Q. L. Kweh (2), T. Ndoro (2), J. Redmond (2), J. Sharafizad (2), and S. Suknunan (2) (Table 8.3). Thus, if we analyse only a few of the scholars in the table, we see that EE in higher education is still a relatively new concept. Table 8.4 lists the pioneering authors in the field of EE scholarship in terms of Scopus citations. P. M. Le Blanc, E. Ouweneel, W. B. Schaufeli, and C. I. Van Wijhe are ranked highest in terms of Scopus citations of their documents.

Table 8.3. Pioneer Authors on EE in Higher Education Scholarship.

Ranking	Author Name	Nationality	Documents	Scopus Citations
	Ranking Based on the Number of Documents			
1	M. S. Abdullahi	Nigeria	4	6
2	K. Raman	Malaysia	4	6
3	S. A. Solarin	Malaysia	4	6
4	N. Chaiear	South Africa	2	9
5	J. Redmond	Thailand	2	6
6	J. Sharafizad	Malaysia	2	6
7	T. Ndoro	Dubai	2	4
8	S. H. Juan	South Africa	2	3
9	Q. L. Kweh	Australia	2	3
10	I. W. K. Ting	Australia	2	3
11	L. Yao	South Africa	2	3
12	A. Bhana	Malaysia	2	1
13	S. Suknunan	China	2	1

Source: Authors' compilation.

Table 8.4. Ranking of Authors on the Basis of Scopus Citations.

	Ranking Based on Scopus Citations		
Ranking	Author Name	Documents	Scopus Citations
1	P. M. Le Blanc	1	125
2	E. Ouweneel	1	125
3	W. B. Schaufeli	1	125
4	C. I. Van Wijhe	1	125
5	D. H. Arnold	1	104
6	J. Fratzl	1	104
7	R. Mckay	1	104
8	R. Thomas	1	104
9	W. G. Mangold	1	72
10	S. J. Miles	1	72

Source: Authors' compilation.

3.4 Keywords and Emerging Themes

Fig. 8.6 illustrates the most frequently discussed associated keywords in the area of EE in higher education using the network visualisation mode in the VOS viewer. As can be seen, several large nodes characterise the field's primary terms or topics: job satisfaction, work environment, social exchange theory, organisation culture, and EE (Baturina & Simakov, 2023; Juliana et al., 2022; Sood et al., 2022).

Even so, it should always be observed that certain themes are in their initial stage and are making inroads despite their small node size; this also denotes the

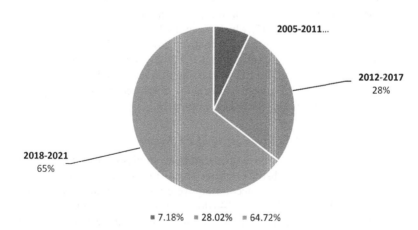

Fig. 8.5. Emerging Themes in EE. *Source*: Authors' compilation.

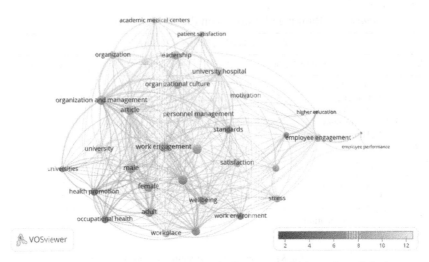

Fig. 8.6.   Associated Keywords. *Source*: Authors' compilation using VOS viewer.

niche area (Fig. 8.4). Occupational health, leadership, motivation, total quality management, and top management commitment are among these topics
(Baturina & Simakov, 2023; Juliana et al., 2022; Sood et al., 2022).

Likewise, the author noted rising trends in EE studies. In Fig. 8.5, between
2005 and 2011, the author separated the articles into three sections between
2005 and 2011, 2012–2017, and 2018–2021. In the early years of EE, from 2005
to 2011, which accounted for 7% of the overall number of papers, and in the
middle years, from 2012 to 2017, which accounted for 28% of the total number
of documents, Finally, the pioneering years from 2018 to 2021, which account for
65% of the total length of publications on EE in higher education, as well as until
now in 2021, emerging trends on EE scholarship that require additional attention
are those relating to how EE transforms negative employee attitudes into positive
ones and helps organisations retain their employees.

3.5 Popular Areas of EE Research

After thoroughly examining the Scopus database, studies on EE in higher education were classified into distinct subject areas (Fig. 8.7). The social sciences
and business, management, and accounting were the most frequently published
subject areas in EE scholarship, with 140 documents published between 2005 and
2021, followed by medicine (18), arts and humanities (17), and economics, econometrics, and finance (17). This demonstrates the need for additional research in
health professions, materials science, and mathematics.

Publications by Subject area

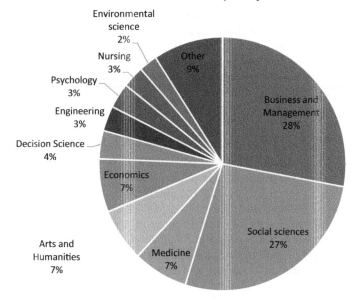

Fig. 8.7.   Documents by Subject Area. *Source*: Authors' compilation using
Scopus database.

4. CONCLUSION

The research discusses theme distribution, author-related features such as geography and sources, academic affiliation, and the network structure of the researchers. Using data from the Scopus database, this study shed light on a bibliometric analysis of EE scholarship from 2005 to 2021. This chapter summarises the research on EE in higher education to identify research trends and important topics. Cluster analysis confirms the separation of research across topics and regional borders. Few authors, nations, and sources dominate the topic, despite a steady publication growth from 2018 to 2020. Thus, this study provides direction for scholars interested in studying EE, along with historical information, the current state of the field, and future advancements in the field of EE, to enable the development of conceptual and theoretical models.

Additionally, this chapter analyses the trends in the EE scholarship, highlighting the pioneering years of 2018, 2019, and 2020. Additionally, we identified recent EE-related topics such as leadership, motivation, top management commitment, employee retention, job satisfaction, and social exchange theory. While most research has been conducted in developed countries, developing countries have also aided in the increase in knowledge. Cooperation between nations will enable a more complete picture of the EE scholarship to be painted. While EE's primary focus is on business and management, the central theme of EE in higher education is to engage higher education institutions' employees. As a result, journals devoted to higher education had the most documents, such as *Journal of Applied Research in Higher Education*. Additionally, our study demonstrates that research on EE in higher education is still in its infancy, originating in the social sciences, business, and management.

5. LIMITATIONS AND FUTURE RESEARCH

The study shows the distribution of themes and author-related variables such as the location and sources, academic origin and the network structure of writers. Results give a general overview of the discipline and indicate areas for future research. Since 2005, particularly in the last few years, the field of EE has experienced tremendous growth, significantly impacting the literature. According to the findings, the topic of EE is diverse and fragmented, with most writers contributing only one publication to the field's body of knowledge so far. Cluster analysis confirms the separation of research across themes and geographical borders. Only a few authors, nations, and sources dominate the area, even though publication numbers have steadily increased from 2005 to 2021.

To summarise, EE is a relatively new field of study now critically important to academia. Cross-sectoral studies are needed because of the gap in the number of persons studying EE in the developing and developed nations. However, the results discussed in this chapter have limitations. To begin, this review analysis is done on Scopus-indexed publications only. Second, this method needs to address the issue of multiple researchers having the same name. Thirdly, it's worth noting that this study focuses on a specific field: EE in higher education. Therefore, researchers should be cautious in generalising these findings to a broader population. Although citations and co-citation studies have the potential to reveal the evolution of a subject and its citation patterns, they have limits owing to the quantitative structure of management research's bibliometric methodology. Google Scholar and Web of Science can be used to do additional bibliometric analysis, which will provide extra information on this field. Further sociograms can be used to understand better the relationships between variables in the field of EE. By using the Scopus database, the research advanced both broad themes of EE and networks/clusters, notably co-authorship, citation, co-citation, bibliographic coupling, and co-occurrence.

REFERENCES

Baturina, L., & Simakov, A. (2023). Students' attitude towards e-learning in Russia after the pandemic. *Education Science and Management, 1*(1), 1–6.

Chandani, A., Mehta, M., Mall, A., & Khokhar, V. (2016). Employee engagement: A review paper on factors affecting employee engagement. *Indian Journal of Science and Technology, 9*(15). https://doi.org/10.17485/IJST/2016/V9I15/92145

Ellegaard, O., & Wallin, J. A. (2015). The bibliometric analysis of scholarly production: How great is the impact? *Scientometrics, 105*(3), 1809–1831. https://doi.org/10.1007/S11192-015-1645-Z/TABLES/9

Harter, J. K., Schmidt, F. L., Agrawal, S., Plowman, S. K., & Blue, A. (2013). *The relationship between engagement at work and organizational outcomes.* Gallup Poll Consulting University Press.

Jan van Eck, N., & Waltman, L. (n.d.). *Software survey: VOSviewer, a computer program for bibliometric mapping.* https://doi.org/10.1007/s11192-009-0146-3

Juliana, A. P., Lemy, D. M., Pramono, R., Djakasaputra, A., & Purwanto, A. (2022). Hotel performance in the digital era: Roles of digital marketing, perceived quality and trust. *Journal of Intelligent Management Decision, 1*(1), 36–45.

Kahn, W. A. (1990). Psychological conditions of personal engagement and disengagement at work. *Academy of Management Journal, 33*(4), 692–724.

Luthans, F., & Peterson, S. J. (2002). Employee engagement and manager self-efficacy: Implications for managerial effectiveness and development. *Journal of Management Development, 21*(5), 376–387. https://doi.org/10.1108/02621710210426862

Manuel, K. (2002). Teaching information literacy to generation. *Journal of Library Administration, 36*(1–2), 195–217, doi: 10.1300/J111v36n01_12

Ngobeni, E. K., & Bezuidenhout, A. (2011). Engaging employees for improved retention at a higher education institution in South Africa. *African Journal of Business Management, 5*(23), 9961–9970. https://doi.org/10.5897/AJBM11.1381

Rueda, G., Gerdsri, P., & Kocaoglu, D. F. (2007, August). Bibliometrics and social network analysis of the nanotechnology field. In *PICMET'07-2007 Portland international conference on management of engineering & technology* (pp. 2905–2911). IEEE.

Saks, A. M. (2006). Antecedents and consequences of employee engagement. *Journal of Managerial Psychology, 21*(7), 600–619. https://doi.org/10.1108/02683940610690169/FULL/XML

Sood, K., Kaur, B., & Grima, S. (2022). Revamping Indian Non-Life Insurance Industry with a trusted network: Blockchain technology. In K. Sood, R. K. Dhanaraj, B. Balamurugan, S. Grima, R. Uma Maheshwari (Eds.), *Big Data: A game changer for insurance industry* (pp. 213–228). Emerald Publishing Limited.

van Eck, N. J., & Waltman, L. (2010). Software survey: VOSviewer, a computer program for bibliometric mapping. *Scientometrics, 84*(2), 523–538. https://doi.org/10.1007/S11192-009-0146-3/FIGURES/7

Vance, R. J. (2006). Engagement and commitment. In *SHRM foundation's effective practice guidelines* (pp. 1–45). https://www.shrm.org/hr-today/trends-and-forecasting/special-reports-and-expert-views/Documents/Employee-Engagement-Commitment.pdf

Ventura, A. B. (2021). Employees retention in business organizations: Literature review. *GSJ, 9*(7). www.globalscientificjournal.com

White, H. D., & McCain, K. W. (1998). Visualizing a discipline: An author co-citation analysis of information science, 1972–1995. *Journal of the American Society for Information Science, 49*(4), 327–355.

CHAPTER 9

SKILLS GAPS AND SHORTAGES IN THE INDIAN LABOUR MARKET DUE TO CHANGING DYNAMICS OF EMPLOYABILITY

Manju Dahiya, Ritu Singh and Mallik Arjun Ahluwalia

Department of Economics, Galgotias University, Dankaur, UP, India

ABSTRACT

Purpose: *This chapter explores the changing global dynamics of employability and the current skill gaps among college students. Employability is defined as the measure of how desirable an individual is in the workforce, that is, their skills and knowledge. This chapter is centred on the students' existing skills, missing skills, and the skill requirements of different industries.*

Methodology: *For this study, both primary and secondary data have been collected. Case studies have been used to analyse the skill gaps among students and industry requirements. Primary data has been collected from Indian students and case studies from other countries.*

Findings: *After conducting primary surveys and analysing case studies, we were able to conclude that there are serious skill gaps among students – especially in industries related to new emerging technologies. Educational institutes are not keeping pace with technological changes, and, in some cases, are not taking care of students' interests. This is a serious problem for unemployed youth around the world.*

Contemporary Challenges in Social Science Management
Skills Gaps and Shortages in the Labour Market
Contemporary Studies in Economic and Financial Analysis, Volume 112A, 151–166
Copyright © 2024 by Manju Dahiya, Ritu Singh and Mallik Arjun Ahluwalia
Published under exclusive licence by Emerald Publishing Limited
ISSN: 1569-3759/doi:10.1108/S1569-37592024000112A022

Practical Implications: *This chapter will help design the curriculum, addressing core issues of skill shortages in the labour market in developing and underdeveloped countries, decreasing the labour shortage and increasing employment, and helping countries' national income.*

Significance: *This study is important as it addresses the issue of unemployment by providing a clear understanding of the present needs of industries. Educational institutions and the government will be able to design the best curriculum and education policies to provide the youth with all the necessary skills to help them fulfil the needs of industries.*

Keywords: Labour market; employability; education; skill gap; educational institutes; youth employments

INTRODUCTION

With the changing world economy and demand, industry requirements are constantly changing. In the labour market, traditional hiring processes are no longer used. Unemployment impacted 67.6 million young people worldwide, accounting for 13.6% of the youth labour force. Millions of other people lacked employment, education, or training (Lee et al., 2020). Now, more than a degree is needed; students need quality education and experience. According to research, college and workplace success correlates with deeper learning outcomes, including communication, critical thinking, teamwork, self-management, problem solving, and persistence (Lathram et al., 2019). Education still matters, but higher costs of education and stagnant wages afterwards have produced a lower return on educational investment, which means 'don't go until you're ready' and 'don't leave without a degree'.

Educational institutions should change their outlook on competencies and abilities as firms strive to rethink their hiring standards to locate suitable people and fill open positions. Creating jobs and boosting productivity are top priorities for policy makers around the world. Too many workers worldwide need more time to be ready to meet the requirements of businesses, particularly in industries characterised by competition and expansion. Training systems are frequently afflicted with poor administration and incentives, rendering them undependable or inefficient. Furthermore, in several countries, education systems need to provide the younger demographic with the fundamental cognitive and behavioural skills required for optimal performance in the place of work (Tandon et al., 2011).

This chapter sheds light on the issue of the skill gap in three countries, namely, India, one of the most rapidly growing economies and the fifth largest in the world (World Economic Forum, 2022); the United States, the largest economy in the world; and Indonesia, a rapidly growing middle-income country. The primary survey is conducted only for India. For other countries, case studies and secondary data have been used.

LITERATURE REVIEW

Unemployment among youth is now a concern for every country, especially in emerging markets around the globe. Many studies have been conducted to find the reasons for unemployment among youth. Adermon and Hensvik (2022) suggest that recruiters prefer candidates with any experience. The most preferable is traditional job experience over gig experience. This study was conducted to examine the usefulness of work experience in traditional wage jobs in Sweden by pitting the callback rates of recent high school graduates against people with (i) gig experience, (ii) traditional job experience, and (iii) a history of unemployment, found that gig experience increased the callback rate by around 2% (or 11%, in contrast to with those with a history of unemployment), where the influence of conventional wage jobs is around twice as large.

Similarly, Malik and Venkatraman (2017) reviewed available literature to understand why the increasing skill gap exists among India's young population. The study stated that one of the key causes of the wide skill gap is the absence of industry–academia collaboration and the static curriculum of educational institutes. This chapter advised the Indian government to open various institutes in urban and rural areas to introduce young students to new emerging technologies and promote research projects. This chapter also raised the need to design a platform where industry and government agencies can meet up routinely to update the curriculum and introduce new skills.

Internships are mandatory in many educational institutes because they are believed to reap benefits for the students. Some research has also been conducted to examine this (Stebleton & Kaler, 2020; Kathuria, Kedia, Varma, Bagchi, & Khullar, 2017). Examine the complex future of a changing workplace and how the increasing use of machines will influence job trends. This chapter concludes that attendees of higher educational institutions should be encouraged to engage in experiential learning to get practical experience through internships, project work, etc. Similarly, Margaryan et al. (2019) study the causal effect of internship experience on getting a job. The result shows that students who have done internships during graduation have a lower risk of unemployment. It also suggests that industry experience attained using student internships at firms expands earnings by around 6% in the short or medium term.

The major skill gaps that Indian students and possibly students from other emerging economies might face are digital and technical skills. According to *The Economic Times* (2022), India's rise in literacy has been hampered by rising unemployment. In India, unemployment is not caused by a lack of employment opportunities but by a lack of talented employees, particularly in IT, engineering services, and sales. University education is primarily concerned with imparting theoretical knowledge. Unemployment is rising due to the youth's lack of practical knowledge and the industry's unwillingness to provide 'on-the-job training' and 'shadowing'. Also, Unni (2022) addressed the increasing skill discord among education and job requirements in India. Policies encouraging non-graduate technical and non-graduate technical diploma/certificate holders to enter lower graduate-intensity occupations would contribute to bridging the skill gap and relieving the weight on graduate higher education.

India: Skill Gap and Employability

In India, the unemployment rate has remained around 5% since 1991, but it grew instantly in 2020 because of COVID-19 (see Table 9.1 and Fig. 9.1). During the COVID period, all work was done in virtual mode. Working from home became the new normal. Classes were also moved to the internet in academia. The COVID period has increased the demand for labourers who have technical knowledge.

Since skilled workers enjoy exceptional career progress and help grow their organisations in a similar fashion to their less skilled counterparts, several organisations now prefer skilled workers to less skilled ones. Skills highly elevate productivity and the quality of work to yield more impactful results. According to the World Trade Organization (WTO) estimates, if India focuses on skill development and training, its GDP might rise by 3–5% by 2035. India must impart the required training and skills to its youth to develop holistically.

Table 9.1.   Unemployment Data of India (as % of Total Labour Force).

Year	Unemployment (% of the Total Labour Force)
1991	6.73699999
1992	6.81500006
1993	6.79799986
1994	6.82999992
1995	7.01399994
1996	7.18100023
1997	7.27899981
1998	7.48699999
1999	7.70900011
2000	7.76999998
2001	7.95699978
2002	8.10200024
2003	8.35999966
2004	8.53100014
2005	8.69999981
2006	8.625
2007	8.53600025
2008	8.35400009
2009	8.38399982
2010	8.31900024
2011	8.16800022
2012	8.09500027
2013	8.0369997
2014	7.98099995
2015	7.91499996
2016	7.84200001
2017	7.7329998
2018	7.6500001
2019	6.51000023
2020	10.1949997
2021	7.71299982

Source: Unemployment, total (% of total labor force) (modeled ILO estimate) – India | Data (2023).

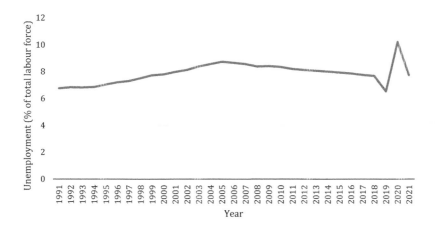

Fig. 9.1. Unemployment in India as a Percentage of the Total Labour Force.
Source: Author's compilation.

Only 25% of the Indian workforce, according to *Skill Development and Employment Opportunity* (2020), has partaken in skill development programmes, notwithstanding its necessity for a more expansive base of trained workers.

Following 2018, banking, financial services, and insurance remained India's top hiring sectors (Wheebox, 2022, p. 25). Maharashtra, Uttar Pradesh, and Kerala have the most employable talent. Since 2016, Uttar Pradesh has remained the top supplier of employable talents (Wheebox, 2022, p. 26).

According to Wheebox (2022), only 48.7% of youth have employability talent. This has increased by 2.8% from last year. West Bengal, Uttar Pradesh, and Tamil Nadu procured a mention in the list of the top states regarding English as a second language, which fuels global connectivity and digitalisation across industries.

According to the recent trend in job market data analysis, data visualisation, vocational training, market research, product design, and creative imagination are highly demanded.

Observing the employable skills of graduates of different courses, B.Tech graduates are highly employable with 55.1% employability, followed by MBA graduates with 55.09%, B.Pharma graduates with 44.62%, and B.Arts graduates with 44.02% employability (Wheebox, 2022).

Considering that India's average age demographic is predominantly young, the fast-paced changes in the economy's needs should be confronted via skilling initiatives, education, training, and enabling job opportunities using infrastructure growth (Ministry of Human Resource Development, 2020).

In India, unemployment among those with advanced education is higher than among the general labour force (see Table 9.2). This indicates that there exist skill gaps in the population, which prevent them from finding work. The general method for bridging the skill gap is to train people for specific roles. With an expanding number of fresh graduates and an increasing number of skilled career prospects, scaling skill training for custom profiles is a challenge.

Table 9.2. Unemployment in India as a Percentage of the Total Labour Force
With Advanced Education.

Year	Unemployment (% of the Total Labour Force With Advanced Education)
1994	10.97
2000	10.31
2005	10.19
2010	7.5
2012	8.09
2018	16.51
2019	15.72
2020	17.90

Source: Unemployment with advanced education (% of total labor force with advanced education) –
India | Data (2023).

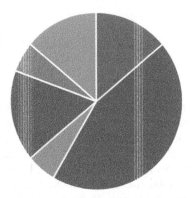

- Old curriculum
- Not focused on student interest
- Need for trained professors
- Lack of practical knowledge
- Lack of skill development program
- Focused on marks only

Fig. 9.2. Student Response to Problems in Educational Institutes.
Source: Author's compilation.

The results of the primary survey of students in this chapter are identical to
that in 'Bridging India's Gaping Skill Gap' (2022). Table 9.5 shows the work experience of our respondents.

Some of the comments made by the students on the question of problems in
educational institutions are (see Fig. 9.2):

(a) 'Lack of practical knowledge'
(b) 'Static syllabus'
(c) 'Focused only on academic excellence and expansion rather than co-curriculum
    excellence and expansion'.

(d) 'Fewer values of new ideas and concepts and limits of thought range'.
(e) 'The Indian educational system depends on books. We should focus on extracurricular activities to enhance our skills and knowledge. In today's corporate world, we focus on skills rather than degrees, so that's why only academic education is not enough'.

As per the survey, 44.4% of students believe that educational institutes need to provide practical knowledge, 13.9% of respondents think that educational institutes follow an old and static curriculum. It needs to be revised, 6.5% of students think that their interests are not considered, whereas 13.9% of students responded that educational institutes focus only on marks, and 5.6% believe that they need more trained and professional professors in institutions. In addition, 16.7% believe that educational institutes don't conduct skill development programmes (Baturina & Simakov, 2023; Juliana et al., 2022; Sood et al., 2022).

In the survey, we asked students if academic education is enough to get employed. In response to this, 76.1% disagreed, while 23.9% said that academic education is enough for them to get a job. A similar study was conducted in Sweden (Adermon & Hensvik, 2022). Its findings suggest that gig experience during education is more valuable than no experience.

Question. Do you think academic education is enough to get a job?

Table 9.3. Students' Views on the Adequacy of Academic Education to Get Employment.

Response	Responses (%)
Yes	23.9
No	76.1

Source: Author's survey.

Question. How much do educational institutions have helped you develop technical skills and project-based experience?

Table 9.4. Students' Views on the Contribution of Educational Institutes in Providing Technical Skills and Project-based Experience to the Students.

Response	Responses (%)
All skills have been gained from educational institute	6.5
Most skills have been gained from educational institute	19.6
Only some skills have been gained from educational institute	65.2
No skill has been gained from educational institute	8.7

Source: Author's survey.

For practical knowledge and work experience, students mostly rely on freelancing and internships. From January 2019 to January 2021, the Indian freelance market saw a 22% increase in available jobs (Wheebox, 2022, p. 39). This is a growing trend. As shown in Fig. 9.3 and Table 9.4, only 6.3% of students think that educational institutes provide all the required skills, whereas 65.2% of students believe that they gain some limited skills from educational institutes.

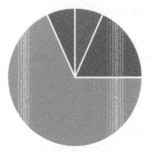

■ All skills have been gained from educational institutes

■ Most skills have been gained from educational institutes

■ Only some skills have been gained from educational institutes

■ No skills have been gained from educational institutes

Fig. 9.3. Student Response on How Much Skills Have Been Gained From Educational Institutes. *Source*: Author's survey.

Table 9.5. Respondents With Work Experience.

Respondents who have already done freelance jobs or internships	80.4%
Respondents who are currently working as interns/part-time	23.9%

Source: Author's survey.

Question. Would an internship/freelancing or other kinds of work experience help you land a job?

Table 9.6. Students' Views on the Significance of Internships, Freelancing, or Other Kind of Work Experience in Securing Jobs.

Response	Response (%)
Yes	50.0
No	11.4
Maybe	38.6

Source: Authors' survey.

Among our survey respondents, 80.4% of students have done internships or other types of freelance work during higher education. Additionally, 50.0% of students believe that work experience gained through internships or freelancing

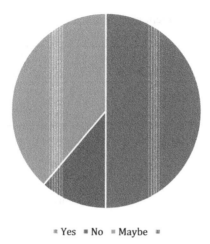

≡ Yes ▪ No ≡ Maybe ≡

Fig. 9.4.   Student Response on Whether an Internship, Freelancing, Gig, or Other Types of Work Experience Will Help Them Get a Job. *Source*: Author's compilation.

will help them get a job; 38.6% were not sure, and 11.4% don't believe that it will (see Fig. 9.4 and Table 9.6).

'Skill initiatives' work to close the chasm between skills and employability (*Skills for Employability*, n.d.). The NASSCOM Foundation collaborates closely with the NASSCOM SSC, the IT Sector Skills Council. All training curriculum adheres to the SSC's 'Qualification Packs' for similar skills. The Indian government has started to provide vocational training to the youth for employability. The Modular Employable Skills (MES), a scheme under the Skill Development Initiative (SDI) (n.d.), is one such step. The recent 'New Education Policy, 2020' is another significant step in ensuring overall student skill.

UNITED STATES: SKILL GAP AND EMPLOYABILITY

The skill gap in America has received a lot of attention. Not surprisingly, COVID-19 exacerbated the problem, and there are still nearly as many unoccupied jobs as there were in a recession, despite near-record unemployment (see Table 9.7 and Fig. 9.5). When the rate of unemployment rose in the spring of 2020, jobs that require a graduate degree decreased more than those that did not, and fresh college graduates suffered the most damage. The job postings for bachelor's level jobs fell the most, furthest, and fastest (Song, 2021).

Over the next decade, the skill gap is projected to cost the US economy $1.2 trillion in GDP CEOs are concerned that the shortage of available talent has risen from 56% in 2011 to 79% in 2019. Their desired skills have also changed, and organisations are currently struggling to find tech-savvy employees (Song, 2021).

Table 9.7.   Unemployment in the United States as a Percentage of the
Total Labour Force.

Year	Unemployment, Total (% of the Total Labour Force)
1991	6.80000019
1992	7.5
1993	6.9000001
1994	6.11999989
1995	5.6500001
1996	5.44999981
1997	5
1998	4.51000023
1999	4.21999979
2000	3.99000001
2001	4.73000002
2002	5.78000021
2003	5.98999977
2004	5.53000021
2005	5.07999992
2006	4.61999989
2007	4.61999989
2008	5.78000021
2009	9.25
2010	9.63000011
2011	8.94999981
2012	8.06999969
2013	7.36999989
2014	6.17000008
2015	5.28000021
2016	4.86999989
2017	4.36000013
2018	3.9000001
2019	3.67000008
2020	8.05000019
2021	5.3499999

Source: Unemployment, total (% of total labor force) (modeled ILO estimate) – India | Data (2023).

One of the important aspects is that in the United States, college graduates have a lower unemployment rate than workers without a bachelor's degree. Only 1.9% of college graduates, aged 25 and older, were suffering from unemployment in February 2020, right before the COVID-19 pandemic spread its wings in the United States, compared to 3.1% of workers who earned some college degree but not a 4-year degree and 3.7% of workers who were only high school graduates. By June 2020, 6.8% of college graduates, 10.8% of workers with some college degree, and 12.2% of high school graduates were unemployed as a result of the pandemic. By March 2022, the unemployment rate for college graduates almost bounced back to levels preceding the COVID era (2%), but dropped to 3% for those lacking a 4-year college degree but not college, and 4% for those who were only high school graduates (Schaeffer, 2022).

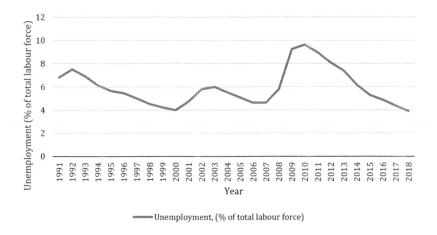

Fig. 9.5.   Unemployment in the United States as a Percentage of the Total Labour Force.
Source: Author's compilation.

The problem in the United States is the low literacy rate among adult popula-tion (Adult Literacy in the United States, 2019). According to World Population data on Literacy Statistics, 21% of them are illiterate. Fifty-four per cent of adults have literacy levels below the 6th grade. One in every 5 adults finds it difficult to read and write basic sentences. As per the *Washington Post*, students with poor reading and maths skills are at a greater risk of being laid off. Several firms denied adults with low literacy during COVID-19. Illiterate people earn 35% lower than their educated counterparts, as per the World Literacy Foundation.

Hiring in the Modern Talent Marketplace (2019) has conducted a skill gap survey that substantiates (Modestino, Shoag, & Ballance, 2016) that skill require-ment has been shot up in the U.S. market. Hiring managers in the United States face a wide range of challenges across industries and within their organisations. Employers indicated that finding the 'right' candidate is difficult. Fifty-nine per cent of the respondents said that it is now harder to find suitable employees than it was 3 years ago. A survey found that 80% of executives are concerned about a digi-tal skills gap (Craig, 2019). Only 41 million American jobs, according to Brookings, do not need notable digital skills; about 100 million do. Two-thirds of the jobs created in the past 10 years required either advanced or intermediate digital skills.

Regardless of the new ways to gain skills and enter the workforce, higher edu-cation is still one of the most important factors in the hiring process.

Three-quarters of respondents (74%) said that their company requires the sub-mission of a credential as part of the hiring process. This traditional approach extends to how employers use this data when hiring. Only one-quarter (26%) of the respondents reported that the credentials are analysed and integrated into a comprehensive picture of the candidate. The majority (41%) believe that creden-tials are mostly used to verify skills.

The majority of respondents (78%) concur that to locate individuals to fill open positions, employers will need to reexamine their recruiting criteria.

Employing decision makers anticipate that skill tests will become more significant when evaluating candidates as skills become a more prominent consideration in the employment process. In the upcoming year, more than two-thirds of respondents (67%) predict that the usage of skill evaluations in interviewing will rise.

According to *Hiring in the Modern Talent Marketplace* (2019, p. 9), when considering a possible applicant, competency is valued more highly by employers than a formal degree.

Respondents of the *Hiring in the Modern Talent Marketplace* (2019) ranked critical thinking skills as the most important when asked to rank various types of skills, such as critical thinking and problem-solving skills, digital skills, communication skills, technical skills, and other interpersonal or soft skills in importance to their company when hiring. Even though the digital economy and market have received much attention, respondents were most likely to consider digital skills to be the least important when hiring.

In the 2019 *Hiring in the Modern Talent Marketplace* survey, improvements to the organisation's hiring procedure are reportedly a priority in nearly half of the respondents (45%) organisations and HR departments (49%).

According to HR experts, changing the talent market begins with partnerships in the workplace and education. Respondents' strongest message is to combine educational, workforce, and training activities, as media narratives increasingly aim to contrast them.

Over half (61%) of the respondents' organisations ranked maintaining or enhancing education and workforce collaborations as a priority.

The respondents have mentioned the top three potential solutions to fix the skill gap, namely, increased internal initiatives to upskill existing personnel, more educational and career technical education (CTE) initiatives (e.g. partnerships with post-secondary institutions, programmes with neighbourhood schools) to create talent pipelines, and increased compatibility between the knowledge and abilities provided in CTE and educational programmes and those in demand in the labour market (Baturina & Simakov, 2023; Juliana et al., 2022; Sood et al., 2022).

Indonesia: Skill Gap and Unemployability

Indonesia is a rapidly growing middle-income country with a literacy rate of 96% (measured in 2020), according to World Bank data. Even after accounting for socioeconomic factors and the country's high literacy rate, Indonesia still performs poorly on international examinations of student achievement. Indonesia has the Asia-Pacific region's second-highest youth unemployment rate (ILO Regional Office for Asia and the Pacific, 2018). The rate of participation in Indonesia's labour force fell from 67.8% in 2000 to 67.0% in 2017. In contrast, the employment-to-population ratio has risen from 63.6% in 2000 to 64.2% in 2017. The unemployment rate significantly decreased to 4.2% in 2017 from 6.1% in 2000. Similarly, the youth unemployment rate decreased from 19.9% in 2000 to 15.6% in 2017. The job market in Indonesia appears to value theoretical and practical job knowledge. According to the 2008 Employer Skill Survey (Tandon et al., 2011, p. 5) both theoretical and practical knowledge acquired via primary schooling and on-the-job training are essential for technical abilities. Indonesia is expected to benefit from a 'demographic bonus' between 2030 and 2040. During this time, a great chunk of Indonesia's population will be between the ages of 15 and 64 (Bappenas, Badan Pusat Statistik, & UNFPA, 2013). Additionally, as the dependence ratio continues to decline, Indonesia is anticipated to enjoy a demographic dividend by about 2030, according to Asian Development Bank (2018). Over the following 10–15 years, this will open the door for quicker economic development. Because of the increased labour supply, there may be more women pursuing secondary and higher education, better savings rates, and higher earning potential, all of which may lead to higher growth rates. To take advantage of the potential of the demographic transition, the Indonesian government has developed a number of policy and programme initiatives focused on human capital development (Indonesia Ministry of National Development Planning and the United Nations Children's Fund, 2017). The Bappenas, Badan Pusat Statistik, and UNFPA (2013) structure the learning process around students and seek to improve their fundamental skills in addition to developing transferable skills. Personal empowerment is also promoted through school activities. For instance, extracurricular activities are meant to give students the opportunity to pursue their interests and hobbies. In an effort to provide more individuals with access to training and skill development opportunities and equip more than 2 million people with the skills necessary for the job market, the Indonesian government has also introduced a pre-employment card (Asian Development Bank & OECD, 2020).

There is an inconsistency between educational qualifications and work requirements in Indonesia. Between 2006 and 2016, there were indications that job seekers and workers, particularly in urban areas, were unaware of vacancies and current job prospects. Despite large advances in educational attainment, the Indonesian education system is struggling to supply labour- and market-required skills. The number of workers with senior secondary and higher education increased by 1 and 2 millions, respectively, between 2010 and 2015; however, the standard of tertiary education remained low, and most students' learning achievement is inadequate. In some disciplines, the education system fails to generate enough graduates, and, in others, graduates lack the necessary skills (Asian Development Bank & OECD, 2020). The vast majority of Indonesian employees lack access to education, and worker skill development initiatives are infrequently carried out. According to the ILO, workers with insufficient qualifications will fill approximately 63% of high-skilled jobs by 2025. To put it another way, there are skill gaps between qualifications and credentials, job prerequisites, and employer expectations (Allen & Kim, 2014). One study found that overqualified individuals were employed in low-skilled jobs. According to the National Labour Force Survey, there was a labour deficit for administrative and technical personnel (e.g. technicians, operators, and labourers) and skilled labour (e.g. accountants and managers) in 2012. Skilled labour was also in short supply in agriculture, transportation, and communication (APEC Human Resources Development Working Group, 2014). Despite the labour surplus, there are skill gaps in the workforce, with workers frequently lacking the fundamental skills needed to meet industry standards.

Both formal vocational and general secondary schools have advantages and disadvantages that must be addressed immediately. Quality and relevance gaps are especially pronounced in secondary education (Tandon et al., 2011, p. 22).

CONCLUSION

Skill gaps are a major concern for all countries, whether developed or developing. Literacy and skill are not even that satisfactory in advanced countries like the United States.

In recent years, India has placed a greater emphasis on the education, skill development, and overall development of its youth. According to the Indian government's budget expenditure for 2020–2021, the education sector will receive 3.5% of the GDP. However, much more is required to successfully launch all skill development programmes and the New Education Policy. The government should also increase its research spending.

Total expenditures on educational institutions in the United States in 2018 amounted to 3.5% of GDP at the elementary/secondary level, according to COE – Education Expenditures by Country (2022) data. This figure exceeded the OECD average (3.4%). Still, the United States must examine its literacy rate and the skills of its youth.

Indonesia has a high literacy rate, but the problem is that literacy rates vary by region. Some parts of Indonesia have a higher level of education than others (Nambiar et al., 2019). Indonesia can become a great resource for economic development if policies addressing the aforementioned challenges are developed quickly and implemented properly.

We can now conclude that there are serious skill gaps among students, particularly those related to new emerging technologies, after successfully conducting primary surveys and analysing case studies. Educational institutes are not keeping up with technological changes, and in some cases, educational institutes are not looking after the interests of students. This is a major issue for unemployed youth all over the world. Most graduates are completely unqualified for employment.

To overcome the issue of a skill gap among youth, the government needs to launch vocational courses and activities, as suggested by Lathram et al. (2019). Also, educational institutes need to focus on the student's interests.

REFERENCES

Adermon, A., & Hensvik, L. (2022). Gig jobs: Stepping stones or dead ends? *Labour Economics, 76*, 1–24.

Adult Literacy in the United States. (2019). NCES.

Allen, E., & Kim, K. B. (2014). *Indonesia: Labour market information systems and services.* Jakarta: Korea/ILO Partnership Programme.

APEC Human Resources Development Working Group. (2014). A Report on the APEC Region Labour Market: Evidence of Skills Shortages and General Trends in Employment and the Value of Better Labour Market Information Systems. Asia-Pacific Economic Cooperation Secretariat.

Asian Development Bank. (2018). Indonesia enhancing productivity through quality jobs. In E. Ginting, C. Manning, & K. Taniguchi (Eds.) Philippines: Asian Development Bank.

Asian Development Bank & OECD. (2020). Employment and skills strategies in Indonesia. OECD Reviews on Local Job Creation, OECD Publishing, Paris.

Bappenas, Badan Pusat Statistik, and UNFPA (2013). Indonesia Population Projection 2010-2035. Jakarta: BPS – Statistics Indonesia.

Baturina, L., & Simakov, A. (2023). Students' attitude towards e-learning in Russia after pandemic. *Education Science Management, 1*(1), 1–6.

Bridging India's Gaping Skill Gap. (2022, March 14). *The Economic Times.* https://economictimes.indiatimes.com/industry/services/education/bridging-indias-gaping-skill-gap/articleshow/90208286.cms

COE – Education Expenditures by Country. (2022). National Center for Education Statistics.

Craig, R. (2019, March). America's skills gap: Why it's real, and why it matters. Washington, DC: Progressive Policy Institute.

Hiring in the Modern Talent Marketplace. (2019). U.S. Chamber of Commerce Foundation.

ILO Regional Office for Asia and the Pacific. (2018). Asia-Pacific Employment and Social Outlook 2018: *Advancing decent work for sustainable development.* Bangkok: ILO.

India Skills Report 2022. (2022). Gurgaon: Wheebox. https://wheebox.com/assets/pdf/ISR_Report_2022.pdf

Indonesia Ministry of National Development Planning and the United Nations Children's Fund. (2017). *SDG Baseline Report on Children in Indonesia.* Jakarta: BAPPENAS and UNICEF.

Juliana, A. P., Lemy, D. M., Pramono, R., Djakasaputra, A., & Purwanto, A. (2022). Hotel performance in the digital era: Roles of digital marketing, perceived quality and trust. *Journal of Intelligent Management Decision, 1*(1), 36–45.

Kathuria, R., Kedia, M., Varma, G., Bagchi, K., & Khullar, S. (2017, December). *Future of work in a Digital Era: The potential and challenges for online freelancing and microwork in India.* Indian Council for Research on International Economics.

Lathram, B., Lenz, B., & Ark, T. V. (2019). Preparing students for a project-based world. Novato: Getting Smart, Buck Institute for Education.

Lee, S., Verick, S., & Schmidt-Klau, D. (2020, October 6). The labour market impacts of the COVID-19: A global perspective. *The Indian Journal of Labour Economics, 63,* 11–15.

Malik, G., & Venkatraman, A. (2017). "The great divide": Skill gap between the employer's expectations and skills possessed by employees. *Industrial and Commercial Training, 49*(4), 175–182.

Margaryan, S., Saniter, N., Schumann, M., & Siedler, T. (2019). Do Internships Pay Off? The Effects of Student Internships on Earnings. *IZA – Institute of Labor Economics, Discussion Paper No. 12478.* Bonn.

Modestino, A. S., Shoag, D., & Ballance, J. (2016). Upskilling: Do employers demand greater skill when workers are plentiful? Federal Reserve Bank of Boston, (14–17). Boston.

Ministry of Human Resource Development. (2020). *National Education Policy 2020.* New Delhi: Government of India.

Modestino, A. S., Shoag, D., & Ballance, J. (2016). *Upskilling: Do employers demand greater skill when workers are plentiful?* HKS Faculty Research Working Paper (14-17). Boston.

Modular Employable Skill (M.E.S.) Under Skill Development Initiative (S.D.I.) Scheme. (n.d.). Directorate of Employment and Craftsmen Training.

Nambiar, D., Karki, S., Rahardiani, D., Putri, M., & Singh, K. (2019, July). *Study on skills for the future in Indonesia.* Oxford Policy Management.

Schaeffer, K. (2022, April 12). *Key facts about U.S. college graduates.* Pew Research Center.

Skill Development and Employment Opportunity. (2020, February 11). MyGov Blog.

Skills for Employability. (n.d.). Nasscom Foundation.

Song, V. (2021, February 1). *COVID-19 has widened the skills gap. But it also presents an opportunity to close it.* EdSurge.

Sood, K., Kaur, B., & Grima, S. (2022). Revamping Indian Non-Life Insurance Industry with a trusted network: Blockchain technology. In K. Sood, R. K. Dhanaraj, B. Balamurugan, S. Grima, R. U. Maheshwari (Eds.), *Big Data: A game changer for insurance industry* (pp. 213–228). Emerald Publishing Limited.

Stebleton, M. J., & Kaler, L. S. (2020). Preparing college students for the end of work: The role of meaning. *Journal of College and Character*, *21*(2) 132–139.

Tandon, P., Kruse, A., & Di Gropello, E. (2011). *Skills for the labor market in Indonesia: Trends in demand, gaps, and supply*. World Bank.

The Economic Times. (2022, October 27). Bridging India's gaping skill gap. *The Economic Times*.

Unemployment, total (% of the total labor force) (modeled ILO estimate) – India | Data. (2023). World Bank Data.

Unemployment, total (% of the total labor force) (modeled ILO estimate) – United States | Data. (2023). World Bank Data.

Unemployment with advanced education (% of the total labor force with advanced education) – India | Data. (2023). World Bank Data.

Unni, J. (2022, January). Skill gaps and employability: Higher education in India. *Journal of Development Policy and Practice*, *1*(1) 1–17.

Wheebox. (2022). India Skills Report 2022.

World Economic Forum. (2022). India overtakes UK as the world's fifth-largest economy | World Economic Forum. *The World Economic Forum*. https://www.weforum.org/agenda/2022/09/india-uk-fifth-largest-economy-world/

CHAPTER 10

LABOUR MARKET TRENDS AND SKILLS MISMATCHES IN TRANSITION ECONOMIES: THE CASE OF KOSOVO

Theranda Beqiri[a] and Simon Grima[b]

[a] University Haxhi Zeka, Peja, Kosovo
[b] University of Malta, Malta

ABSTRACT

Purpose: *This chapter addresses the skills shortages in Kosovo's labour market, emphasising the service sector. The labour market economy is very dynamic, and Kosovo, with the youngest population in Europe, also has the highest unemployment level among youths. Therefore, we aim to analyse the mismatches of the skills demand in the labour market.*

Methodology: *The scientific methods used in this chapter are quantitative methods applying analytical and critical approaches based on economic theory. In this chapter, we analysed secondary data from Labour Force Surveys (LFS) and official reports such as the World Bank and UNDP. We have also conducted primary research with the employees of SMEs in the service sector, with specifically related questionnaires for descriptive issues.*

Findings: *The logit model used in this research has shown goodness of fit and yielded significant results. Based on the empirical findings, we have found a need for some main soft skills such as communication skills, language skills, ICT skills, and additional training to help gain employability skills. These findings suggest*

Contemporary Challenges in Social Science Management
Skills Gaps and Shortages in the Labour Market
Contemporary Studies in Economic and Financial Analysis, Volume 112A, 167–181
Copyright © 2024 by Theranda Beqiri and Simon Grima
Published under exclusive licence by Emerald Publishing Limited
ISSN: 1569-3759/doi:10.1108/S1569-37592024000112A023

that there is a need for more skills in the service sector, significantly impacting the employees' job performance and the job seeker's level of employability.

Significance: *Noticeably, countries that are still in the transition process face inequalities in the labour market and have a very high level of unemployment. The findings can be used in analysing demand-side management of the labour market and mismatching of skills in transition economies by policy makers.*

Keywords: Labour market; mismatch of skills; training; education; unemployment; employment; youth

1. INTRODUCTION

1.1. Labour Market in Transition

The labour market in a market economy operates through supply and demand in the market. In this market, the labour demand is also the firm demand for employees, while the supply is the employees' offer of the skills needed for the required work. The job offer also includes the growth of the population level, the participation levels of the active population, as well as the level of education. Whereas labour demand also contains the factors that affect the labour costs, such as the minimum payment and the payment for the level of productivity.

Education and level of education are related and have been the focus of many studies. The difference in employment for the same level of education is usually very small, but this part also gives us enough information. The impact before entering the labour market can impact human capital depending on how much is invested in it before entering the labour market, and it has to do with the skills required in the labour market.

The labour market coordinates the labour force from entry to exit from the labour market. The actions that take place in the labour market depend on that country's economic and social situation as well as the institutional policies that are implemented by that country. The labour market is a dynamic process since it depends on many factors that directly impact it, such as competition in the capital market, investments, technology development, and from the side of competition of human capital and labour force activity.

Progress can only be achieved by educating and working based on industrial age models to prepare students for the knowledge-based workplace. Therefore, there is a lifelong learning approach whose main duties are to reduce the gap between learning in school and the workplace.

Many countries in transition experience a need for more skills in the labour force, which means that youngsters have a high level of unemployment or are employed below their level of education. As a result, education produces profiles that need to be aligned with the labour market's requirements. This underlying skill gap is a significant obstacle to the country's economic development, resulting in a discrepancy between the skills the graduate workforce possesses and the skills required by the real sector (Ziberi et al., 2021).

Kosovo's low participation and employment rate characterises the youth labour market. The development of the private sector has become parallel to the formalisation of the economy. All societies in transition go through this phenomenon of the labour market, where the ratios between the legal and the illegal economy change in certain periods.

Lack of work experience, low education skills, and inappropriate work attitudes are the main defects of the employability debate in Kosovo. The implication is the need for education and training to increase employability. Based on the fact that many positions that are difficult to fill are concentrated in certain professions and industries and certain regions, it appears that an approach with a sectoral and regional focus would be appropriate. At the same time, it has been accepted by employers that a group of reasons is related to the lack of attractive skills in some jobs, low salary offers, lack of career prospects, insufficient people interested in work, and the small number of job seekers (Brancatelli et al., 2020). The need for skills and abilities is fluid, meaning that the required skills will change as certain sectors expand and enterprises experience changing environmental impacts.

The transition economies have experienced much greater labour market changes than industrialised countries, whose skills gaps are largely due to globalisation and technological innovation. The economic systems' overall transformation and structural changes to an open economy have led to far more intense changes in the labour market in these countries.

In Kosovo, there are still labour market challenges that derive from the working-age youth entering the labour market and the job creation, the persistently low participation of women, and generally unstable employment opportunities regarding the employment contract (Gashi & Williams, 2019).

In Kosovo, Youth unemployment was 15–24 with 49.1% in 2020 (Table 10.1), particularly among women. According to the LFS results from the Kosovo Labour Force Statistics (2020), the unemployment rate was 25.9%.

Unemployment was highest among females at 32.3%, compared to males at 23.5%. The highest unemployment rate is in the age group, according to the results of LFS. In 2020 inactive labour force is quite high at 61.7%, with a particular focus on females at 79.2%, compared to males at 44.0%.

Precarious conditions for young people result from demographic pressures, joblessness growth patterns, emigration trends, and poor education.

Reforms in the labour market in transition economies, oriented towards competition, have influenced the increase in the level of unemployment among the economically active population. The reforms have affected women more than men; some have even left the workforce. Kosovo's high official unemployment, estimated by the Kosovo Statistics Agency as 25.9% in 2020, is a symptom of the difficult business environment and a perennial political concern. The difficult labour market conditions affect youth and women disproportionately and risk undermining the country's social fabric. A large informal economy exists, which is difficult to be captured in official data. Inactivity is also related to employers' perceptions of the low quality of formal education and vocational training institutions that are seen as not equipping employees with skills that are in demand. One outcome of low skills mismatches is that hiring remains highly informal and

Table 10.1. Key Labour Market Indicators Divided by Year, Gender, and Youth.

Labour Market Indicators	Age	2018			2019			2020		
		Male	Female	Total	Male	Female	Total	Male	Female	Total
Labour force participation rate (%)	15–64	63.3	18.4	40.9	59.7	21.1	40.5	56.0	20.8	38.3
Inactive population (%)	15–64	36.7	81.6	59.1	40.3	78.9	59.5	44.0	79.2	61.7
Unemployment rate (%)	15–64	28.5	33.4	29.6	22.6	34.4	25.7	23.5	32.3	25.9
Unemployment rate (%)	15–24	51.5	64.7	55.4	44.1	60.3	49.4	45.2	57.2	49.1
Employment to population ratio (%)	15–64	45.3	12.3	28.8	46.2	13.9	30.1	42.8	14.1	28.4
Share of status category in total employment (%)	Employee	70.3	80.7	70.1	83.3	73.1	69.6	84.8	73.4	73.4
	Self-employed with employees	9.4	2.2	9.6	2.9	8.1	11.4	4.2	9.6	9.6
Self-employed	Own-account worker or freelancer	14.7	11.6	14.9	8.9	13.5	14.6	6.1	12.5	12.5
	Unpaid family worker	5.7	5.5	5.4	4.9	5.3	4.4	4.9	4.5	4.5

Source: Kosovo Labour Force Statistics.

reliant on personal contacts. Economic issues in a developing country, such as Kosovo, political changes with political instability, and low institutional trust impact the prevailing desire to migrate (Krasniqi, 2019). Remittances, the high level of emigration in Kosovo is further undermining growth prospects, even if it temporarily relieves labour market pressures from the growing labour force. Regarding migration findings by Beqiri and Hoxha (2022) suggest that respondents with economic, cultural, and security concerns have a statistically significant higher propensity to migrate compared to the respondents without these concerns. Despite these challenges, Kosovo's relatively young population, low labour costs, and abundant natural resources have attracted several significant investments and several international firms and franchises which are present in the market.

2. AIM OF THE STUDY

The literature review and introduction showed that the labour market dynamics in Kosovo are very challenging, and the issue of the high level of unemployment, especially for youngsters and females in Kosovo. The level of unemployment is an issue that might decrease with the increase of the solutions in the level of education and the skills pieces of training needed in Kosovo's labour market. The quality of education is the critical factor since the graduates that enter the labour market are expected to have knowledge of academic issues and a more general variety of soft skills to find a job Wilton (2012). Therefore, this study aims to see the perceptions employees working in the service sector have of additional skills, except those gained through formal education. Identifying the skills that helped them gain a job and whether they needed additional training to maintain the job and further their careers in the service sector. The questionnaire was structured by asking what types of skills need to be improved for service sector employees.

According to Cojocaru (2017), high informality makes it harder to measure economic activity accurately, and some informal employment cannot be recorded. Nonetheless, inactivity is high, particularly among women owing to family responsibilities, poor provision of child and elderly care services, and employers' biases. Findings from Horodnic et al. (2020) regarding undeclared work in the service sector show that compared with the service sector in hotels and restaurants, the competitors in transport and information technology are considerably more likely to notice that their business is affected by undeclared work.

Based on ILO (2022), it is important to identify and anticipate skills based on social dialogue and labour market information to adapt skills provision and promote employability and productivity. The ability to adapt curricula effectively is supported by information regarding current and future skills needs and an awareness of the skills required by employers on the job by learners. A skill intelligence approach reduces the possibility of skills mismatch (overqualification, underqualification, gap in skills, shortages of skills, and obsolescence of skills).

According to the European Commission (2022), skills are divided into basic skills – literacy, numeracy, and transferable skills, such as foreign language science – and digital skills. According to ILO (2022), basic skills are literacy and numeracy, and personal skills are honesty, integrity, and work ethics. Transferable skills are learning to learn, communication (including oral, information technology communication, and written skills), problem-solving, and team working skills.

Given the importance of the services sector in Kosovo, these skills will likely be of increasing importance going forward. Businesses in the service sector are growing at different levels in Kosovo and have needs for different skills. Sometimes businesses need help finding the right staff and filling in their vacancies. Therefore, we have conducted research in service-oriented businesses to gain more knowledge on the gap between the skills and mismatch in this particular sector.

3. LITERATURE REVIEW

There is no accepted theory regarding skill mismatch, and although it is related to education training, it is also related to the personal characteristics of the workers. Measuring skill mismatch is particularly challenging, mostly due to the need for more direct information about workers' skills and job requirements (Leuven & Oosterbeek, 2011). Employability skills will not secure you the job but will allow you to advance in your career and achieve organisational objectives (Ismail et al., 2011). Becker (1962) introduced the human capital theory, which states that each worker will be paid their marginal value in the labour market and that investment in human capital increases earnings.

Educational over-investment is explained in the job competition model, telling that individuals invest in education to achieve their goals and take better positions in the labour market (Di Pietro & Urwin, 2006; Sala, 2011). There are indications that the higher level of formal schooling in the workforce results in the increased average formal schooling level of employees, positively affecting the education and job matches in the labour market (Lichy & Khvatova, 2019). Similar results are also found by Cabus and Somers (2018); from their research, an increase in companies' workforce average schooling level decreases the probability that companies report mismatch.

Rapid technology growth and the changing nature of work led to more opportunities and risks, leading to more insurance and financial needs (Sood, Kaur et al., 2022), which subsequently requires higher skills in this sector.

According to screening theory, potential employees and employees are selected and rewarded according to assumptions based on their skills from their education, experience, or training. Hence, a huge percentage of employees work in jobs incompatible with their education, which often results that them being higher in jobs below their capabilities and qualifications (Senkrua, 2021). The categorisation is based on offering jobs below the skills and qualifications of the job searchers; therefore, they result in working in jobs with lower wages than their qualifications.

Globalisation, including technological developments, has been allied with an increasing variety of occupational professions, which can cause the need for new skills and increase skill shortages in the labour market (Brunello & Wruuck, 2021).

Unlike developed countries, where the key source of the increasing skill gaps can be related to the globalisation process and technological innovation, the transition economies have faced far more intense labour market changes caused by the overall transformation and the structural changes of the economic systems (Stanković et al., 2021). Skills mismatch has an impact on job satisfaction and the level of net income. Findings from Veselinović et al. (2020) strongly support that self-reported education-job mismatch has a 13–15% impact on net income among workers.

Wilton (2008) states that employees with graduate degrees, additional training, and globally recognised certificates can give employers a competitive advantage in the local and international markets. Skills and knowledge required to remain competitive will be changing at an accelerating rate in the service and information sectors competitive. Traditional education and training models are insufficient to meet this increasingly important need (Fischer, 2000). The business cycle is also important, and there is a decline because low-quality jobs are also declining, while the matches with employee skills increase (Brunello & Wruuck, 2021). Due to frequent changes in the business environment these days, graduates are expected to have more skills than those they received through formal academic schooling. They are expected to have soft skills and communication skills (Coetzee, 2014; Hernández-March et al., 2009; Jackson, 2016; Jusufi, 2020). Matching employees' skills is the aim of every educational institution.

Nevertheless, the mismatch of skills is present. According to ILO (2022), these transformations can benefit workers and enterprises but could also be disruptive, leading to unemployment, underemployment, difficult transitions of youth into the labour market, skills mismatches, skills gaps, and skills gaps shortages, inequalities, and inefficiencies (Desjardins & Rubenson, 2011). Effective and inclusive skills and lifelong learning systems promote better responsiveness of skills supply to current and future labour market needs and thus serve as key enablers of human development, full, productive, and freely chosen employment, and decent work for all. Lifelong learning is a significant part of the working life of employees. It is also important for employers to invest in improving working skills through formal and non-formal education for their increased effectiveness and better business results (Beqiri & Mazreku, 2020). Communication skills competencies are vital skills for employees, and they show their professional competence and the ability to perform their day-to-day tasks. Obtaining communication skills starts with education, their first experience, and additional pieces of training (Koval et al., 2018). From the employee's perspective, Berlingieri and Erdsiek (2012) identify and argue that their perception is different from the theory, taking into account that some workers do not prefer to work where there is maximum productivity; they distinguish the work by the job characteristics and attributes, as well as the location of the job and mobility costs. According to Brunello and Wruuck (2021),

> Skill requirements and the quality of matches are identified by asking employees whether they have the skills required to do a more demanding job than their current one or whether training is needed to carry out the job in a satisfactory way.

Although, findings from the 'Skills Towards Employment and Productivity Survey' in Kosovo (World Bank Group, 2019) also scoring high on certain socio-emotional characteristics or skills is positively linked to the probability of being employed (Baturina & Simakov, 2023; Juliana et al., 2022; Sood, Seth et al., 2022).

4. RESEARCH QUESTIONS AND HYPOTHESIS

In this research, we have developed questionnaires about their skills with related questions for the employees. To understand the skills they gained during their education and what additional skills and training they had to obtain to find a job or have a career in their field. Therefore, we have concentrated our research questions on finding the self-reported mismatch among the employees and the additional training they need to do their jobs adequately. We have also incorporated the transferable skills questions according to ILO definitions explained above in the text. During the research, the respondents from the service sector companies are chosen randomly from all the positions in the organisation to have a variety of opinions starting from employees, lower level managers, middle managers, and workers with higher positions managers.

1. How long was the transition from finishing your studies to finding a job after your bachelor studies?
2. Did you need additional skills to get a job after your studies?
3. Did the knowledge of a foreign language help you in gaining your job?
4. Do you need additional training to fulfil your job requirements?
5. Do you think that teamwork is important to do your job satisfactorily?
6. Do you think that your presentation skills help you achieve better results at your job?
7. Is there an impact on communication skills and employee performance in the organisation?

When it comes to *H1*, we have developed the following hypothesis:

H1. There is no difference between additional training regarding employability skills and increased efficiency of the employees in doing the job.

5. METHODOLOGY

5.1. Scope, Sample, and Period of the Study

This research explores the mismatch of skills in the service sector in the labour market of Kosovo. The questionnaires were developed with relevant questions regarding transferable skills. They were distributed to employees to gain better knowledge of which skills they think are needed to be employed and gain a competitive job.

The Kosovo Business Registration Agency (KBRA) operates within the Ministry of Trade and Industry, the only institution for registering Kosovo businesses. Of the registered service companies in the **KBRA**, there were 1,283 registered travel agencies, although we can say that around 10% are passive, financial services 264, and ICT software 587 companies.

The sample and data used in this chapter are based on the independent research survey conducted by authors during the second part of 2022 in the service sector companies in Kosovo. We have mainly concentrated on travel agencies, financial and security companies, and ICT companies. The sample was randomly selected from the business and comprised 110 companies with 250 respondents.

5.2. Data Analysis

To attain the study's objectives, we have used some descriptive analysis according to the responses we received from our questionaries' and the results derived from the SPSS. We have also used the Pearson correlation matrix of the main indicators studied to see the relevance and the proportion of correlation between different variables. For testing the *H1*, we have used the logit model. Logistic models have typically been interpreted in terms of odds ratios; for continuous predictors, a 1-unit increase in a predictor value indicates the change in odds expressed by the displayed odds ratio.

6. RESULTS AND INTERPRETATION

In this research, we have replies from 250 participants from the 110 service organisations, shown in Fig. 10.1, where 46.4% are responses from employees in Travel Agencies, 37.6% are employees from Financial Services, and 16% from ICT Software Developer institutions.

Regarding the education level of the employees in the service sector in Kosovo, we can say that from the results, they are highly educated, are shown in Fig. 10.2. In ICT enterprises, 75% of employees have a master's degree, 15% with a bachelor's degree, and 10% have additional training. In travel agencies, 45% are with a bachelor's degree, 35% with a master, around 5% with high school, and 15% had additional training before getting the job. While in financial institutions, 48.5% are with master's degrees, 30% with bachelor's degrees, and 21.5% need additional training before getting the job.

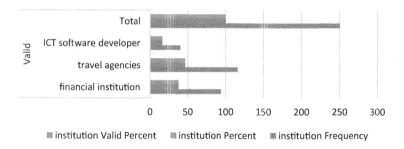

Fig. 10.1. Service Sector. *Source*: Authors' calculation.

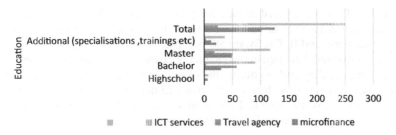

Fig. 10.2.   Education of Workers in the Service Sector. *Source:* Authors' calculation.

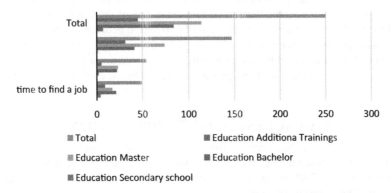

Fig. 10.3.   Transition From School to Job. *Source:* Authors' calculation.

The transition from school degree to job from our respondents in Fig. 10.3 are as follows, 64.8% of respondents with master's degrees found their jobs within 6 months after they finished their studies, 20.1% needed a year to find a job, and 14.1% more than a year. 48.8% of respondents with a bachelor's degree found their jobs within 6 months after their degree, and 26.1% with a bachelor's found their job in less than a year, while 25.6% searched for 1–2 years to find a job. 68.8% of the employees interviewed obtained additional training during or after their education and then found a job within 6 months, 20% of the employees in the service sector that had additional training found their job in less than a year, and 11.2% had to search for jobs within 1–2 years.

To find out the impact and any correlation between employees' performance and the employable or transferable skills in the service sector concerning our research questions, we have used the Pearson correlation matrix generated from SPSS. The Pearson correlation test in Table 10.2 gives us significant results without considering means and distribution levels. Employee performance is positively correlated with on-job training at 0.451%, oral communication skills at 0.302%, ICT skills at 0.187%, and presentation skills at 0.267. It is not related to written communication skills, which seem less important according to the employee

Table 10.2. Correlations Matrix.

		Age	Exp	EP	OJT	OS	FLS	ICT	PS	WS
Age	Pearson Correlation	1	0.250**	-0.120	-0.050	-0.115	0.156*	0.214**	-0.064	0.220**
	Sig. (Two-tailed)		0.000	0.059	0.429	0.070	0.014	0.001	0.316	0.000
	N	250	250	250	250	250	250	249	250	250
Experience	Pearson Correlation	0.250**	1	-0.033	-0.013	0.032	0.405**	0.036	-0.094	0.092
	Sig. (Two-tailed)	0.000		0.600	0.841	0.613	0.000	0.567	0.137	0.147
	N		250							
Empl performance	Pearson Correlation	-0.120	-0.033	1	0.451**	0.302**	0.100	0.187**	0.267**	-0.118
	Sig. (Two-tailed)	0.059	0.600		0.000	0.000	0.100	0.003	0.000	0.063
On job training	Pearson Correlation	-0.050	-0.013	0.451**	1	0.182**	0.077	0.076	0.120	-0.125*
	Sig. (Two-tailed)	0.429	0.841	0.000		0.004	0.226	0.229	0.058	0.049
Oral communication skills	Pearson Correlation	-0.115	0.032	0.302**	0.182**	1	-0.043	0.191**	0.313**	-0.117
	Sig. (Two-tailed)	0.070	0.613	0.000	0.004		0.503	0.003	0.000	0.066
Foreign language skills	Pearson Correlation	0.156*	0.405**	0.100	0.077	-0.043	1	0.005	0.002	0.146*
	Sig. (Two-tailed)	0.014	0.000	0.116	0.226	0.503		0.940	0.969	0.021
ICT skills	Pearson Correlation	0.214**	0.036	0.187**	0.076	0.191**	0.005	1	0.359**	0.047
	Sig. (Two-tailed)	0.001	0.567	0.003	0.229	0.003	0.940		0.000	0.047
Presentation skills	Pearson Correlation	-0.064	-0.094	0.267**	0.120	0.313**	0.002	0.359**	1	0.041
	Sig. (Two-tailed)	0.316	0.137	0.000	0.058	0.000	0.969	0.000		0.523
Written communication	Pearson Correlation	0.220**	0.092	-0.118	-0.125*	-0.117	0.146*	0.047	0.041	1
	Sig. (Two-tailed)	0.000	0.147	0.063	0.049	0.066	0.021	0.459	0.523	

Source: Authors' calculation.

*Correlation is significant at the 0.05 level (two-tailed).

**Correlation is significant at the 0.01 level (two-tailed).

respondents in the service sector. Experience is correlated with age at the level of 0.01 (two-tailed), which is expected.

Logistic regression is a very useful analytical tool because of the simplicity of the relationship between the coefficients and odds ratio, where the odds ratio is usually very easy to explain and interpret (Hosmer et al., 2013). According to Sperandei (2014), the logistic regression's main advantage is that it avoids perplexing effects since it analyses the association of all variables.

Omnibus Tests of Model Coefficients explain the variance in the outcome. Here the Chi-square is highly significant Chi-square = 84.443 df = 7, p-value 0.000 which indicates the goodness of fit of independent variables in the model.

The variables in the equation output show us that the regression equation is:

$$\text{Log}(p/1 - p) = \beta 0 + \beta 1 {}^* X1 + \beta 2 {}^* X2 + \beta 3 {}^* X3$$
$$+ \beta 4 {}^* X4 + \beta 5 {}^* X5 + \beta 6 {}^* X6 + \beta 7 {}^* X7$$

Independent variables are: $X1$, on job training; $X2$, oral communication skills; $X3$, language skills; $X4$, ICT skills; $X5$, written skills; $X6$, teamwork skills; and $X7$, level of education, while the dependent variable is extra training that they had after the education for skills to get the job.

These are the logistic regression equation values for predicting the dependent variable from the independent variable. They are in log-odds units.

$$\text{Ln(odds)} = 4.130 + 2.029\text{OJT} + 0.971\text{OCS} + 0.364\text{LS}$$
$$+ 0.645 \text{ ICT} - 0.372\text{WS} - 0.217\text{TW} + 0.589\text{EDU}$$

The variables in the equation output also give us the exponential function of the regression Exp(B). This is better known as the odds ratio predicted by the model. This odds ratio can be computed by raising the base of the natural log to the bth power, where b is the slope from our logistic regression equation. The Exp(B) column odds ratio tells us that variable on-the-job training has a score of 1.766 which tells us that the model predicts the odds for employees that have on-the-job training increase their skills for 7.609 higher than those that do not have on-job training, keeping everything else equal. Additional training in oral communication skills has an impact of having efficiency for 2.641 higher than those employees that do not have this training. For employees that do know a foreign language the odds of being employed and having a career is 1.439 higher than for those that do not know the foreign languages, although the significance in this variable is on the margin of significance. ICT skills are significant and the odds of finding a job and having an advancement in career is 1.905 higher than for those that do not have these skills. Education is significant and the odds of getting a job with more years of education is 0.555 higher for each degree keeping everything else equal. There is an interesting result for other transferable skills such as written skills and teamwork that the employees in the service sector in Kosovo do not find relevant to getting a job or for their advancement in their current jobs, since they did not result significantly in our research.

From the results of Table 10.3 and the interpretation of their results, we can reject $H1$. 'There is no difference between additional training regarding

Table 10.3. Logit Model Estimated Coefficients Variables in the Equation.

		B	SE	Wald	df	Sig.	Exp(B)
Step 1[a]	On-job training	2.029	0.331	37.648	1	0.000	7.609
	Oral communication skills	0.971	0.327	8.830	1	0.003	2.641
	Language skills	0.364	0.206	3.121	1	0.077	1.439
	ICT skills	0.645	0.320	4.051	1	0.044	1.905
	Written skills	−0.371	0.314	1.400	1	0.237	0.690
	Teamwork	−0.217	0.343	0.399	1	0.528	0.805
	Education	0.589	0.219	7.243	1	0.007	0.555
	Constant	4.130	1.280	10.411	1	0.001	0.016
	Omnibus Tests of Model Coefficients	Chi-square	84.443	df	7	Sig.	0.000
	Model Summary	2 Log likelihood	254.114[a]	Cox & Snell R^2	0.289	Nagelkerke R^2	0.388

Source: Authors' calculation.
[a]Variable(s) entered on Step 1: job training, oral communication skills, language skills, ICT skills, written communication skills, teamwork, and education.

employability skills and increased efficiency of the employees in doing the job'. Therefore, we can say that the additional communication training increases employability and transferable skills and impacts the employees' increased performance.

7. CONCLUSION

The study aims to comprehend the employee's perspective on the employability skills gained during their formal education and their opinions of the mismatch of skills in their jobs. Our research concludes that most employees need additional training to find a job during or after their studies. Indicates a mismatch of skills between skills needed in the labour market and those gained in formal education. From the results regarding communication skills, we found a positive correlation between the employees' performance and oral communication skills, presentation skills, and ICT skills. Although, also education is very important, and the odds of finding a job and having a good performance in your job in the service sector increase with each degree by 0.55 higher than for those with less education. Around 70% of the employees in this research found their job within 6 months when they had additional communication skills training during or after their education.

Regarding skills, we have seen that additional training has increased the skills for employability and increased performance. Therefore, some of the employees can organise training for their workers since results in the correlation and logit model above clearly indicate that job training is very important for the employees and, in their perception, increases their skills in doing the job well in their workplace environment. Policy makers and respective ministries responsible for education curricula are updating the curricula considering labour market needs, but they are still transitioning. Policy makers and educational institutions should respond faster to the changes in the labour market needs to decrease the level of skills mismatch and reduce the inefficiency in the labour market. Some of the skills the employees found important, such as presentation skills, ICT, and oral skills, can be easily incorporated into their teaching curricula.

On the other hand, the graduates that have been more proactive and participated in non-formal education have shown better performance in their jobs. The limitation of this study is that it is developed only in selected institutions in the service sector. However, we can say that it is a good starting point to generate further research in this field.

REFERENCES

Baturina, L., & Simakov, A. (2023). Students' attitude towards e-learning in Russia after the pandemic. *Education Science and Management*, 1(1), 1–6.

Becker, G. S. (1962). Investment in human capital: A theoretical analysis. *Journal of Political Economy*, 70(5, Part 2), 9–49.

Beqiri, T., & Hoxha, A. (2022). The propensity of youth to migrate: Evidence from Kosovo. *Economic Studies*, 31(6), 120–132.

Beqiri, T., & Mazreku, I. (2020). Lifelong learning, training, and development of employee's perspective. *Journal of Educational and Social Research*, 10(2), 94.

Berlingieri, F., & Erdsiek, D. (2012). *How relevant is job mismatch for German graduates?* ZEW-Centre for European Economic Research Discussion Paper (12-075). https://d-nb.info/1193583993/34

Brancatelli, C., Marguerie, A. C., & Brodmann, S. (2020). *Job creation and demand for skills in Kosovo: What can we learn from job portal data?* World Bank Policy Research Working Paper, (9266). Washington, DC: World Bank. http://hdl.handle.net/10986/33850

Brunello, G., & Wruuck, P. (2021). Skill shortages and skill mismatch: A review of the literature. *Journal of Economic Surveys*, 35(4), 1145–1167.

Cabus, S. J., & Somers, M. A. (2018). A mismatch between education and the labour market in the Netherlands: Is it a reality or a myth? The employers' perspective. *Studies in Higher Education*, 43(11), 1854–1867.

Coetzee, M. (2014). Measuring student graduateness: Reliability and construct validity of the Graduate Skills and Attributes Scale. *Higher Education Research & Development*, 33(5), 887–902.

Cojocaru, A. (2017). *Kosovo jobs diagnostic (No. 27173)* (pp. 1–71). The World Bank Group.

Desjardins, R., & Rubenson, K. (2011). *An analysis of skill mismatch using direct measures of skills.* OECD Education Working Papers No. 63. OECD Publishing (pp. 1–88). http://dx.doi.org/10.1787/5kg3nh9h52g5-en. https://doi.org/10.2767/997479KE-04-22-265-EN-N. ISBN: 978-92-76-60085-5

Di Pietro, G., & Urwin, P. (2006). Education and skills mismatch in the Italian graduate labour market. *Applied Economics*, 38(1), 79–93.

European Commission. (2022). *Study supporting the evaluation of the council recommendation on upskilling pathways: New opportunities for adults.* https://ec.europa.eu/social/main.jsp?catId=1146&langId=en.

Fischer, G. (2000). Lifelong learning—More than training. *Journal of Interactive Learning Research*, 11(3), 265–294.

Gashi, A., & Williams, C. C. (2019). Evaluating the prevalence and distribution of unregistered employment in Kosovo: Lessons from a 2017 survey. *The South East European Journal of Economics and Business*, 14(1), 7–20.

Hernández-March, J., Martin del Peso, M., & Leguey, S. (2009). Graduates' skills and higher education: The employers' perspective. *Tertiary Education and Management*, 15, 1–16.

Horodnic, I. A., Williams, C. C., Manolică, A., Roman, C. T., & Boldureanu, G. (2020). Employer perspectives on undeclared work in the service sector: Impacts and policy responses. *The Service Industries Journal*, 43(5–6), 358–377.

Hosmer, D. W., Jr, Lemeshow, S., & Sturdivant, R. X. (2013). *Applied logistic regression* (Vol. 398). John Wiley & Sons.

Ismail, R., Yussof, I., & Sieng, L. W. (2011). Employers' perceptions on graduates in the Malaysian services sector. *International Business Management*, 5(3), 184–193.

Jackson, D. (2016). Modelling graduate skill transfer from university to the workplace. *Journal of Education and Work, 29*(2), 199–231.

Juliana, A. P., Lemy, D. M., Pramono, R., Djakasaputra, A., & Purwanto, A. (2022). Hotel performance in the digital era: Roles of digital marketing, perceived quality and trust. *Journal of Intelligent Management Decision, 1*(1), 36–45.

Jusufi, N. (2020, November). *Skills gap analysis in retail industry* (pp. 1–47). Kosovo Retail Association. https://helvetas-ks.org/eye/file/repository/Skills_gap_Analysis_in_Retail_Industry.pdf

Kosovo Labour Force Statistics. (2018). Labour Force Survey 2018. KAS. https://www.ilo.org/surveyLib/index.php/catalog/5693/related-materials

Kosovo Labour Force Statistics. (2019). *Labour Force Surveys for 2019*. KAS. https://www.ilo.org/surveyLib/index.php/catalog/7628

Kosovo Labour Force Statistics. (2020). *Kosovo Labour Force Survey*. https://www.ilo.org/surveyLib/index.php/catalog/5692

Kosovo Business Registration Agency (KBRA). https://arbk.rks-gov.net/page.aspx?id=2,1

Koval, V., Polyezhayev, Y., & Bezkhlibna, A. (2018). Communicative competencies in enhancing regional competitiveness in the labour market. *Baltic Journal of Economic Studies, 4*(5), 105–113.

Krasniqi, B. (2019). *IESB Institute: Labour market and skills needs analysis; Perspective for the future* (pp. 1–57). Publication of "Aligning Education and Training with Labour Market Needs 2" ALLED. https://www.researchgate.net/publication/336349866_Labour_Market_and_Skills_Needs_Analysis_in_Kosovo_Perspective_for_the_future. ISBN: 978-9951-8990-0-0.

Leuven, E., & Oosterbeek, H. (2011). Overeducation and mismatch in the labour market. *Handbook of the Economics of Education, 4*, 283–326.

Lichy, J., & Khvatova, T. (2019). Rethinking solutions for re-balancing the education–job mismatch. *The Journal of Management Development, 38*(9), 733–754.

Sala, G. (2011). Approaches to a skills mismatch in the labour market: A literature review. *Papers: Revista de Sociologia, 96*(4), 1025–1045.

Senkrua, A. (2021). A review paper on skills mismatch in developed and developing countries. *International Journal of Sustainable Development & World Policy, 10*(1), 8–24.

Sood, K., Kaur, B., & Grima, S. (2022). Revamping Indian Non-Life Insurance Industry with a trusted network: Blockchain technology. In K. Sood, R. K. Dhanaraj, B. Balamurugan, S. Grima, & R. U. Maheshwari (Eds.), *Big Data: A game changer for insurance industry* (pp. 213–228). Emerald Publishing Limited.

Sood, K., Seth, N., & Grima, S. (2022). Portfolio performance of Public Sector General Insurance companies in India: A comparative analysis. In S. Grima, E. Özen, & I. Romānova (Eds.), *Managing risk and decision making in times of economic distress, Part B* (pp. 215–230). Emerald Publishing Limited.

Sperandei, S. (2014). Understanding logistic regression analysis. *Biochemia Medica, 24*(1), 12–18.

Stanković, J. J., Džunić, M., & Marinković, S. (2021, December). Urban employment in post-transition economies: Skill mismatch in the local labour market. *Journal of Economics and Business, 39*, 279–297. ISSN: 1331-8004; 1846-7520 (Online).

The ILO strategy on skills and lifelong learning for 2022–30, the conclusions adopted by the International Labour Conference in December 2021, October 2022, pp. 1–17. https://www.ilo.org/wcmsp5/groups/public/--ed_norm/--relconf/documents/meetingdocument/wcms_857706.pdf

Veselinović, L., Mangafić, J., & Turulja, L. (2020). The effect of education-job mismatch on net income: Evidence from a developing country. *Economic Research, 33*(1), 2648–2669.

Wilton, N. (2008). Business graduates and management jobs: An employability match made in heaven? *Journal of Education and Work, 21*(2), 143–158.

Wilton, N. (2012). The impact of work placements on skills development and career outcomes for business and management graduates. *Studies in Higher Education, 37*(5), 603–620.

World Bank Group. (2019). *Kosovo Country Report: Findings from the skills towards employment and productivity survey*. World Bank. https://elibrary.worldbank.org/doi/abs/10.1596/31720

Ziberi, B., Rexha, D., & Ukshini, K. (2021). Skills mismatch in the labour market: The future of work from the viewpoint of enterprises in case of Kosovo. *Journal of Governance & Regulation, 10*(3), 104–116. https://doi.org/10.22495/jgrv10i3art9

CHAPTER 11

BRIDGING THE SKILL GAP OF INDIAN HANDICRAFT INDUSTRY WORKERS: AN ANALYSIS OF THE PROBLEMS AND REMEDIES FOR HANDICRAFT ARTISANS

Uma Shankar Yadav,[a] Rashmi Aggarwal,[b] Ravindra Tripathi[a] and Ashish Kumar[a]

[a]DHSS, Motilal Nehru National Institute of Technology Allahabad, Pryagraj, India
[b]Chitkara Business School, Chitkara University, Punjab, India

ABSTRACT

Purpose: *This chapter investigates the current skill gap in small-scale industries, the need for skill development and digital training in micro, small, and medium enterprises (MSME), and reviews policies for skill development and solutions.*

Need for the Study: *While the legislature and organisations have initiated various considerations for the successful implementation of the Skill Development System in the country's MSMEs, there are significant challenges that must be addressed quickly to fill the skill gap in workers in this digital era.*

Research Methodology: *Secondary data has been used for the chapter review. Analysis has been done based on review data from women handloom and handicraft workers in the micro or craft industry who received a Star rating from the National Skill Development Corporation (NSDC) partners in Lucknow.*

Contemporary Challenges in Social Science Management
Skills Gaps and Shortages in the Labour Market
Contemporary Studies in Economic and Financial Analysis, Volume 112A, 183–202
Copyright © 2024 by Uma Shankar Yadav, Rashmi Aggarwal, Ravindra Tripathi and Ashish Kumar
Published under exclusive licence by Emerald Publishing Limited
ISSN: 1569-3759/doi:10.1108/S1569-37592024000112A024

For data collection, a questionnaire based on random sampling was used. The data were analysed using a rudimentary weighted average and a percentage technique.

Findings: *The studies provide answers to some fundamental problems: are small industry employees indeed mobilised to be skilled outside the official schooling system? Is the training delivery mechanism adequate to prepare pupils for employment? Would industries be willing to reduce minimum qualification criteria to foster skill development?*

Practical Implication: *Non-technical aptitudes digital and soft skills for workers in this sector should be emphasised in MSMEs, and significant reforms in MSME sectors and capacity-building education and training programmes should be implemented in the Indian industry to generate small and medium enterprises production and employment.*

Keywords: Micro, small, and medium enterprises; handicraft sector; digital skill; capacity building; vocational education; small industry labours; skill development

Abbreviations:

MSME	micro, small, and medium enterprises
NSDC	National Skill Development Corporation
PIB	Press Information Bureau
GDP	gross domestic product
OECD	Organization of Economic Cooperation and Development
CBSE	Central Board of Secondary Education
NGO	Non-governmental Organisation
ITI	Industrial Training Institute
IT	Information Technology
TUFS	Total Unit Funding Services

1. INTRODUCTION

The population's skill set propels a country's economic growth, social development, technical progress, degree of education (from elementary to graduate), and cultural norms. It has been highlighted in several international publications that nations with higher and more advanced levels of education and skills are better able to overcome challenges and make the most of their resources. They can also make significant progress towards sustainable growth by taking advantage of the chances given by the dynamic and ever-evolving macroenvironment.

India confronts a massive difficulty in its efforts to skill its people since only 4.69% of the overall workforce has undergone formal skill training, in comparison to the United Kingdom (68%), Germany (75%), the United States (52%), Japan (80%), and South Korea (96%). The Department of National Skill Development

Corporation (NSDC) studied the skills gap between 2010 and 2014. The subject matter experts deliberated on the magnitude of the skill requirements necessary for the various industries and the job roles. In addition to that, this study shed light on the market for skilled labour (demand and supply side). According to what was found, India will require an additional 109.73 million trained workers by 2022 in the 24 main areas selected for skilling India. The projection is that about 16.16 million people will enter the labour force, considering the workforce participation rate of 90% for males and 30% for females (Elborgh-Woytek et al., 2013; Yadav et al., 2023b). Those interested in furthering their education but lacking the necessary abilities will not be eligible. If this new skill acquisition method is implemented, 104.62 million people are expected to acquire such skills over the next 7 years. The problem for India is far from done; in the next 7 years, 104.62 million new workers will enter the workforce, and they will all be expected to have some training. As a country, we must invest in training infrastructure, including centres, instructors, and divisions by industry, geographic distribution, and employability tracking to meet our trainees' needs.

With so many people working in the country's unofficial economy, India's informal sector has a formidable challenge regarding training and education. Because the informal sector, which employs men and women in the workforce despite being outside the purview of the legal framework, is joint in medium and small industries, it is challenging to map existing skills and measure the additional skills required concerning the industry. Compared to the formal sector, the informal sector receives more attention at the macrolevel in India regarding the emphasis on generating jobs. According to the statistics from the census, the percentage of working women in urban areas fell from 17.8% to 15.5% between 2004 and 2011, while their involvement in the workforce in rural areas fell from 33.3% to 26.5% during the same period. As the informal sector has a significant economic impact in industries like textiles, food processing, export houses, and information technologies (ITes), it is impossible to ignore its contribution to the gross domestic product (GDP). These are also the key exporting regions. That's why providing workers with the training they need to increase output across the board and ensure the sector's long-term success is crucial.

It's common knowledge that most women in the workforce in this country are toiling away in the low-paying informal economy. Women who enter labour and work in the informal sector face several disadvantages, including the possibility of acquiring lower-quality skills, having no access to social security benefits, and having their daily salary rates capped at the minimum required amount. Women employees have fewer employment prospects than men because they lack essential industrial skills. This low involvement in the workforce directly results from the wrong working circumstances that women workers face. The majority of women employees who are employed in the informal sector do not have the necessary skills and do not have a formal education.

The percentage of women actively participating in the labour force in India is much lower than that of male workers. A gender breakdown of the labour force shows that men comprise 74.4% of the workforce, while women comprise only 25.8% among those aged 15 and above. Compared to many other developing economies, where the percentage of women actively participating in the workforce is higher than 50%, this percentage is significantly lower than 50% in India. Increasing workplace sensitivity to gender issues and providing training for skills suitable to non-traditional jobs are two steps towards mainstreaming gender roles. This will allow for increased productivity and a faster rate of economic growth. In the informal sector, the certification of the abilities of the women employed there would further boost women's engagement. Inclusion in economic growth and development is necessary to achieve sustainable growth.

Women's participation in the Indian labour force, despite being a crucial portion of the market, is falling. Female labour force participation dropped from 39% in 2000 to 30% in 2010. While 82% of Chinese women aged 25–45 participated in the labour force, only 72% of Brazilian women did the same. Yet, just 39.5% of women in India were economically active simultaneously. Due to the fact that fewer women are choosing to be active participants in the labour force in our country, women are under-represented in the labour force. Because of this, it would be a significant obstacle to finding a way to tap into the potential of the youthful population of Indian women who are of working age. These data point to the necessity of providing skill training for women to earn consistent earnings, have positive job outcomes, join forces, and grow into productive members of society who add to the nation's wealth (Tripathi et al., 2022; Rana & Bhargava, 2017).

According to the Organisation of Economic Cooperation and Development (OECD) Economic Survey from November 2014, India ranks poorly regarding women's participation in the labour force. Currently, women only contribute a pitiful 24% to the economy. Still, if more women employees could find jobs and contribute to their full potential, the Indian GDP might grow by an additional 4.2 percentage points. As a result, the rate of economic expansion can be sped up by increasing the number and quality of employment possibilities available to women in the labour market. A female labour force that is better educated and more talented would be more attentive to the importance of achieving sustainable development goals.

1.1. Research Problems

With about 54% of the overall population under the age of 25, the percentage of India's working-age population is among the world's highest (Elborgh-Woytek et al., 2013). Because of this, India has one of the youngest populations of people of working age in the world. To avoid this demographic dividend becoming a demographic nightmare over the next 25 years, training this workforce with marketable skills and ensuring that they contribute significantly to social and economic growth is critical. It's anticipated that this demographic bonus will continue for some time. As a result, their abilities should match the priority areas of the government's initiatives, such as 'Made in India' and 'Skills India'.

1.2. Defining the Nature of the Issue

One might argue that there is a talent shortage in the current job market in several ways. The most severe problem is the widespread belief that foreseeable future employees have significant gaps in necessary skills. Many point fingers at the education system, namely public education beginning with the Central Board of Secondary Education (CBSE) board and continuing through high school, for failing to teach students these vital skills. Due to its usage in policy discussions, the phrase 'skills gap' has been adopted to describe the situation.

In the second part of the topic, we go deeper into the specific abilities required for various jobs. For instance, one common claim is that India suffers from insufficiently qualified engineers and information technology (IT) professionals. When we say that people's skills are limited, this is what we mean.

One additional concern expressed more frequently in nations other than the country is the idea that there is always the possibility of an imbalance between the supply and demand for talent. This worry is much more prevalent in countries other than India. This scenario will conceivably play out in specific labour markets, but it is typically not the case regarding educational qualifications.

To begin evaluating the assertions concerning skills shortages, the first obstacle is to develop a conceptual framework that will allow one to comprehend the connection between employees and their abilities and employers' requirements. One theory, long associated with discussions of internal labour markets and the study of human resources (and personnel), holds that employers have the most trouble determining if a candidate's experience and education are a good fit for a given position. Over time, employers have begun to internalise the supply of labour, choosing candidates for entry-level positions based on their broad talents and then educating and developing workers throughout their working lives to fulfil the specific skill requirements of the company (Rana & Bhargava, 2017). This strategy seems to have suffered significant setbacks in recent years (e.g. Kaur et al., 2023b), a topic will discuss later in this chapter.

This alternate approach prioritises the labour market as the primary means of meeting the needs of potential employers in terms of skill sets. The idea of connecting job searchers with businesses rests on the premise that job seekers actively seek employment opportunities and employers seek out candidates with the requisite abilities. On an actual two-way street, the employer and the applicant are looking for a position that works for them. When there is a close fit between the applicants' talents and the requirements of the position, and when there is neither a shortage nor an abundance of skills compared to the organisation's needs, we have a good match.

In economics textbooks, the job-search process is generally modelled as reasonably passive. If a job applicant receives an offer from a potential employer that meets or surpasses their reservation price, they will accept the position. When there is a shortage of qualified applicants, businesses may increase pay to attract them, but if there is an oversupply, they may reduce pay to remain competitive. The prospect of scarcity is not incorporated into this model, as in other economic models. The common perception is that shortages only occur when there is some market failure, like wage freezes during wartime or restrictions on mobility and that they are only temporary until hiring procedures are adjusted.

The reality is that companies may broaden their net through recruitment and intelligent selection and that job seeker can broaden their net by becoming informed about open openings. Both sides can search more thoroughly. Furthermore, we know that the quantity of suitably qualified applicants is critical in determining the volume of job openings; when demand exceeds supply, corporations must resort to capital substitution to generate new jobs requiring fewer specialised skills. Employers have been shown to lower skill requirements for particular jobs during the periods of labour shortage and raise them during the periods of labour surplus (Kaur et al., 2023a; Tripathi et al., 2022).

1.3. Skills Gap As Well As a Skills Shortage

1.3.1. The Concept of the Talent Gap

The term 'skill gap' refers to the widespread lack of skills in the population, regardless of one's definition of 'skills'. This is the broadest and most detailed criticism of competence ever spoken. It is commonly argued that the reduction is related to the lacklustre skill set of recent high school and college grads, with school failure often being blamed as the root cause of pupils' sagging grades. So, the reduction is linked to the lack of preparedness among recent graduates.

Problems of a similar nature in India may have their origins in the Cold War and the National Defence Strategy rule of 2010 (Elborgh-Woytek et al., 2013). This statute increased scientific and engineering education funding to stay competitive with developing countries like India. National Council on Excellence in Education's 1983 study, 'A Nation at Risk', detailed the widespread decreases in student achievement throughout the 1970s. Long after its publication, this report contributed to the public's perception that US schools were inadequate.

The survey indicated that just 5% of businesses were experiencing skill shortages, but this low percentage was linked to businesses not implementing high-performance work methods. The group recommended, among other things, that students be held to national standards for education that align with international norms.

Promoting women's educational attainment and development and acquiring skills appropriate in the macroeconomic environment can go a long way towards achieving this goal through increasing women's economic involvement as workforce members. The challenge resides in improving the quality of skill training offered in India and the significant increase in training facilities for skill training.

Although NSDC has made great strides in removing, more must be done to remove impediments to women's employment in India's informal sector of the economy. Poor quality skills, low productivity, lack of access to higher education due to economic constraints, gender limits, geographical immobility, and inadequate excellent quality skills training are a few of the difficulties society faces today. If India wants to realise the full potential of women's employment participation, a revolution in the world of work is urgently necessary in addition to educational and skill development revolutions. Only then will women in the workforce reach their full potential. Women have more significant social and economic aspirations than males, so an increase in women's educational attainment would immediately enhance the economic engagement of such women in the labour force. If the quality of the skills taught to female workers is worse, the NSDC's and other businesses and Non-governmental Organisations' (NGOs') efforts to close the skills gap will be in vain by 2025.

Institutions of higher learning, vocational schools, and other training centres must also conduct in-depth analyses of the quality of skills training to conform to the new, all-encompassing norm. Hence, it is crucial to identify the necessary skills gap and provide the female labour force with the necessary resources with high-quality training to empower women to the point where they are competent to enter the formal economy and participate in mainstream employment, both of which would lead to a sustainable way of life.

In addition, the current initiatives geared towards enhancing the employability of women require a quality-centric approach that includes a balanced blend of education, counselling, and social support. Yet, existing skill development programmes and initiatives must close the gap in the delivery of breadth and depth of skills critical to the employability of the intended audience. To close the gender skill gap and boost the quality of training for women in the informal economy, the government must take decisive action. This is so people may get the training they need to find steady work, earn a living income, participate in social security, among other benefits.

This research will help bridge the gap between the quality standards of formal and informal skill training for women in training and women working in the informal sector. The research will also yield a skill mapping technique that can be used to fill in the gaps between current and ideal training for specific talents.

2. REVIEW AND OVERVIEW OF LITERATURE

Small, disorganised businesses in the food processing industry are being forced to close as large, well-funded corporations from the United States and abroad enter the market, as noted in the study by Renana and Sinha (2001). Put another way, the rise of multinational firms is killing mom-and-pop shops. More women than men are employed in India's food processing industry. More than 3.10 million women are working in the food processing business, the equivalent of 0.35% of all female workers. Female workers constitute the vast majority in the informal sector. Compared to larger competitors, smaller food processors may not have the resources to invest in state-of-the-art equipment and elaborate quality control labs (Tripathi et al., 2022). These units cannot produce new inventive items that would attract a broad consumer base and cannot fulfil the high-quality standards necessary for the business. Both of these factors prevent them from competing effectively in the market. Since 1981 although women continue to make up a growing share of the workforce overall, recent years have shown a decline in the proportion of women actively seeking employment. However, that percentage was slightly uptick in 1992 and 1993.

Similarly, there has been a general downward trend in the ratio of females to males. The average number of female workers in manufacturing units fell from 21.7 in 1981 to 14.8 in 1982. This represents a reduction from the 1981 figure. With these numbers in hand, it's easy to see how the food processing industry's push towards modernisation will disproportionately hurt female workers.

Report on a World Bank Project from 2007: Specified India that at the core of the country's many training systems are Industrial Training Institutes (ITI) and Industrial Training Centres, both operated by private sector organisations

(Commey et al., 2020). Various trades can be learned at these institutions and centres over up to 2 years. One of the most significant problems with these is their restricted employability, which is caused by the rigidity of their curricula and the lack of market response that results from poor industry–institution links. In 2006, a study commissioned by the World Bank and carried out by tracer revealed that fewer than 30% of graduates from the ITI could find jobs and that companies desired different technical capabilities and better 'soft' skills, teamwork, and innovativeness.

A study by Monk et al. (2008) compared the incomes of people who participated in traditional apprenticeships and vocational training programmes to those who did not. Although the programmes contributed significantly to the likelihood of women participants getting employment, their research demonstrated that the programmes had a far more significant effect on the earnings of male participants than on female participants (Rushita et al., 2023). Men were trained in disciplines like carpentry, mechanics, metal workers, tailoring, and craft labour, while women were relegated to less productive occupations like hairstyling and tailoring. Since women were compelled to labour in these less effective forms of training, their earnings were inevitably lower than men (Cuberes & Teignier, 2012).

Elizabeth Katz (2008) showed that Latin American countries implemented a new strategy to encourage more women to enter the workforce. There, a youth employment programme that provided training in vocational courses worked in conjunction with decentralised training institutions to encourage programme participants to enrol in vocational programmes. The local businesses' requirements and necessities were considered when developing the course material for the training programme (Census of India, 2011). The training included both classroom instruction and training while performing the job duties. Successfully promoting and luring women into employment, these programmes were able to do so because of their much-targeted nature and their foundation in demand for labour in the private sector (Baturina & Simakov, 2023; Klasen & Lamanna, 2008). All the remarkable opportunities these programmes give to young working women. These benefits include equal opportunity, a stipend to help with childcare costs and training in non-traditional skill areas. There has been a rise in the proportion of 'Latin American' countries where women are employed and the amount of money they make due to this new approach to vocational training (Agenor et al., 2021; Chakravarty et al., 2014; Commey et al., 2020).

According to Törnqvist and Schmitz's (2009) research, education is both a driving force and an essential instrument in women gaining greater autonomy. It provides women with the abilities, information, self-assurance, and knowledge necessary to seek economic independence through gainful employment. The young girls have been given financial incentives in the form of fee subsidies, which has led to a practical improvement in their enrolment and a reduction in dropout rates, which has led to an increase in completion rates. The school's proximity to residents, the calibre of its teaching staff, the safety of its facilities, and the availability of adequate restrooms are all factors that contribute to increased female student enrolments (Commey et al., 2020). According to the study, receiving vocational training increases workers' compensation. It reduces the likelihood that a woman will only engage in labour that requires a low level of ability and salary (Balakrishnan, 2014).

In Liberia, Chakravarty et al. (2014) found that a two-stage training programme focused on teaching women six specific skills while addressing job placement issues. According to the results, the training considerably impacted the respondents' subsequent employment and income. Because they were the ones getting training, apprentices (both men and women) from a wide range of occupations were the ones who filled out the survey (Elborgh-Woytek et al., 2013).

Advancing the conversation through experimental analysis of gender variations in labour participation's impact on productivity and welfare, as done by Cuberes and Teigner (2014). Based on Cuberes and Teigner's (2014) work, we used various agents to investigate a career preference model via simulation. The agents' implementation of several restrictions hindered women's economic engagement, such as low wages, gender disparities in entrepreneurial activity, and reduced per capita income. The wage disparity between men and women in India caused a reduction of around 26% in the country's per capita income. According to their research findings, Maitra and Mani (2015) found a high likelihood of employment in India for women actively engaged in and trained in sewing. They possessed particular qualities, such as long working hours, and made more money in the short and medium terms.

Ages of childhood, working life, and retirement were all factored into the calculations. It was hypothesised that public policies, such as public investment in infrastructure and the efficacy of expenditures spent on health and education, would positively affect economic growth and participation. This hypothesis was tested using a model with overlapping generations. These stages were a part of this model. Research conducted by the author indicates that the governmental policies discussed above contributed to a rise in the proportion of women in the labour force. Its inclusion could be very beneficial to the tune of 1.5–2.4% yearly economic growth (Rushita et al., 2023).

2.1. Overview of Literature

The sector is not getting the number of qualified workers that it expects from vocational schools, polytechnics, and other official and informal training institutions. Many in the business world look down on the graduates of these schools because they don't think they're prepared for the workforce, especially women. Because of the improvements in transportation and communication brought on by the food processing industry's technological and infrastructure upgrades, women are seeing a structural shift in their jobs that is facilitating their mobility across different informal sectors. Women who wish to maintain gainful employment must either acquire new skills according to the industry's needs or look for a job elsewhere (MSME, 2015).

Another illustration would be a study in India on women who participated in a sewing training programme. According to the study, women participating in the programme were more likely to be employed, work more weekly hours, and have higher short- and medium-term earnings (World Bank, 2007).

Evidence from the academic literature suggests that training institutions are falling short of industry standards when imparting necessary skills. So, it is vital to identify the needs gap and offer ways to overcome it to move forward. In particular, for women, the benefits of receiving skill training through structured pedagogy include better pay and a higher standard of living as a result of better inputs of skills, transformations of those skills in terms of equipping the beneficiary, and better pay and a higher standard of living as a result of better skills. The gender gap in the workforce has serious economic, social, and environmental consequences that must be addressed (Kaur et al., 2023b; Yadav et al., 2023a).

2.2. Research Gap

Even though there are many sources and, journals, government sites data available which have explained the skill development gap and skill shortage in different sectors, there is limited data or fewer data available for the skill gap in the miniature industry, especially in the handicraft sector and how to bridge the gap for enhancing the skill, knowledge of artisans. So in this chapter, we have focused on the skill gap in the handicraft sector and different strategies to bridge the gap and increase the skill of artisans.

2.3. Framework

From a socioeconomic and demographic standpoint, India must invest in its people's skill sets. It's a vital tool for enhancing productivity and earning potential, which in turn helps reduce poverty. Boosting people's skills can help the government achieve its 'Skilling India' goal and our prime minister's goal of expanding manufacturing in India.

Most of the population is under 25, which benefits the country's continued economic and social development thanks to the demographic dividend. India's strategic advantage lies in its enormous pool of young workers. Still, the fact that most of these new workers lack the necessary skills makes it difficult for the country to fill available positions. As of 2014, the NSDC had been charged with overseeing the Ministry of Skill Development and Entrepreneurship (NSDC) and found that there would be an increased requirement of 109.73 million trained personnel in 24 selected industries by 2022. According to the Economic Survey of 2014–2015, just a pitiful 3% of India's workforce has received training in skills, despite the country adding over 12 million people to the labour market annually. That's a rather significant discrepancy. With such a gap, it's clear that the country's workforce needs immediate access to targeted skill training that will help them find gainful employment and contribute meaningfully to the country's economic development and social cohesion (Agenor et al., 2021). Some trained individuals who have found employment in the organised sector struggle to maintain their positions and need additional training to upgrade their abilities to match the needs of the industry. This isn't easy since cutting-edge knowledge is required to succeed in this field. There are now 11,964 ITIs in India, with total enrolments of 16.92 lakh students as of 2014.

Although acquiring new skills would be beneficial, there is no assurance that the training will be of sufficient quality, yield the desired outcomes, or meet the standards of the relevant industry. Notwithstanding this, we will keep providing this kind of instruction, as we know its value. Thus, we need a method to assess the skills training programme regularly and provide helpful input to the relevant training institutions and other stakeholder (Esteve-Volart, 2004). There's also a requirement for training institutions to be flexible enough to change with the times. Timely upgrades to training programmes, instructors, course materials, research methods, and other supporting infrastructure can help achieve this goal. As a result, the employment rates of recent college grads in structured industries will rise, whether public or private (Katz, 2008).

A Framework for the Inputs and Outcomes of the Skills Training Process. By the end of the day, this framework will help us identify the quality gap in skills training and develop strategies to close it, which are necessary for sustaining employment prospects. When transmitting or acquiring skills, all parties involved, including the trainer and the learner, must always consider quality. In the long term, only this approach will result in economic gains (Baturina & Simakov, 2023; Juliana et al., 2022; Sood et al., 2022).

At first, a depiction of the process of training skills has been provided. The input–output methodology, used by most institutions currently involved in the skill training industry, serves as the foundation for the process. The trainees may take part in official training supplied by formal training provided by institutions like Vocational Institutes, Polytechnics, and Engineering Schools or informally through methods like learning at home or through speciality shops that teach specific skills (Katz, 2008). Whether formal or informal, stakeholder training is supposed to result in trainees picking up valuable skills. When it comes to industry, this manifests as the hiring of a skilled employee who should be productive on the very first day of their economic engagement or work and who makes a sizeable contribution to the revenues of the business by reducing the amount of time, money, and waste produced (Rana & Bhargava, 2017).

The outcome of the training procedure has been incorporated into the framework (Table 11.1) recommended in this study. Hence, it is founded on the input–output strategy, which should bring about sustainability and reduce structural unemployment. According to Endris and Kassegn (2023), the quality of the inputs (what is given to trainees), the quality of the training techniques (both formal and informal training), the quality of the output, the skills obtained, and the quality of the outcome are all included in the framework. The result will take the form of employment in either the formal or informal economy, depending on the quality of the skills training received. The lack of a job would be a distinct possibility if the quality of the skills training were poor (Balakrishnan, 2014).

So, including quality in the skill training can significantly impact the outcome. It may prove to be a more all-encompassing strategy for guaranteeing long-term employability, thinking about everyone with a vested interest (Rana & Bhargava, 2017). Skill India should not lose sight of the importance of a high-quality education system, as seen by the rising aspirations of young people,

Table 11.1. Function and Level in the Handicraft Sector and
Skill Requirement.

Function	Level	Skill Required	Skill Gaps
Bidding/ Procurement	Import Mediator/ Buyer Maintenance	Understanding of different varieties of cotton in terms of their pile lengths and whether or not they are suitable for the type of yarns that are wanted	There is a lack of understanding regarding the maintenance requirements of diverse machinery
		Familiarity with the many different kinds of cotton flaws. For example, a cotton crop harvested after exposure to rain would not only have a drab appearance but may also be dotted with small black spots	A lack of adequate information regarding skills in process improvement, including waste management, finding solutions to maintenance and engineering-related problems, and working without much supervision because most units don't have one
		Have an impact on the overall quality of the yarn. The quality of the cotton will affect the quality of all of the products that are produced downstream	Modern machinery
		Knowledge of the most recent developments in the industry and the ability to foresee the impact these trends will have on procurement. For instance, if there is an expectation of a decrease in cotton production, this would lead to an increase in price, and as a result, there would be a requirement to build up the raw material inventory	An understanding of the upkeep requirements specific to the various textile machines. For instance, the capability to maintain various machinery utilised in a spinning unit, such as carding machines, draw frames, speed frames, ring frames, and auto covers

(Continued)

Table 11.1. (*Continued*)

Function	Level	Skill Required	Skill Gaps
			Be sure you know modern machine tools and that spare parts are readily available
			Capacity for effective communication with machinery producers to understand the specific needs that diverse machines place on their upkeep
			Plan and oversee the maintenance of the machinery to guarantee that there will be as little downtime as possible. This is necessary for spinning machines, known for their heavy reliance on technology

Source: Table compiled by authors.
Report of the Committee to examine the requirement of human resources in the textile sector.

even as underemployment forces many of them to work in less formal settings, especially women (Government of India, 2009).

2.3. Necessary Abilities and Existing Skills

In Table 11.1, we've laid out precisely what sorts of abilities are needed and where there are gaps in the spinning industry.

The majority of the instruction provided in the ITIs is concentrated on the following occupations: (1) Bleaching, (2) Dyeing, (3) Block Printing, (4) Cutting and Tailoring, (5) Dress Making, (6) Embroidery, (7) Hand Weaving of Niwar Tape, (8) Durries, (9) Carpet, (10) Knitting with Hand Operated Machine, (11) Weaving of Silk and Woolen Fabrics, etc.

The garment industry faces significant challenges regarding the availability of skilled labourers. Up to 50,000 individuals receive annual training through the ATDC, ITIs, and NIFT. A few participants from the private sector also offer training that is particular to the garment industry. Training while an employee is working fulfils a significant percentage of the requirements for human resources at the operator level. Hence, training at the operator level is a significant improvement area. Poaching is a problem caused by an acute shortage of trained human resources, making it difficult to justify spending money on in-house training initiatives (Endris & Kassegn, 2023).

3. OBJECTIVE

This chapter focused on the three main objectives of study are:

- To study the skill gap among handicraft workers and other sectors.
- To study the briefing of the skill gap with other sectors to compete with other sectors.
- To review the whole chapter and suggest some ideas about skill development in the handicraft sector.

4. RESEARCH METHODOLOGY

This chapter's review is based on secondary data from past research studies and data from the Indian MSME and NSDC. The discussion and recommendations in the next section are based on the findings, and the consequences of the research are also discussed in the chapter's final section.

5. DISCUSSION AND RESULT

5.1. Emerging Trends in Skill Requirements

5.1.1. Technology

There would be significant changes to the types of players participating due to technological advances. As was mentioned before, just 2–4% of looms in India's textile industry are shuttle-less, which is a considerable drop from the worldwide average of 16.9%. As a result, it's safe to assume that the Indian weaving industry is woefully behind the times. Nonetheless, despite significant modernisation, in India's spinning industry still, around 60% of the spindles installed are older than 10 years, and open-end (OE) rotors make up only 1% of the total spindles installed. India has a far smaller investment in special-purpose machines than other countries in the garment industry (Kaur et al., 2023b; Yadav et al., 2023b; Kumar et al., 2023). These machines have very specialised tasks and add value to the end product. A tiny percentage of export firms have purchased cutting equipment and finishing machines. Although government incentives like total unit funding services (TUFS) and the industry's generally low level of technology would drive modernisation, the power costs inside the business would be prohibitive (World Bank, 2007).

The upgrading of the technology would call for the human resource to be trained in the operation of modern machinery in addition to an increase in the amount spent internally on training. Because of the labour shortage and the rising pay rate, there will be a further push towards increased automation, ultimately resulting in increased productivity. For instance, due to modernisation, the number of operating hours required to produce one quintal of yarn has dropped from 77 to 25, and this trend is expected to continue. In addition, the number of employees needed to complete post-spinning operations has decreased due to the introduction of automatic cone-winding machines.

Maintenance personnel for modern machinery need to be highly trained and knowledgeable about the specifics of the field in which they work. The industry's performance would be considerably impacted by machine downtime and the high cost of spare components, making appropriate maintenance necessary.

5.1.2. Procedures Regarding Quality
There would be a greater emphasis placed on and adoption of procedures that are relevant to quality and the environment, such as the textile sector does not prioritise research and development in any way. For the sector to continue to be competitive in terms of its products and prices, additional research and development funding for processes and products will be required. To accomplish this, firms must put forth individual R&D efforts and collaborate with academic institutions.

5.1.3. Labour Laws for Handmade Industries
Adaptable work requirements will have a positive effect on the market. The T&C sector is governed by the Contract Labour Act of 1970, which prohibits the employment of contract labour for ongoing activities. For this reason, exporters often struggle to meet the demand due to seasonal changes and custom orders. Alterations to the way the regulations are now written could result in the creation of more job openings. Also, under the rules that are now in place, women are not permitted to work night shifts. The relaxation of these restrictions, accompanied by appropriate protections, has the potential to increase the number of women who participate in the business while also contributing to the solution of the talent gap in the sector (MSME, 2015).

5.2. Having To Do With Human Resources
Technological modernisation will require more technical proficiency in manufacturing and upkeep throughout the textile industry's value chain. Multitasking and a wide variety of abilities are required at the operator level in this industry. Personnel in upper echelons and areas like procurement must be well-versed in a wide range of equipment and up-to-date on technological developments. Functions like procurement significantly benefit from this kind of attention to detail (Rana & Bhargava, 2017).

The growth of the global garment industry will be a significant factor in the increased demand for workers in the textile industry. Operators with a deep familiarity with sewing machine features and the many kinds of seams and stitches will be responsible for meeting the bulk of the demand for labour resources. Although line systems of operations will continue to be the backbone of the business, 'make through' operations systems will be necessary to export designer and high-end clothing. Operators will need to be able to stitch the entire garment, even if the industry will continue to rely heavily on online methods of operations. Possessing readily available talents in merchandising and design is crucial for expanding exports and tapping into new markets.

5.3. Regions That Will Drive Human Resource Requirements

The states of Tamil Nadu, West Bengal, Karnataka, Maharashtra, and Gujarat are likely to be the most influential in creating these new jobs across India. An estimated 30% of the textile industry's jobs will be in Tamil Nadu.

We see some interesting patterns emerge when we examine how women are represented in the workforce across different informal economic sectors. As an illustration, the agricultural industry employs 68.4% of women, whereas the service sector employs 15.6% of women. Over the past two and a half decades, women's employment has shifted dramatically from the informal sector, which required little formal education or training, to the more specialised sectors, which can do (World Bank, 2007). This shift has taken place in the employment opportunities available to women. This move could contribute to the decrease of women in agriculture at the national level, which has decreased by 15%. However, their participation has grown in every other area. Similar increases have been seen in the percentage of women working in the service sector (23% higher) and manufacturing (60%) over the same period. With a few significant exceptions, this trend is visible throughout a wide range of regions (Report on Employment–Unemployment Survey, 2014).

The government has attempted to offer a basic level of subsistence through incomes through numerous programmes, including the Pradhan Mantri Gram Sadak Yojana, Indira Awaas Yojana, Swarnjayanti Gram Swarozgar Yojana, and many more. As a result of completing a sectoral study of the many different areas highlighted by the government's 'Make in India' Program, the sectors can be grouped into the following four groups, illustrated in Table 11.1 (Rushita et al., 2023; PIB, 2022; Rana & Bhargava, 2017).

Industries such as Defence, Electronics, and Aviation predominantly depend on output from other countries, whereas the nature of their domestic consumption is that of a domestic market. It may be possible to generate growth in these industries by reducing reliance on imported goods and strengthening policies and regulations. Hence, for women to obtain the skills necessary for working in these sectors, the relevant industries should educate them on the documentation processes and the most effective ways to use and transfer imported technology (PIB, 2022).

5.4. Suggestion for Skill Development Priorities for the National Skills Development Council

From what has been said, it is evident that the following should be NSDC's primary focus areas for developing skills in the T&C industry.

(a) Technicians who run the machinery used in the textile industry.
(b) People in the Textile Manufacturing Sector Who Operate Sewing Machines.

Based on our discussions with key players in the T&C sector, we've identified the following broad areas for skill development in which NSDC can concentrate its efforts. Table 11.3 illustrates the focus areas for NSDC for skill building. Please see Table 11.2 for content and skill building in the handicraft sector.

Different segments and courses have been given in tabular form for skill building in a small industry in Table 11.3.

Table 11.2. Important Skill Building in the Handicraft Sector.

Segment	Course Type	Content Areas for Skill Building
Fabric Manufacturing	Power Loom Operations	• Dobby weaving expertise, jacquard loom operation, threading a loom, and the ability to switch patterns on a loom • Weaving with synthetic silk, water jet looms, high-speed looms, and rapier looms • Production of artificial silk with the use of looms • Preventative measures and scheduled appointments for maintenance • Adherence to quality standards
Garments	Apparel Manufacturing	• Making patterns • Making patterns • Computer-based tools • Computers for planning • Controlling production
Garments	Fashion Design	• Styling and illustration for the fashion industry • Merchandising; activities in the design studio
Garments and Fabric Manufacturing	Quality Assurance	• Construction of garments and the making of patterns • Technical auditing and computer skills • Defects in fabrics and garments and possible solutions • Processes and inspections related to quality control

Source: Table compiled by authors.

Table 11.3. Segment and Courses and Different Content Areas of Skill Building.

Segment	Content	Content Areas for Skill Building
Garments	Knitwear Manufacturing	• Creating patterns for knitted items quality control time and motion studies • Computer-based tools computers for planning and controlling production
Garments and Fabric Manufacturing	Production Supervision and Quality Control	• Techniques for inspection • Quality Assurance Systems Skills for Sewing and Supervision
Garments	Sewing Machine Technician	• The operation and maintenance of high-speed sewing machines • Chain stitch, button stitch • Chain stitch, button stitch • Maintenance and precautions
Garments	Sewing Machine Operators	• Controlling the fundamentals of a sewing machine; threading the needle; stitching a variety of forms; and adhering to quality standards • Preventative measures for the sewing machine

Source: Elborgh-Woytek et al. (2013).

5.5. Essential Skill Sets

Listed below are some of the Mainstream T&C industry's most in-demand skill sets as of late. Some advanced substantial amount of competence in both analytical work and consultancy, which is supported by the following capabilities:

- Knowledge of how policies are formulated at a high level.
- Comprehensive and well-organised database covering a variety of fields (Rana & Bhargava, 2017).
- Understanding the most critical aspects contributing to success in various initiatives and programmers.
- Capability to research developing trends in the economy as a whole as well as in particular industries.
- A deeper understanding of the various organisational programmes and procedures.
- In a nutshell, you need to be able to analyse data, construct mathematical and financial models to foresee outcomes, and identify problematic areas to make necessary adjustments.
- Capability of recognising the numerous types of dangers that could occur and recommending suitable preventative measures for each one.

6. CONCLUSION

Because almost every sector of the economy relies on them, from textiles to vehicles to electronics to chemicals and chemical goods, etc., and have the potential to act as sourcing destinations for other countries. It requires diverse skill sets to generate employment and increase efficiency. There is a lot of room for improvement in these fields, especially for female labour in the informal economy, through the correct imparting of skills and quality assurance, as well as the global move from Made in China to Made in India. As a result of the multifaceted nature of the transformation goal for India, the country has the potential to achieve success on par with that of Japan and Korea in the middle of the 1950s, as well as China in the middle of the 1990s and after that. Agriculture, railroads, infrastructure construction, the hospitality and tourism industries, and so on are all examples of consumer markets where the emphasis is placed on domestic production for domestic consumption, and the skills necessary to boost productivity and implement mechanisation must be disseminated. Improve medium and small businesses by educating workers in a variety of skills in a concentrated manner; this should also help to solve the issue of structural unemployment. Considering consumer relations, skills are essential to success in export-oriented industries, such as textiles, IT services, gems and jewellery, and food processing. Despite their lack of education or training, women make up a sizeable portion of India's informal workforce and contribute significantly to the country's raw material resources and competitive labour force.

6.1. The Implication of the Research

Skills training for women in the informal workforce would have far-reaching consequences, ranging from the microlevel of individual workers to the macrolevel policy ramifications for the long-term success of women in the informal economy, including the need to track the results of skill building programmes and ensure their quality. That's because it's generally accepted that if women acquire marketable skills through education, they'll be more likely to keep their positions. Women will gain confidence in themselves and their abilities, and as a result, they will make more remarkable contributions to their households, communities, and countries.

6.2. Limitation and Further Scope

Even this chapter has focused on the skill or talent gap and bridging skills with small industries, especially in the handicraft sector. They were so tried to solve many problems. But it has focussed on only the handicraft sector, especially women involved in this sector, so this chapter needs further exploration to explore ideas and work in this sector. So researcher and academician can enhance their knowledge and do better research in the handicrafts sector with digital technology awareness.

ACKNOWLEDGEMENT

I am thankful to all my co-authors who contributed to chapter writing and other data collection, especially secondary data.

REFERENCES

Agenor, P. (2015). Gender equality and economic growth in Britain: An overlapping generations model for India. *European Journal of Economics, 23*(2), 45–56.

Agenor, P., Kumar, S., & Ghosal, I. (2021). Gender equality with skill gap and economic growth: An overlapping generations model for India. *The Indian Economic Letters, 54*(3), 35–43.

Balakrishnan, S. (2014, February 21). 'Bridging the gap between the campus and the corporate: Increasing employability' – Challenges, opportunities and methods. *7th National Management Convention (NMC)* (25 pp.).

Baturina, L., & Simakov, A. (2023). Students' attitude towards e-learning in Russia after the pandemic. *Education Science Management, 1*(1), 1–6.

Census of India. (2011). Office of the Registrar General and Census Commissioner, India, Ministry of Home Affairs, Government of India.

Chakravarty, S., Jr, Korkoyah, Lundberg, M., Adoho, F., & Tasneem, A. (2014). *The impact of an adolescent girls employment program: The EPAG Project in Liberia.* WPS6832. The World Bank.

Commey, V., Kokt, D., & Hattingh, J. (2020). Innovative human resources management: Critical competencies expected from hospitality graduates in Ghana. *Journal of Sustainable Tourism and Entrepreneurship, 1*(4), 279–291.

Cuberes, D., & Teignier, M. (2012). *Gender gaps in the labor market and aggregate productivity.* Sheffield Economic Research Paper SERP 2012017. Sarge institute of economic policy, Durban

Cuberes, D., & Teignier, M. (2014). Gender inequality and economic growth: A critical review. *Journal of International Development, 26,* 260–276.

Elborgh-Woytek, M. K., Newiak, M. M., Kochhar, M. K., Fabrizio, M. S., Kpodar, M. K., Wingender, M. P., … & Schwartz, M. G. (2013). *Women, work, and the economy: Macroeconomic gains from gender equity.* International Monetary Fund

Endris, E., & Kassegn, A. (2023). Analysis of growth and constraints of agricultural micro- and small-scale enterprises in North Wollo Zone, Amhara Regional State, Ethiopia. *Cogent Social Sciences, 9*(1), 2197291.

Esteve-Volart, B. (2004). *Gender discrimination and growth: Theory and evidence from India.* STICERD Development Economics Papers 42. Suntory and Toyota International Centres for Economics and Related Disciplines, London School of Economics.

Government of India. (2009). *Skill formation and employment assurance in the unorganized sector.* National Commission for Enterprises in the Unorganized Sector.

Juliana, A. P., Lemy, D. M., Pramono, R., Djakasaputra, A., & Purwanto, A. (2022). Hotel performance in the digital era: Digital marketing roles, perceived quality and trust. *Journal of Intelligent Management Decision, 1*(1), 36–45.

Kaur, H., Sodhi, D., Aggarwal, R., & Yadav, U. S. (2023a). Managing human resources in digital marketing. In *digital transformation, strategic resilience, cyber security and risk management* (pp. 155–162). Emerald Publishing Limited. https://ideas.repec.org/h/eme/csefzz/s1569-37592023000111c009.html

Kaur, H., Sood, K., Yadav, U. S., & Grima, S. (2023b). Sustainable solutions for insurance and risk management. *The Impact of Climate Change and Sustainability Standards on the Insurance Market*, 359–372. https://onlinelibrary.wiley.com/doi/pdf/10.1002/9781394167944.ch23

Klasen, S., & Lamanna, F. (2008). *The impact of gender inequality in education and employment on economic growth in developing countries: Updates and extensions.* Discussion Papers 175. Ibero-America Institute for Economic Research.

Kumar A., Yadav, U. S., Yadav, G. P., & Tripathi, R. (2023). New sustainable ideas for materialistic solutions of a smart city in India: A review from Allahabad city. *Materials Today: Proceedings, 34*(3), 23–33. https://www.sciencedirect.com/science/article/abs/pii/S2214785323043092

Maitra, P., & Mani, S. (2015). Learning and earning: Evidence from a randomized evaluation in India. *Labour Economics, 45*, 116–130.

Monk, C., Sandefur, J., & Teal, F. (2008). *Does doing an apprenticeship pay off? Evidence from Ghana.* RECOUP Working Paper 12. University of Oxford, Oxford.

MSME. (2015, June). *National Policy for skill development and entrepreneurship* (pp. 167–169). Ministry of Skill Development and Entrepreneurship Press.

PIB. (2022). *2022 Year Ender Review: Ministry of Skill Development and Entrepreneurship.* https://pib.gov.in/PressReleasePage.aspx?PRID=1887602

Rana, R., & Bhargava, S. (2017). Bridging the skills gap of women workers of informal sector in India for sustainable development. *International Journal of Economic Research, 23*(2), 761–772.

Renana, J., & Sinha, S. (2001). "Liberalization and the woman worker", Self Employed Women's Association (SEWA). *Journal of Women Society, 34*(3), 39–98.

Report on Employment–Unemployment Survey. (2014). Ministry of Labour and Employment, Labour Bureau, Government of India, Chandigarh.

Rushita, D., Sood, K., & Yadav, U. S. (2023). Cryptocurrency and digital money in the new era. In *digital transformation, strategic resilience, cyber security and risk management* (Vol. 111, pp. 179–190). Emerald Publishing Limited.

Sood, K., Kaur, B., & Grima, S. (2022). Revamping Indian Non-Life Insurance industry with a trusted network: Blockchain technology. In K. Sood, R. K. Dhanaraj, B. Balamurugan, S. Grima, & R. U. Maheshwari (Eds.), *Big Data: A game changer for insurance industry* (pp. 213–228). Emerald Publishing Limited.

Törnqvist, A., & Schmitz, C. (2009). Women's economic empowerment: Scope for Sida's engagement, in women's economic empowerment. *Journal of Economic Policy, 24*(3), 231–329.

Tripathi, M. A., Tripathi, R., Yadav, U. S., & Shastri, R. K. (2022). Gig economy: A paradigm shift towards Digital HRM practices. *Journal of Positive School Psychology, 6*(2), 5609–5617.

World Bank. (2007). Project appraisal document on vocational training improvement project. *World Bank Press, 89*(2), 345–356.

Yadav, U. S., Sood, K., Tripathi, R., Grima, S., Yadav, N. (2023b). Entrepreneurship in India's handicraft industry with the support of digital technology and creativity during natural calamities. *International Journal of Sustainable Development and Planning, 18*(6), 1777–1791.

Yadav, U. S., Tripathi, R., Tripathi, M. A., Ghosal, I., Kumar, A., Mandal, M., & Singh, A. (2023a). Digital and innovative entrepreneurship in the Indian handicraft sector after the COVID-19 pandemic: Challenges and opportunities. *Journal of Innovation and Entrepreneurship, 12*(1), 69.

INDEX

Note: Page numbers followed by "n" with numbers refer to endnotes.